P9-DVV-214

Where's the Learning in Service-Learning?

Janet Eyler
Dwight E. Giles, Jr.

Foreword by Alexander W. Astin

Where's the Learning in Service-Learning?

Jossey-Bass Publishers
San Francisco

Chapter 7 epigraph excerpted from *The Meaning of It All* by Richard Feynman. Copyright © 1998 by Michelle Feynman and Carl Feynman. Reprinted by permission of Perseus Books Publishers, a member of Perseus Books, L.L.C.

Excerpt from "Little Gidding" in *Four Quartets*, copyright 1943 by T.S. Eliot and renewed 1971 by Esme Valerie Eliot, reprinted by permission of Harcourt Brace & Company.

Jossey-Bass books and products are available through most bookstores. To contact Jossey-Bass directly, call (888) 378-2537, fax to (800) 605-2665, or visit our website at www.josseybass.com.

Substantial discounts on bulk quantities of Jossey-Bass books are available to corporations, professional associations, and other organizations. For details and discount information, contact the special sales department at Jossey-Bass.

Manufactured in the United States of America on Lyons Falls Turin Book. This paper is acid-free and 100 percent totally chlorine-free.

Library of Congress Cataloging-in-Publication Data

Eyler, Janet.
  Where's the learning in service-learning? / Janet Eyler, Dwight E. Giles, Jr.; foreword by Alexander W. Astin.—1st ed.
    p.   cm.—(The Jossey-Bass higher and adult education series)
  Includes bibliographical references and index.
  ISBN 0-7879-4483-1 (hard : perm paper)
  1. Student service—United States.   2. College students—United States.   I. Giles, Dwight E., Jr.   II. Title.   III. Series.
  LC220.5.E95   1999
  378'.015'0973—dc21   99-6120

HB Printing   10 9 8 7 6 5 4 3 2 1   FIRST EDITION

The Jossey-Bass
Higher and Adult Education Series

Contents

Foreword

Many of us who are enthusiastic advocates of service-learning have tended to emphasize its "service" benefits: we promote more widespread adoption of service-learning in higher education because we see it as a powerful means of preparing students to become more caring and responsible parents and citizens and of helping colleges and universities to make good on their pledge to "serve society." This wonderful and much needed book by Janet Eyler and Dwight E. Giles, Jr., addresses the "other" benefit of service-learning: its enormous potential for enhancing the learning process. The authors also show us that "cognitive" learning and "affective" service can, in fact, be closely connected and thereby mutually reinforcing and that an "affective" outcome like "commitment to service" also has important cognitive components. Indeed, this book helps to underscore an important reality about higher education: while we classroom teachers typically believe that we are dealing only with the cognitive side of student development, the learning process is inescapably cognitive *and* affective. In this connection, Eyler and Giles raise important and challenging questions about how we have traditionally gone about defining and assessing student "learning."

While the authors are themselves strong supporters of service-learning, they have buttressed their advocacy with a wealth of quantitative and qualitative research evidence gleaned from surveys of more than fifteen hundred students together with a number of personal interviews, including problem-solving interviews completed by students before and after service-learning and one-time interviews where other students evaluated their experiences with reflection during service-learning. The conclusions about student learning have been enhanced by examining changes in the quality of problem analysis and critical thinking over the course of a semester of service-learning. And the credibility of the students' views about service-learning has been strengthened by the authors' sensitivity to the possibility that the high level of enthusiasm for service-learning that characterizes many participants may discourage critical commentary from other students. At the same time, the quantitative evidence has been strengthened by the inclusion, within the same courses, of students who did and did not participate in a service experience.

A particular strength of this book is that it focuses on both the outcomes *and* the process of service-learning. The coverage of outcomes is extensive: personal and interpersonal (Chapter Two), understanding and application (Chapters Three and Four), critical thinking (Chapter Five), perspective transformation (Chapter Six), and citizenship outcomes (Chapter Seven). College teachers and administrators will be particularly interested in Chapters Eight and Nine, in which the authors provide a wealth of useful information on what makes a service-learning program or experience particularly effective. Moreover, most of the other chapters provide important information on the complex connection between process and outcomes. Reflection, which proves to be one of the most powerful process variables, is treated at length throughout the book, and an excellent summary of reflection principles is included in Chapter Eight.

Reading this book should prove to be an illuminating and valuable experience not only for faculty and staff who are already engaged in service-learning work but also for those who may be new to the field or who might be considering getting involved in this very exciting form of pedagogy.

February 1999   ALEXANDER W. ASTIN
Los Angeles, California

Preface

Our passion for doing this research grew out of our experiences as teachers and community practitioners. We saw how powerful service-learning was for our students, and we experienced it ourselves as well. Often the power of this experience to stimulate our own learning surprised us. We had not really expected to learn much more about HIV policy, for example, when we accompanied students in an intensive AIDS outreach program. Although the issue was a new one for us, we had spent a lot of time becoming knowledgeable about the history of AIDS policy in America and felt well equipped to assist teams of students as they explored the issues. We had planned a series of service opportunities for students to provide assistance and to learn about the complexity of the lives of people living with AIDS. We did not realize how much we also had to learn until the day we worked with students to clean an apartment, wrestle with the public health bureaucracy to obtain a hospital bed, and then bring a man who seemed far too weak to be on his own home from the hospital. But sitting there and sharing a pizza with this man and knowing that when we left he would be vulnerable to stronger neighbors who had been circling with an eye on his stuff and that he would be perhaps unable to walk from the couch to the bed made it clear to us how little we had understood about the struggles of people living with HIV. We knew about gaps in the safety net, and we knew about the difficulties of policy implementation; but when we left that day, we understood these things in new ways and had a new set of questions about HIV policy. As our students repeatedly told us, "When you see an issue in someone's life, you want to know more, and it makes it so much more important to do something about it." Just as combining study of subject matter with community service provokes curiosity to know more in our students, participating in service-learning made us want to know more about how to design and implement better service-learning programs.

The learning we saw in our service-learning students was deeper than merely acquiring and spitting back a series of facts about a subject; it engaged our students' hearts as well as their heads and helped them understand the complexity of what they were studying. It also provided opportunities to apply what they learned and think critically about assumptions they had never questioned before. We have been impressed by the ability of students to bring the information and skills learned in the classroom to bear on a project and help a community group achieve an important goal. We have been impressed by the power of service to motivate students to want to know more. We have been impressed by the ways in which service-learning creates connections—between feelings and thought, between studies and life, between self and others, and between college and community. It is clear to us that these programs lead to better learning and that the learning leads to more effective community service.

Although we were convinced of the power of service-learning through our experience, we were aware that outside the community of true believers, there is some considerable doubt as to the value of service-learning as an approach to academic learning. And we were aware through our work with colleagues around the country that service-learning programs tend to be somewhat marginal in most academic institutions. There is a constant struggle to find the resources necessary to support and sustain programs. One of the common experiences of pioneers in the field has been cancellation of programs and lost jobs (Stanton, Giles, and Cruz, 1999).

This marginal status is partly due to the fact that service-learning has not been embraced by academic departments as a legitimate instructional method (Zlotkowski, 1996). Skeptics ask whether service-learning, although popular with students, has an impact on what students learn. As we looked at the research, it was clear that little had been directed at academic learning. The few studies that had tried to measure academic learning directly were narrowly focused and used grades to assess the impact of service-learning. These studies had yielded mixed results: service-learning did not hurt achievement, but did not always contribute to higher student grades (Sugar and Livosky, 1988; Markus, Howard, and King, 1993; Miller, 1994; Kendrick, 1996). The handful of studies that attempted to go beyond conventional measures of fact acquisition had been limited to small groups or single institutions (Eyler and Halteman, 1981; Batchelder and Root, 1994). There was a real need to think more clearly about the nature of the learning that can be expected from service-learning and to determine if and under what circumstances these expectations have been met in practice.

Although the research has been limited, the dramatic increase in service-learning programs has created a demand for information to help justify and sustain these programs. Skeptics may be dubious about the learning in service-learning, and even true believers are anxious for information to help refine their practice. This increased interest in research about service-learning has been dramatic over the past decade. As recently as ten years ago only a handful of people showed up for research presentations on this topic at practitioner association conferences such as the National Society for Experiential Education (NSEE); in the past several years there have been many well-attended sessions. These practitioner associations have also seen increasing demand for research-oriented publications. Higher education associations and conferences for college presidents and deans have also added sessions on service-learning research to their national conference agendas. The creation of the *Michigan Journal of Community Service Learning*, the first journal with a focus on service-learning research, reflects this growing interest in research to assess and improve the effectiveness of service-learning.

Our Research

We have conducted a number of small studies of experiential learning and service-learning with our students over the years, and this work led to questions that we felt could be answered only with a major national research project (Eyler and Halteman, 1981; Eyler, 1992, 1993; Giles and Eyler, 1994a). Our need to know more coincided with both growing national demand and the interest of the Fund for the Improvement of Postsecondary Education (FIPSE) and the Corporation for National Service (CNS) to provide more empirically based guidance to the field.

The primary data sources for this book are the material from two national research projects that we conducted over the past several years. Comparing Models of Service-Learning, supported by FIPSE, sought to do for higher education something similar to what Conrad and Hedin (1980) accomplished when they assessed the impact of a variety of experiential and service-learning programs on high school students in a groundbreaking national study conducted in the late 1970s. Our study combines extensive survey data collection with intensive student interviews. It began with pilot focus groups, interviews, and pilot surveys and was extended to include a national survey of over fifteen hundred students from twenty colleges and universities, eleven hundred of whom were involved in service-learning. These surveys, conducted before and after a semester of community service, examine the impact of service-learning on students. The surveys are also used to explore the impact of particular program characteristics on student outcomes. We went beyond survey responses and conducted intensive interviews with sixty-six students at six colleges before and after the service semester; these interviews assess possible changes in students' problem-solving and critical thinking abilities, as well as changes in the complexity of their thinking about social issues.

In a second project, developed for the Corporation for National Service, we interviewed sixty-seven students in seven colleges and universities. These interviews focused on students' experience with reflection in service-learning and led to the publication of A *Practitioner's Guide to Reflection in Service-Learning* (Eyler, Giles, and Schmiede, 1996). These students were from large public universities, small private colleges, a historically black college, and a business-oriented college; some students participated in curriculum-based service-learning classes or programs, while others participated in volunteer activities. We draw on their voices as well as those of students in our problem-solving interviews throughout this book.

This work draws from higher education reform and experiential learning theory with roots in Dewey and recent findings in cognitive science. It is designed to address the major concerns of higher education professionals about the importance of service-learning programs to their academic mission. These rich data sets, which focus on students' assessment of their learning as well as the impact of service-learning on the way students think, are unique. They provide the opportunity to determine what is powerful about service-learning with both qualitative and quantitative data, and they focus on the central goal of higher education: learning.

The learning goals in higher education are complex, and students are affected by many of life's experiences; no single intervention, particularly over the course of a semester, can be expected to have a dramatic impact on student outcomes. Although the effects of service-learning on students that we found in our studies were often significant, they are not large. They are, however, rather consistent. Service-learning makes a difference, and within the group who experience these programs, higher-quality service-learning makes a bigger difference.

Who Will Find This Book Useful?

This book will interest anyone who has ever been curious about the impact of service-learning—both skeptics who suspect that service-learning is just another pedagogical fad and believers who have experienced the power of service-learning and want to know more about what makes it effective. It is designed to be relevant to the many different constituencies in higher education.

Faculty

When faculty members are contemplating adding a service-learning component to their courses, they want to know if it will add enough to student learning to make it worth the effort. The heart of this book is a series of chapters that define some important learning outcomes and provide evidence of the effect of service-learning participation on achieving those outcomes. Faculty members will find this book useful in helping them reflect on their goals for instruction. It also provides data that suggest what kinds of features they may want to build into their service-learning courses to achieve these goals.

Directors of Campus Community Service Centers

Directors of service-learning, coordinators of community service-learning, or directors of community programs and others who work to provide service opportunities for students continuously struggle for resources. This book may be useful in that process in several ways.

For people trying to recruit faculty to include service in their classes, this book provides evidence of the kinds of goals that can be furthered and evidence about the kinds of program characteristics that are important to increase impact. This same information may also be useful in dialogue with campus administrators. The quality of the service placement was shown to be a consistent factor in the impact of service-learning on students in our studies, information that supports the importance of these efforts to obtain resources for developing effective community partnerships and successfully placing students.

Presidents and Deans

One of the benefits of service-learning is that it is a pedagogy with multiple payoffs. Presidents and deans are under pressure to foster good community relations. Service-learning can help accomplish this by meeting a demand for community outreach in a way that also simultaneously helps achieve the academic goals of the institution. It is an approach to learning that prepares students with the teamwork skills demanded by employers, prepares students who are used to applying what they have learned, and may develop the problem-solving and critical thinking skills that prepare them for citizenship (Ehrlich, 1997). Service-learning is about connections—some of them intensely personal and others involving connections among the many stakeholders in the modern college or university. Service-learning may be a vehicle for strengthening the bonds between the college and the community, between students and faculty, and between students and their college.

Students

One of the most enjoyable parts of these projects for us was the chance to meet with students from across the country, in focus groups and later in intensive interviews, about their community service. We have found students to be intensely interested in both the goals and the processes of service-learning. Many of these students plan future work in community agencies, as teachers, or in higher education student affairs. Every once in a while we run into a former student who is now a director of a campus service-learning center or working with an agency. We hope this book will be interesting and useful for students who have a serious interest and perhaps future in service-learning. It may serve as a useful text for higher education courses that include this focus.

Staff of Community Agencies

The service is central to the value of service-learning. Agency staff with an understanding of how service fits into the curriculum and what kinds of service experiences work best for students may be in a better position to build college-community partnerships that work well for them. Many students are filled with enthusiasm about continuing their community service, and students who have good academic experiences with service-learning are in a position to provide thoughtful service in the community. Although the focus of this research is on what students take from the service-learning process, there is reason to think that the experiences that make good learning also lead to effective service.

Researchers

Serious academic research about service-learning is in its early stages. We hope that this work will be a jumping-off place for future researchers, particularly those who want to focus their attention on academic learning. With our problem-solving interviews we have taken a step in the direction of identifying and measuring reasonable performance outcomes for service-learning, and we think our experiences will be useful for researchers who are planning their studies. We hope that others will continue to develop more finely grained assessments of student learning more closely tied to specific experiences and subject matter.

Plan of the Book

In the following chapters, we unfold the evidence for this learning using both student voices and statistical data. We begin in Chapter One with an overview of the main themes of the book and outline some of the ways in which service-learning helps students achieve important outcomes of a college education. Chapters Two through Seven develop these outcomes and show how service-learning and particular characteristics of service-learning make a difference.

Chapter Eight shifts the focus from student outcomes to program characteristics and summarizes the impact of key characteristics on the outcomes identified in Chapters Two through Seven. Finally we put forward some implications for practice in Chapter Nine.

We have accepted the challenge of writing for two types of readers: those who want the statistics and those who want the stories. In order to do this, we have put all of the data analysis tables in resource sections at the end of the book. For those who wish to see the regression results and beta weights, they are there. For those who wish to skip them, they can rest assured that when we report findings, we are doing so at least at a .05 level of significance. Throughout we have illustrated the findings about the impact of service-learning with quotations from student interviews. We hope that readers will find their journey through the book as useful to their work as we have found the process of creating it useful to ours.

February 1999   JANET EYLER
Nashville, Tennessee   DWIGHT E. GILES, JR.

Acknowledgments

This book represents the culmination of two national research projects that involved several thousand people. Indeed this book was possible only with the generous assistance of so many people; because of this large-scale involvement, it is probably impossible to acknowledge everyone who assisted us over the past five years. With that caveat and an advance apology to anyone we may have omitted, we have combed our records and our memories so we can acknowledge and thank those who helped us in this venture.

First and foremost, we thank the over twenty-five hundred college and university students from all over the United States who filled out survey questionnaires, told us their stories through interviews, and sat through our focus groups. Without their willingness to share their learning with us, there would have been no project.

A project of this scope requires substantial financial resources. We are grateful to the U.S. Department of Education's Fund for the Improvement of Postsecondary Education (FIPSE) for major grant support. In addition to the financial assistance, we benefited greatly from the wisdom and support of Jay Donahue, our FIPSE program officer over the four-year period of the grant. We also received grant support from the Corporation for National Service and are grateful for Goodwin Liu's vision and trust in awarding us the grant. Marilyn Smith, Bob Seidel, Amy Cohen, Hugh Bailey, and Bev Roberts also provided valuable assistance from the Corporation for National Service. Our home base, Peabody College of Vanderbilt University, provided much support for the whole range of activities associated with the data gathering and analysis.

We are especially grateful to our successive department chairs, Dave Cordray, Bob Innes, and Joe Murphy, who supported us in many ways. Our colleague Ed Martin invited us into his community service laboratory course for data gathering beginning in fall 1993, thus providing us with valuable insights both before the project began and though all four years of national data gathering. Our colleague John Bransford provided valuable insights as we sought to incorporate expert and novice theory into our problem-solving interviews, and our colleague John Braxton provided consultation on data analysis. We are grateful to Connie Lee McGahey and Mildred Tyler for providing us with administrative and clerical support. Special thanks are due to Angela Schmiede, who provided expertise on focus groups, made numerous presentations of our interim findings, and helped write one of the earlier products of our work, "A Practitioner's Guide to Reflection in Service-Learning."

Lizette Tucker and Barbara Clinton of the Student Health Coalition at Vanderbilt University Medical College gathered data from their student volunteers during the first phase of the project.

At various points of the project, colleagues from other schools joined us during their sabbaticals or summer breaks to serve as research fellows or research associates. We thank Sue Root, Garry Hesser, and Julianne Price for this valuable assistance. We also appreciate the numerous interviews at various schools that Jim Keith and Jackie Schmidt-Posner did. Independent scholar Cindy Lynch provided valuable assistance in developing and scoring the problem-solving and critical thinking interviews.

Over the course of the project, many graduate students worked long, hard hours to attend to the details of our grand ideas and plans. Foremost among these is Sabrena Yoder, who managed the project's fieldwork with precision and grace for three years and kept her good humor throughout. Scott Gilmer, Heather Gard, Sharon Powell, Doug Taylor, Emily Bergen, Char Gray, and Michele Teper served as graduate research assistants at various points in the project. Our project intern, Kate Eyler-Walker, provided hours of coding and thematic data analysis. JoAnn Johnson and Jill Trump provided professional transcription services.

During the first, pilot year of the FIPSE grant, intensive efforts to gather data and to structure the project were provided by Mary Edens, Esther Onaga, and Phil Smith at Michigan State. At Stanford, Tim Stanton, Jackie Schmidt-Posner, and Janet Luce gave us crucial assistance during the first year of the project. In the spring of 1994, BreakAway, the national alternative break office, provided us with access to alternative spring break groups at Covenant and Augsburg colleges, the University of Michigan, Michigan State, University of Cincinnati, and Indiana University. During the fall 1994 semester, Bonner Scholars Program directors at Guilford, Rhodes, Maryville, De Pauw, Concord, Morehouse, Earlham, Oberlin, Antioch, Berry, Carson-Newman, and College of the Ozarks helped gather data.

We appreciate the input of our advisory board for the final interview study; Robert Bringle, David Cooper, Mary Edens, Thomas Ehrlich, and Susan Root provided useful guidance.

The large-scale surveys, the problem-solving interviews, and the reflection interviews were the largest phases of the data gathering in 1995 and 1996. Over a hundred faculty, service-learning program directors, and staff distributed our surveys to their students, encouraged student participation in interviews and focus groups, and then went the extra mile to make sure we received the data. In no particular order, we thank all of these collaborators:

Robert Newbrough, Carl Lutrin, Sam Lutrin, Angela Schmiede, Anne Takemoto, John Saltmarsh, Kristine Samuelson, Romy Kozak, David Cantrell, Douglas E. Booth, Joyce Solochek, Michael Vater,

Andrew Tallon, Mary Anne Siderits, Thomas Hughson, Holyn Wilson, Christine Firer-Hinze, Jim Weil, Ana Maria M. Guzman, Janet K. Boles, Eve Wildi, Gary Nothnagle, Phyllis M. Ladrigan, Joseph DaBoll-Lavoie, Harry Murray, Lindsay Reading Korth, Seana S. Lowe, David Cooper, Marie J. Corey, Cyrus Stewart, Virginia David, Dennis Ritchie, Leslie Townsend, Gina Petonito, Mark McCarthy, Trace Haythorn, Karl Mattson, Susan Root, Judith Goode, Don Tobias, Ruth Bounnous, Deanna Terzian, Dale Topp, Gail Gunst Heffner, W. D. Brown, Ralph Sorenson, Kay Tracy, Amelia Trevelyan, L. M. Glennon, M. McLaren, Chris Skelley, Ken Taylor, Joseph Siry, Tim Rupe, Cynthia Petterson, Nancy Cushing-Daniels, Ingrid Martinez-Rico, Lou Hammann, Lynn Collins, Mary MacMahon, Linda Marshall, Jane Fleischman, Cindy Hartlaub, Diane Davis, Jason Edwards, Chris Cupoli, David Crowner, Timothy Owens, Robert Davis, V. F. Childers, Twila Yates Papay, Rick Bernsten, Laura Julier, Bob Innes, Fred Montague, Douglas D. Perkins, Cathleen D. Zick, Maggie Jones, Sarah Rosenthal, Amber La Croix, Myrna Snider, Sarah MaHaffy, S. J. Manuel, Nicole Sault, George Westermark, Katie Culbertson, Stephanie Doley, Tim Stanton, Lynn Torin, Ann Watters, Carole Pertofsky, Marjorie Ford, Stuart Tannock, Jackie Schmidt-Posner, Joanna Levin, Bob Basil, Dean Duncan, Alan Paulson, James R. Scarritt, Bob Bringle, Julie Hatcher, Bobbi Timberlake, Irene Fisher, Steve Cochrane, Marian Penn, Bill Head, Marsha Moroh, Al Cabral, Edward Zlotkowski, Jim Ostrow, Amy Kenworthy, Bill Denton, Beryl Mitchel, Gaia Mica, Deborah White, Judy Rauner, Kim Johnson-Bogart, and Shelly Fields.

Andy Furco and Liz Hollander provided helpful comments on an early draft of the manuscript for this book. John Saltmarsh provided the national service-learning statistics from Campus Compact.

Finally, for moving the project from a mountain of data to this book, we thank our editor, Gale Erlandson, for her input, encouragement, and needed critical feedback. Her insights about service-learning and higher education constantly challenged us to remember our audience. David Brightman, editorial assistant at Jossey-Bass, helped with publishing details at every step of the way.

February 1999 JANET EYLER
Nashville, Tennessee DWIGHT E. GILES, JR.

We are grateful for the support of our families
throughout this project and for their working
alongside us in our communities—
sandbagging flooded rivers,
serving as a foster family, building houses,
answering volunteer firefighting calls,
and rescuing animals in need.

We dedicate this book to

Edwin Walker
and
Zachary and Katherine Eyler-Walker

and to

Karen Giles

The Authors

JANET EYLER is associate professor of the practice of education, Peabody College of Vanderbilt University. She has been on the faculty at Peabody since 1976, where she has served as an associate dean and has chaired the Department of Human Resources. She teaches public policy, organizational theory, adult learning, and program evaluation and has taught a variety of service-learning courses, including integrating a week-long alternative spring break experience into a public policy class.

Eyler's scholarly work has focused on experiential learning, and she has a number of publications on internships and service-learning. With Dwight E. Giles, Jr., at Vanderbilt, she has codirected a national service-learning research project funded by the Fund for the Improvement of Postsecondary Education and a Corporation for National Service research project on learning outcomes for college students. The work in this book is drawn primarily from these two studies. Eyler is the coauthor, with Giles and Angela Schmiede, of *A Practitioner's Guide to Reflection in Service Learning: Student Voices and Reflections* (1996).

Eyler has served as a consultant in program evaluation for businesses and universities as well as a consultant in service-learning practice and evaluation for colleges and universities, foundations, and professional societies. She has served on the board of the

National Society for Experiential Education and chaired its research committee.

She and Giles were given the Outstanding Research Award in 1998 by the National Society for Experiential Education for their collaborative research work in service-learning.

DWIGHT E. GILES, JR., is professor of the practice of human and organizational development and director of internships at Peabody College of Vanderbilt University. Before coming to Vanderbilt, he was a faculty member and program director at Cornell University for twelve years, where he taught fieldwork preparation and field study courses and was instrumental in the establishment of the university's Public Service Center.

Giles's scholarly interests include volunteerism, service-learning, and experiential learning. In addition to the FIPSE and CNS projects described above, he and Janet Eyler have published a number of articles and chapters on service-learning. Giles is also a coauthor of *Service-Learning: A Movement's Pioneers Reflect on Its Origins, Practice, and Future* (Jossey-Bass, 1999).

Giles has served as a national and international consultant in experiential learning and service-learning for colleges and universities, foundations, and professional societies. He served on the board of the National Society for Experiential Education and chaired the research committee for five years. He is a member of the academic advisory board of the Institute for Experiential Learning in Washington, D.C., and serves as the North American academic consultant for UK Centres for Experiential Learning. He co-organized the national Wingspread conference in 1991 to develop a research agenda for service-learning and is currently part of the Campus Compact working group on developing a national strategy for service-learning research.

Where's the Learning in Service-Learning?

Identifying the Learning
Outcomes of Service

*I can honestly say that I've learned more in this last
year in [service-learning] than I probably have learned
in all four years of college. I have learned so much,
maybe because I found something that I'm really passionate about, and it makes you care more to learn
about it—and to get involved and do more. You're
not just studying to take a test and forget about it.
You're learning, and the experiences we have are
staying with us. It's not cram for a test the night
before. I know when I take a test that I just want to
get it over with. That doesn't happen with service; it
stays with you.*

*We learn these theories in school and ideas, but until
we really apply them or see them in action, they're
not real. And we come out of school, if we haven't
done something like this, not understanding.*

Students like service-learning. When we sit down with a group
of students to discuss service-learning experiences, their enthusiasm is unmistakable. Although skeptics sometimes dismiss the programs that evoke this student excitement as "fluffy, feel-good stuff"
without "one iota of scientific research that says that this has made

a difference in a student's education" (Markus, Howard, and King, 1993, p. 411), the students clearly do not agree. These discussions come back again and again to how much they learned through this experience. And when they talk about their learning, it is clear that they believe that what they gain from service-learning differs qualitatively from what they often derive from more traditional instruction. As the opening quotations reflect, these students value the connection of their passion to their learning; when the personal and intellectual are connected, they can go beyond cramming for tests to acquiring information that has meaning to them and stays with them. Because they are learning and applying information in complex real-world contexts, they believe that the quality of their understanding is increased.

Student enthusiasm and accompanying faculty belief in the power of service to enhance learning have helped to create a surge of interest in service-learning opportunities on campuses. Several factors have bolstered this interest. Recent findings about learning published by cognitive scientists call for practices remarkably similar to those embodied in service-learning (Bransford, 1993; Resnick, 1987b). The goals and practices of service-learning also address criticisms of the passive, compartmentalized nature of much of the instruction in higher education.

Although the goals and processes of service-learning have been a good fit for addressing current concerns about higher education, "some critics of 'service learning' question the quality of the service and rigor of the learning" (Gose, 1997, p. A45). For these programs to be integrated into the curricula in colleges and universities, key stakeholders, including academic deans and faculty, need to join students in being convinced of their academic worth. Indeed any academic innovation ultimately must face the test of its impact on the central academic mission of higher education (Zlotkowski, 1996). Before we can understand the academic value of service-learning programs, we need a clear idea of what learning might be expected from this approach and the extent to which these outcomes are consistent with the goals of higher education. This book responds to the concerns for evidence of the academic value of service-learning.

This chapter explores the growing popularity of service-learning, the fit between service-learning and the mission of higher education, and the nature of the learning in service-learning. Our view of this learning is broader than the notion of academic learning as a relatively passive acquisition of information. The remaining chapters of the book focus on exploring these learning outcomes in greater detail and examining the impact of different characteristics of service-learning on student outcomes.

What Is Service-Learning?

A lot of energy has been devoted to defining service-learning. In 1990 Jane Kendall wrote that there were 147 definitions in the literature, and there has been no falling away of interest in this endeavor since. We have observed dozens of programs and have been impressed by the diversity of what is labeled service-learning. Schools that have a fall orientation activity with an afternoon of community service may call it service-learning; at the other extreme, there are well-integrated programs within colleges and universities where students spend a year or two in a connected series of courses linked to service projects in the community. In between these one-shot efforts and intensive programs are individual courses that include a service component. These also vary dramatically. Commonly students may elect a service option as extra credit or in lieu of another assignment, and these options are often not incorporated into class discussion in any sustained way. Less often single courses may be built around community service, and reflection on this experience is central to the progress of the course.

Sigmon (1996) described this diversity in service-learning by playing with the graphic presentation of the two concepts that make up the term (see Table 1.1). A course like the community

service lab we observed where students hear a bit about community
agencies but that is primarily focused on getting them into the field
to provide service fits his description of "SERVICE-learning," as do
volunteer service programs with occasional opportunities for reflection. The course where students studying juvenile justice primarily
observed community groups looks more like "service-LEARNING";
there are many courses with limited service, which adds a dimension to an academic experience without being a significant part of
the course. Volunteer programs within colleges and universities that
may have no link to particular academic pursuits but exist alongside the curriculum fit the "service learning" model; service projects
may capture student enthusiasm and interest, but the students are
left to make academic connections themselves. The class in which
students learn to develop program evaluation skills by assisting a
local agency with their evaluation fits Sigmon's "SERVICE-
LEARNING" category; this term applies to programs where the two
foci are in balance, and study and action are explicitly integrated.

In our own practice, we have embraced the position that service-learning should include a balance between service to the community and academic learning and that the hyphen in the phrase
symbolizes the central role of reflection in the process of learning
through community experience. And indeed there is a considerable
best-practices literature of practitioner wisdom that stresses the
importance of reflection as the vital link between service and learning (Honnet and Poulsen, 1989). Many programs do not fit this balanced model; instead the service may dwarf the learning, or the
academic focus dominates. Complicating matters is the evidence
that the quality and quantity of reflection in program descriptions
may not reflect the actual experiences of students; it is not uncommon to find students reporting far less systematic reflection and integration of their service and learning than program directors or
brochures detail.

Given the diversity and complexity of practice, we were not
inclined to use a tight definition to exclude programs that view

Table 1.1. A Service and Learning Typology.

service-LEARNING	Learning goals primary; service outcomes secondary
SERVICE-learning	Service outcomes primary; learning goals secondary
service learning	Service and learning goals separate
SERVICE-LEARNING	Service and learning goals of equal weight; each enhances the other for all participants

Source: Sigmon (1996).

themselves as service-learning efforts from our research studies. It is quite reasonable to suppose that programs with different structures might be effective in their own way at meeting particular academic goals. Although we are interested in an optimal mix of the service and learning, we were not interested in using definitions to drive our understanding. Part of the focus of our research was to explore the various academic outcomes of service-learning and try to identify the types of experience most likely to lead to particular outcomes. Thus we accept that any program that attempts to link academic study with service can be characterized as service-learning; non-course-based programs that include a reflective component and learning goals may also be included under this broad umbrella. Not all service-learning efforts may help students attain all the goals practitioners hope for, but discovering which practices are important to particular outcomes is central to our efforts here.

The Popularity of Service-Learning

All evidence points to a rapid increase in service-learning courses and programs on college and university campuses over the past decade. This pedagogy is now advocated by "students, faculty, presidents of colleges and universities, and even by Congress and the President of the United States" (Stanton, Giles, and Cruz, 1999).

Two major national organizations encourage and support service-learning. Campus Compact, a coalition of college and university presidents, and the Corporation for National Service, a federal government agency, report data that give some indicators of the popularity of service-learning. There are now 575 member campuses participating in Campus Compact, with estimates that about 10,800 faculty members were involved in teaching 11,800 service-learning courses in the most recent survey of members (Campus Compact, 1998). Ninety-six percent of responding institutions reported some faculty involvement, with an average of 8 percent per campus. About 14 percent of schools have what Campus Compact considers advanced levels of faculty involvement—30 percent or more. The average number of courses per campus for member schools is sixteen. In 1994 only 50 percent of campuses reported some form of support for faculty using service-learning; by 1998 fully 85 percent reported one or more forms of support for faculty involvement.

The Rand evaluation of the Corporation for National Service's Learn and Serve Higher Education (LASHE) programs studied the 458 colleges and universities that received LASHE grants. During the three-year period of the evaluation, fiscal years 1995–1997, these schools developed about three thousand new service-learning courses (Gray and others, 1998). In fiscal 1997 these courses served a median number of sixty students per program.

In addition to these suggestive campus statistics, there are many national indicators of the popularity of these programs. Recently a colleague called us with some information that surprised her. She discovered that a recent conference on accounting education had a whole section of sessions in service-learning. The number of publications in the field, both articles and books, has risen from almost none a decade ago to hundreds. The field now has a journal with the inception in 1994 of the *Michigan Journal of Community Service Learning,* and a number of professional associations have begun to incorporate service-learning into annual conferences and publications. For example, the American Association for Higher Education (AAHE) has made service-learning a major focus of conferences and, most important, has issued a series of eighteen monographs that presents models, research, theory, and actual syllabi for service-learning in particular disciplines.

With all this growth there is still the concern that service-learning is marginal to the academic core of the academy (Zlotkowski, 1996). Historically service-oriented instructional programs have had a rough time maintaining institutional support. In order for the emphasis on service-learning to be sustained on college campuses, presidents, deans, and faculty need to be convinced that it is an effective process for achieving the most valued academic goals of higher education.

The Importance of Service-Learning

The recent popularity of service-learning stems partly from its fit with current views of the way people learn best and the changes needed to make higher education more effective. We believe that the clearest and easiest way to understand the nature of service-learning is to highlight what we like to call the central claim of the field: "Service, combined with learning, adds value to each and transforms both" (Honnet and Poulsen, 1989, p. 1). The question for research such as ours is this: exactly what is enhanced and transformed, and how does that occur? Even a cursory review of the service-learning literature reveals some key themes that suggest the breadth of the learning that occurs and the importance of this learning to improved community participation.

Learning from Experience

Service-learning is a form of experiential education whose pedagogy rests on principles established by Dewey and other experiential learning theorists early in this century (Furco, 1996). Learning occurs through a cycle of action and reflection, not simply through being able to recount what has been learned through reading and lecture. Dewey would have agreed with the students whose words begin the chapter that memorizing material from the classroom for reproduction on tests is static and unlikely to be of much use. Knowing and doing cannot be severed. And like these students, Dewey was convinced that learning is a wholehearted affair, linking emotions and intellect; an educative experience is one that fosters student development by capturing student interest—indeed their passion—because it is intrinsically worthwhile and deals with problems that awaken student curiosity and a need to know that extends over a considerable period of time (Giles and Eyler, 1994b). Experience enhances understanding; understanding leads to more effective action. Both learning and service gain value and are transformed when combined in the specific types of activities we call service-learning.

Recently cognitive scientists have come to a series of conclusions about students' learning that are remarkably similar to those long endorsed by scholars and practitioners in the experiential learning tradition. Their focus has been on what Whitehead (1929) first characterized as the inert knowledge problem: the tendency of students to acquire stores of knowledge that are quite useless to them when they are in new situations. Cognitive scientists found that students rarely transferred knowledge and principles learned in classroom instruction to new problems; even students who had been presented with information about solving a problem directly analogous to a new problem often failed to apply it (Bransford, 1993). Only repeated attempts to solve similar problems and support and encouragement to apply what was learned seemed to lead to application. Cognitive scientists, like experiential educators, recognize the barriers presented to developing "knowledge in use" (Schön, 1995) by the decontextualized nature of much classroom instruction and stress the importance of learning in complex contexts and the "active construction of knowledge" (Bransford and Vye, 1989, p. 169).

Lauren Resnick (1987b) described the defects of much classroom learning clearly in her 1987 presidential address before the American Educational Research Association. She contrasted the nature of learning in school and in the community where this learning will be applied, noting that unlike typical classroom learning, real-world learning tends to be more cooperative or communal than individualistic, involves using tools rather than pure thought, is accomplished by addressing genuine problems in complex settings rather than problems in isolation, and involves specific contextualized rather than abstract or generalized knowledge. College learning that more closely approximates the situation in which students will use their knowledge and continue to learn is less likely to be useless or inert.

A colleague of ours worked with a team of students in her class to help find housing and a job for a homeless man in the community. For those students, potentially abstract concepts about economics, sociology, and psychology become vividly concrete as they struggled with the realities of working with social agencies, learned firsthand the difficulties of locating affordable housing near transportation and job opportunities, and dealt with the complex problems faced by and presented by a homeless person. A real person facing real difficulties in an authentic context forces students to a level of understanding that is sometimes not obtained when they read and glibly summarize what they have read about a complex social issue. Service-learning offers students the opportunity to experience the type of learning Resnick described where they can work with others through a process of acting and reflecting to achieve real objectives for the community and deeper understanding and skills for themselves.

A Connected View of Learning

Another central element of service-learning is to link personal and interpersonal development with academic and cognitive development. This linking of head and heart is a holistic approach involving values as well as ideas. One of the goals of service-learning is to connect the multiple dimensions of human development that are often separated on college and university campuses. As Perry (1970) has demonstrated, personal and intellectual development are integral to each other; the development of personal identity and the ability to make committed decisions are connected to advanced levels of thinking. These connections occur within both the learner and the institution. Few efforts in higher education involve the chaplain's office, student affairs, and members of the faculty as service-learning often does. Cognitive as well as personal development occurs through a process of challenge that touches feelings as well as thought (Fischer and Bidell, 1997). Service-learning is also about leadership development as well as traditional information and skill acquisition or "learning to be effective while learning what to be effective about" (Stanton, 1990, p. 336).

When we interviewed students about the reflection practices most useful to them in service-learning, the importance of this connection between the affective and cognitive was apparent. Many of the reflection techniques that students reported clearly combined the personal and the intellectual. These reflection exercises often asked students to reflect on their values and suggest what implications the learning had for action as well as for illuminating the subject matter being studied. For example, a student working with incarcerated juveniles talked about the reflection process used to structure class discussion: "There's three stages to it. The first one was the person's observations...not your feelings about it.... It was difficult, but I think it was necessary to just split that apart because so commonly people put those two together—what they observed and their feelings and come up with something in the middle. And to separate them is difficult, but it aids in introspection and understanding...the last step was an analysis of the experience and how it applied to something" (Eyler, Giles, and Schmiede, 1996).

Social Problem Solving

One of the major forms of service-learning practice from its beginnings has focused not only on learning about social problems, but on addressing them in the community through social action (Stanton, Giles, and Cruz, 1999). One way in which community and classroom are connected is through community action research. In these action research projects students, faculty, and community members take a community problem or issue and attempt to generate data that the community can use (Giles and Freed, 1985; Reardon, 1994, 1997). Students we interviewed gave such examples as conducting a needs assessment for a community attempting to create an after-school care program, providing research for an advocacy group helping legislators draft a bill on homelessness, and helping a community partner research and write a funding proposal. Because the learning was organized around genuine community problems, this action research process has also fostered an interdisciplinary approach to learning. Students developed their inquiry skills and knowledge about the issues under study while also providing needed research support for community groups; learning thus enhanced service to community.

One of the arguments for action research projects as a form of social inquiry is that they link education to citizenship; students function as contributing citizens during the process of study while acquiring skills and knowledge that equip them for later civic participation (Giles and Eyler, 1994b). This approach, which had its inception earlier in the century as part of progressive education, is being advocated today as a way to link the university to democratic citizenship by those who see inquiry not as an arcane occupation for an elite few but as integral to both intellectual development and community action. Service-learning offers the chance of both "researching for democracy and democratizing research" (Ansley and Gaventa, 1997, p. 46). Problem-based learning linked with service-learning and cooperative learning forms an effective set of methods to educate for civic responsibility (Ehrlich, 1997).

Education for Citizenship

Citizenship is often cited as the purpose of education in general and service-learning in particular, and the focus on citizenship as an outcome is closely tied to the process of social problem solving (Ehrlich, 1997). It is in discussions of the role of higher education in preparing students for citizenship that the fit between the concerns of service-learning leaders and those concerned with higher education reform is most obvious. Service-learning advocates like Stanton have noted that "service-based learning is the means for linking the initiative to develop students' social responsibility with the efforts to improve undergraduate education" (1990, p. 186). Higher education reform advocates have come to a similar conclusion, often singling out service or service-learning as examples of how to cultivate civic and social responsibility as part of education for citizenship (Gabelnick, 1997). One of the key proponents of this linkage has been Benjamin Barber, director of the Walt Whitman Center for the Culture and Politics of Democracy at Rutgers University, who has called for civic education that is mandatory and is linked to a community service component (Barber, 1990, 1992; Barber and Battistoni, 1994).

Service-Learning and the Critique of Higher Education

The nature of experiential education in general and service-learning in particular makes it a good fit in addressing some of the concerns raised about higher education in a series of critiques that appeared in the 1980s and 1990s (Boyer, 1987; Association of American Colleges, 1991). These critiques noted a gap between traditional curricular content and society's needs for new competencies for workers and citizens. A common observation was the lack of connectedness in higher education and the related lack of application of what is learned. Lack of connectedness resulted in the compartmentalization of knowledge by discipline, preventing students from experiencing the relationships among various modes of knowledge; subject matter was walled off behind disciplinary borders and not applied in any integrated way in academic study or to social issues. Students also experienced a lack of connection between classroom learning and their personal lives and between classroom learning and public issues and involvement in the wider world. Critics faulted the lack of intellectual links between institutions, noting barriers to connection between secondary and postsecondary education, between college study and the workplace, and between campus and community (Boyer, 1987; Association of American Colleges, 1991).

Service-learning is an obvious response to the reform critics of higher education. The emphasis in service-learning on applying knowledge to community problems and the reciprocal application of community experience to the development of knowledge meets many of the concerns about the lack of connectedness in higher education. Partly in response to these concerns, service-learning programs sprang up without the benefit of a research base or systematic attempts at evaluation. Founded and developed by bright and passionate students, enthusiastic faculty, and community-oriented student services staffs, these programs have flourished but have not become well connected to the academic core of most institutions that house them.

It is no surprise that such programs often come under fire from skeptics who question their educational value. Perhaps because there have been no systematic efforts to establish conditions under which service-learning is most effective and because most of the assessment of academic outcomes has been limited to course grades or student self-report, the research that has focused on academic benefits of service-learning has had mixed results; although students do not learn less by these measures in service-learning classrooms, it is not clear that they learn more (Markus, Howard, and King, 1993; Miller, 1994; Kendrick, 1996; Gray and others, 1998).

Clearly the theories of experiential education on which service-learning rests and the problems identified in recent criticisms of higher education suggest learning outcomes that are far more complex and important than simple acquisition of information to be displayed on end-of-semester tests. Thus the answer to the question, "Where is the learning in service-learning?" may depend to some extent on what it means to learn more. Is the "learning" celebrated by service-learning students important to adequate mastery of the academic goals of a liberal education? In our research studies, we have been concerned with this need to work within a broader conception of academic learning, to identify the range of outcomes important to academic achievement and the conditions under which service-learning may contribute to these diverse outcomes.

What is the Learning in Service-Learning?

As we have explored the impact of service-learning, we have tried to identify the academic benefits that could be reasonably expected from an emphasis on active, connected learning. Service-learning aims to connect the personal and intellectual, to help students acquire knowledge that is useful in understanding the world, build critical thinking capacities, and perhaps lead to fundamental questions about learning and about society and to a commitment to improve both. Service-learning aims to prepare students who are lifelong learners and participants in the world. It is this broader conception of learning outcomes that has driven our studies of the impact of service-learning.

Learning Begins with Personal Connections

The emphasis on helping students become self-directed lifelong learners has become more pronounced in higher education as theories of development have taken on more importance since the pioneering work of William Perry (1970). Although personal development and interpersonal skills are often viewed as secondary to the academic goals of the academy and segregated institutionally into student services and activities, they are where learning begins for service-learning advocates. Passion is personal, and learning begins with passionate interest (Fischer and Bidell, 1997). For many students their first strong interest in service-learning projects develops when they get to know someone whose life differs dramatically from their own. This early constructive engagement with others is commonly found in those who go on to incorporate community service into their lives (Daloz Parks, Keen, Keen, and Parks Daloz, 1996). And the interpersonal skills developed during service are learning outcomes that will be integral to the learning they are likely to do in their future work and community settings. As Lee Shulman (1998), president of the Carnegie Foundation for the Advancement of Teaching, noted in his keynote speech at the American Association for Higher Education, "Learning is the least useful when it is private; it is most useful when it is public and communal."

One of our concerns with the learning in service-learning is in measuring personal attitudes and values, feelings of connectedness and commitment to the community and interpersonal skills. These contribute to personal growth, but they are also tied to further academic learning.

Learning Is Useful

Academic learning is often assessed through test performance or course grades, but understanding is more than the ability to recall information when prompted by a test; understanding is the ability to call it up when it is relevant to a new situation and use it in that situation. Material that is understood has meaning for learners; it helps them make sense of the world. Learning in context and appreciating what the learner brings to the situation are fundamental to experiential education; attention to these two elements helps students master content and skills and makes it possible to use the information effectively. Building a more adequate view of the world does not happen automatically with exposure to new information; it is the product of continuous challenge to old conceptions and reflection on new ways to organize information and use the new material (Bransford and Vye, 1989; Bransford, 1993). Service-learning can provide the rich context in which to resolve challenges to old conceptions and apply new information and skills. Understanding cannot be severed from active use of information; reflective instruction that encourages students to question preconceptions and adjust the way they think about the subject should facilitate more complex understanding.

The purpose of learning is to use what is learned. In order to test adequately for understanding, we need to see how students identify and describe complex problems and how they marshal skills and knowledge in offering tentative solutions to those problems. We are also interested in their practical strategies for addressing those problems within the community—understanding that will be deepened by their interpersonal skills as well as their knowledge of the issues and the community.

Learning Is Developmental

The very nature of the ill-structured problems we face routinely in a complex information-based postindustrial society requires critical thinking capacities above those normally attained by American college students (King, 1992). Ill-structured problems are complex and open ended; their solution creates new conditions and new problems. Such problems require, first and foremost, the ability to recognize that the problems are complicated and are embedded in a complex social context, the ability to evaluate conflicting information and expert views, and the understanding that there is no simple or definitive solution. Critical thinking and problem solving are not simply skills to be acquired through practice; rather they rest on attaining advanced levels of cognitive development (King, 1992). Traditional academic programs, however, have not resulted in moving most college students to the levels necessary to cope with complex issues and information (King and Kitchener, 1994).

Service-learning programs that place students in contexts where their prejudices, previous experiences, and assumptions about the world are challenged may create the circumstances necessary for growth. Service-learning programs that create this cognitive dissonance and also provide the structure in which to confront the challenge and seek further information and experience to help students sort it out provide conditions consistent with what is known about improved cognitive development and problem solving (King and Kitchener, 1994; Lynch, 1996; Perry, 1970). Critical thinking ability is another important academic outcome of higher education that may be affected by service-learning.

Learning Is Transforming

Understanding and application might be likened to coloring within the lines; critical thinking helps students question assumptions— to color outside the lines; transformative learning is about thinking about things in a new way and moving in new directions—creating a new picture without relying on the old lines. Community experiences that challenge student assumptions coupled with thoughtful reflection may lead to fundamental changes in the way the student views service or society. David Lempert (1995) in his book *Escape from the Ivory Tower* gives a powerful example of such a transformative moment in his own experience with community service. While working on a project in the Philippines, he came to see that even doing a good job in the community project was helping to prop up a regime that he deemed responsible for the conditions his work was designed to ameliorate. More fundamental changes in the system were needed to achieve social justice.

Others have suggested that this movement from immediate service to a desire to create broader systemic change is also a characteristic of individual student development. As students mature in their service experience, they tend to move from a focus on charitable activities to a concern for social justice (Delve, Mintz, and Stewart, 1990). With their first exposure to poverty, students may tend to see the issues in terms of individual failings or misfortunes—to blame the victim. With more experience, information, and thought, some begin to see the complexity of factors surrounding these problems. We would not expect all, or even most, students to have experiences powerful enough to transform, but where programs engage students in important work in the community and provide continuous opportunities for reflection, service-learning may be a catalyst for a dramatic redirection of their lives.

Citizenship Rests on Learning

While citizenship, like personal development, is often considered to be an affective or behavioral rather than cognitive goal of higher education, we are persuaded that effective citizenship rests on the learning we have touched on. Thus we have focused our empirical inquiry on understanding the cognitive dimensions of citizenship. Students are unlikely to be effective community participants without the ability to understand complex social issues, apply what they learn, and have the critical thinking ability to make adequate judgments about the information they receive. The linkage between academic outcomes necessary for good citizenship and experiential pedagogies like service-learning was noted recently by Zelda Gamson (1997), editor of a special issue of *Change* titled "Higher Education and Rebuilding Civic Life." She identifies some of the ways to "devise ways of teaching and learning for civic life" as learning communities, collaborative learning, respect for different learning styles, reflective projects, and cooperation among students and between students and faculty. She argues that education for citizenship is basically good undergraduate education that follows the principles for good practice in that education (Chickering and Gamson, 1987).

Finding the Learning in Service-Learning

Our journey of inquiry has spanned six years and is best described by Donald Schön's characterization of the process of discovery where reflection occurs both in and on action and "proceeds from doubt to the resolution of doubt to the generation of new doubt" (1995, p. 31). At each stage we made discoveries about the learning in service-learning, and with each of these discoveries came doubts and new problems to solve. Indeed only publication deadlines have temporarily interrupted this journey. We take comfort that this is the process we and other practitioners of service-learning go though with our students when we confront the messy and ill-structured problems that exist in our communities. We hope that we have followed a model of inquiry for service-learning that respects the values of the field and generates the kind of useful knowledge that our service-learning students reported in their own journeys of inquiry.

In our work with students in the community, we have been continuously struck by the way in which the emotional power of service-learning helps students connect intellectually with what we were doing in the classroom. Indeed our own understanding, like that of our students, has been transformed by community involvement. For many years before we began the two major studies that provide much of the data for this book, we conducted small research studies with internship and service-learning classes in an effort to understand and improve our instruction. The results of these small studies with our own students were encouraging, but we felt that the questions being asked of this field—by both skeptics and believers—demanded a national study reflecting diverse institutions and communities. In 1993 we sought funding from the Fund for the Improvement of Postsecondary Education (FIPSE) for the

Comparing Models of Service-Learning project, which would eventually fund a survey of fifteen hundred college students from over twenty institutions across the United States, as well as a later round of intensive problem-solving interviews with sixty-six students from seven institutions. In both the survey and the interviews, students responded at the start and again at the end of a semester of service-learning. In a second project for the Corporation for National Service (CNS), we conducted single interviews with sixty-seven students from six colleges and universities who were active in service-learning and community service. These students shared their perceptions of the benefits of service and discussed the types of reflective activity that worked best for them. In many of these efforts we were inspired by the pioneering work of Conrad and Hedin (1980), who attempted to measure the impact of varied experiential programs on high school students across the country. No similar national study had been attempted with college students prior to the studies reported here.

Before beginning our larger efforts, we conducted a series of focus groups with a benchmark group of very active service-oriented students at several institutions to help us identify learning outcomes that should be pursued. The views of these students were consistent with our own earlier experience that in addition to personal and social development, service-learning enhanced student learning. These students also made clear the different quality of the learning that resulted from service-learning compared to more traditional methods. With this set of outcomes in mind, we conducted a series of pilot surveys in 1994 to select and develop measurement instruments, attempting to build on efforts underway in the field. During the spring of 1995, we surveyed fifteen hundred students at the beginning and end of a semester where eleven hundred of them were involved in service-learning.

We recognized the limits of a survey for assessing cognitive development and academic learning and attempted to measure problem solving through an essay as well. Expecting students to draft thoughtful essays twice in a semester in the context of completing a somewhat extensive survey questionnaire proved unrealistic, however. This was particularly a problem at the end of the semester, when faculty were rushed for time too; thus we had a high number of incomplete or unscorable essays. As a response to this problem, we developed an intensive problem-solving interview where students spoke with us for about an hour about how they would address a social problem related to their service. Each of the sixty-six students completed two of these interviews, once at the beginning and then at the end of the semester. These interviews were designed to explore their service experience, how they analyze a problem, and, in the context of that problem, how they justify a position and use information. Because we talked with them twice, before and after their service, we could trace the impact of service-learning on changes in their reasoning process. Material from these interviews provided us with insights into issue understanding, application of information, perspective transformation, and critical thinking ability. It also provided insights into whether the outcomes identified earlier in this chapter were influenced by service-learning or the reflective quality of particular service-learning experiences. During the same period as the original survey, we also conducted the reflection interviews for the CNS project. As we heard students describe their views of effective service-learning, we were able to shape some of the questions for the subsequent problem-solving interviews. Thus the inquiry process explored these questions about learning using both quantitative and qualitative methodologies.

In this book we have combined the quantitative pre- and postsemester survey data, the analysis of problem solving and critical thinking from the pre- and postsemester interviews, and the views expressed in our reflection interviews, which were based on a single session with different students. When we talk about these different sets of student responses, we will refer to them as the survey, the problem-solving interviews, and the reflection interviews. A number of our statistical findings are also illustrated with quotations from the students in our two sets of interviews. We believe that this combination of statistical data and student voice provides some useful insights into this complex and wonderful business of service-learning. In the following chapters we share the questions we raised at different stages of this journey of inquiry and the answers we found. All findings presented are statistically significant at at least the .05 level; the statistical material is located in regression tables in the resource sections at the back of the book. A list of the schools that participated in the studies can be found in Resource A, and a more complete discussion of the methodology of the studies is available in Resource B.

We are convinced that learning begins with the impact of service-learning on the personal and interpersonal development of the students who participated in the study, the subject of Chapter Two. Subsequent chapters detail the nature of the different learning outcomes briefly introduced in this chapter and present data about the impact of service-learning on those outcomes. Finally we examine the program characteristics that seemed to make a difference on these important outcomes and discuss implications for practice.

2

Personal and Interpersonal Development

*I suppose I've learned about real life. That's the only
way I can put it. I've encountered people that I never
would have met if I hadn't been a volunteer. I've had
to deal with situations that I would never have been
confronted with if I hadn't been a volunteer. I've been
able to forge friendships with people that I never
would have met.*

One of the facets of service-learning classes that excites students
is the quality of the interpersonal experiences that occur in
the community compared with their usual classroom work. These
diverse interpersonal experiences may help to prepare students to
meet some of the goals of higher education where we currently often
fall short. Thomas Ehrlich noted that when he was president
of Indiana University, "the most frequent criticism... from both
community leaders and employers, was that our graduates were
unprepared to collaborate as members of a team. While most of the
tasks they would be called on to perform in their communities and
workplaces would be as team members, most of their undergraduate
work had been done alone" (Ehrlich, 1997). Service-learning, which
involves different roles for students from those typically encountered
in the classroom, seems like a natural fit for achieving such
goals of higher education as interpersonal competence, personal

development, and increased experience with and tolerance for diversity. Although they are sometimes not seen as the focus of the academic enterprise, these skills and abilities are among those particularly valued in the communities and workplaces where students will spend their future.

Personal and interpersonal development and diversity are higher education goals in and of themselves, but the interpersonal experiences that aid this development are also good pedagogy for attaining other goals, such as the mastery of academic subject matter, critical thinking, and development of citizenship skills and attitudes. In this chapter, our primary focus is on the personal and interpersonal outcomes of service-learning; later chapters will address how service-learning affects academic learning and citizenship. Here we look first at the impact of service-learning on the ability of students to see their common humanity with people different from themselves. We then look at the impact of service-learning on personal and interpersonal development of students and then on its role in helping students to feel connected to community and college. We also discuss some of the ways in which service-learning provides a different context for this personal growth and learning compared to more traditional instruction. Regression tables related to the impact of service-learning are in Resource D; tables related to the impact of program quality are in Resource E.

Identifying Personal and Interpersonal Outcomes

When we looked at our collection of small preliminary studies, our focus groups and interview studies with college students from service-learning programs on campuses across the county, and our survey of fifteen hundred college students who responded before and after a semester of service, one of the things that jumped out at us was that almost irrespective of the type, intensity, or quality of the service or service-learning experience, students report that involvement in community service has a powerful impact on how they see themselves and others. "Meeting people I never would have met" is consistently something students claim as a catalyst for their growth and change. Students often bubble over with stories about the homeless man they helped with dinner, the little girl they watched overcome her shyness during the course of a semester of tutoring, the person living with HIV who taught them the intricacies of obtaining medical care in a complicated system. Learning often begins with a very personal connection to another.

We looked at open-ended student responses to the question, "What did you learn from service-learning?" and created a list of items to which students in the survey could respond. Of the twelve themes that emerged, six related to personal and interpersonal outcomes:

- "I learned the people I served are like me."

- "I learned to appreciate other cultures."

- "I learned to understand myself better."

- "I learned spiritual growth."

- "I learned how rewarding it is to help others."

- "I learned how to work with others effectively."

The other six related to academic learning and are discussed in Chapters Three and Six. Students responded to the items at the end of their service-learning semester.

We also measured several elements of personal or interpersonal development at the start and end of the semester: tolerance, personal efficacy, leadership skill, communication skill, feeling connected to the community, and valuing a career helping others. We sought to trace growth and perhaps tie it to differences in the characteristics of service-learning programs.

Service-Learning and Diversity

The appreciation of different cultures and the reduction of stereotyping is perhaps a first step in the process by which service-learning brings about personal and interpersonal development. As the student in our opening quotation noted, service-learning can provide opportunities for getting to know people one might ordinarily not know. Among our surveyed students who participated in service-learning, 63 percent reported interacting with those receiving services at least fairly often, 60 percent reported frequent interaction with other volunteers, 51 percent felt that professionals at the placement site often took an interest in them, and 57 percent reported that they had frequent chances to work with people from ethnic groups other than their own. Most service-learning students experience the chance to work with a variety of others in the community, and frequently this is the first opportunity they have to work alongside someone quite different from themselves. These experiences may contribute to the impact that service-learning has on reducing stereotypes and increasing tolerance of and appreciation for other cultures.

Achieving the Goals of Diversity

At the heart of the diversity movement in higher education has been the assumption that when people work with those who are different from themselves, the personal friendships that are created will lead to other positive gains for people and communities. Although many would like to take it beyond better human relations to more fundamental changes in college and society, these personal relationships are where the process begins (Rhoads, 1998). As we see in examples throughout this book, a nearly universal outcome of service-learning is the creation of positive interactions. Many of these connections are built while trying to achieve a common objective, but sometimes they are simple moments where two lives touch in ways that are not purposive, but allow for an emotional connection. A sociology student assisting an elderly woman spoke about such a moment: "I take this lady to the store all the time, and first it's kind of like regular chitchat, and then one time she went to the bakery to get some bread, and she came back with these eclairs. And we just sat and talked. And it's like we've become more personalized—more like friends. I wasn't doing it for any reason, but now I was doing it for her. Not that we ever weren't nice, but we just got a little closer. [It was] not the food but the gesture." A simple sharing of food moved this service project from a dutiful to a personal relationship.

We may underestimate how compartmentalized life on campus can be and how informal segregation limits student interaction. The fact that a campus includes a diverse student body may not mean that the individual students experience diversity. Students who takes notes in class, spend most of their time socializing with their own circle of friends, and sit in de facto segregated cafeterias may rarely be involved in any serious discussion with students from other backgrounds or with other interests. Even traditional classes that include students from diverse backgrounds may not afford much opportunity for real connection. Levine and Cureton (1998) noted that only work on compelling common projects seemed to break down the ethnic segregation on campuses; they found this bond in athletic teams and among theater students. Certainly service-learning projects offer similar potential. A student who participated in a multisemester service-learning project with the homeless in Boston commented about the role of service-learning in breaking down these barriers: "It was great because whenever you go into a new school, you wonder what people think about what you are doing. And here, in this class, we had people who were in sororities, fraternities, athletes, people that were really into academics. But for once a week, every week for two years, we all got together and went to the homeless shelter—which is great because you have people that are from all over: California, Boston, Montana, Maine. All had different perspectives, all had different experiences, and we brought it together and got to come together every week and deal with that."

Because this experience was part of a class, there was the added interaction and reflection around the substantive issues raised by the experience: "We would end up driving there talking about what's going to happen, and then coming back, we're all having our own focus group every week or reflection groups every week just for ourselves."

These interactions may break down stereotypes because they provide students with the opportunity to have genuine, informal contact with others on a sustained basis. Not all the learning that goes on is directly related to the project or the subject matter of the class. One student told us about working with a teammate on a rural project. They began to discuss something that had often bothered her in her own schooling and is a perennial topic in diversity programs: the informal racial segregation that occurs in classrooms and lunchrooms in high schools and on campus. Her teammate, "a very strong black activist, was talking about how he sees that it's necessary; for him actually to empower the black community is what his goal is. Segregation is necessary until equality can be attained." She had assumed that she had a wise nonracist position on this matter and was surprised by his point of view: "It's not a view that I had ever listened to. I mean, I can understand the good intentions, but I have always seen that it was evil that we divided up, and if I was ever a teacher—which is what I was thinking about a lot during the summer—that's something that I would want to discourage. And here he was talking about how that's necessary in terms of comfort levels and all this."

When racial issues are discussed in the classroom, the debate is often contentious, with students feeling forced to defend their initial positions or suppress their real feelings; informal conversations between people who are working together may allow a connection that breaks down the typical defensiveness that often attends such discussions. For this student, the conversation led her to some insights about herself: "It was the first time that I had really heard that. And I don't know why. It was only a half-hour debate, but when we pulled in, I wasn't thinking about Peabody Coal, I was just thinking about how I can really see somebody's other side. And even though I still have problems with this, I can really listen, and that was just a big thing. I don't know why, but that always sticks in my mind." So for a student working on an environmental project in an area that had been strip-mined, one of the most memorable learning experiences came from informal discussions with a peer about other personal issues.

These opportunities to work together may also lead to personal friendships that are sustained beyond the service-learning experience. One student noted, "I met a lot of different people from other cultures—like my roommate now is Indian, and I met him through a service project. That's just kind of coincidental." Ultimately it is these close personal connections that have the power to break down stereotypes and build appreciation for the many insights to be gained as a result of cultural diversity.

Service-Learning Reduces Negative Stereotypes

Several of the outcome measures addressed the sense of personal connection with diverse others.

Stereotypes

One of the most consistent outcomes of service-learning is in the reduction of negative stereotypes and the increase in tolerance for diversity. Even in service experiences of limited duration and without much opportunity for reflection, students report, often with surprise, that the people they worked with were very different from their expectations. In our pilot study of fifty-seven freshmen who spent three hours a week working in local service agencies as part of a required community service course, 75 percent wrote more positive descriptions of the people they worked with after their service, 21 percent continued their previously positive view, and a scant 3.5 percent had more negative assessments (Giles and Eyler, 1994a). One student wrote that she had expected the children she worked with to be "very bad children who didn't want to accomplish anything except to be thugs." She came to see them as "intelligent and kind, and I made some great friends when I got to know them personally and stop stereotyping."

Students in our interview studies also commented frequently on the impact of their service-learning on stereotyping. A common stereotype about poor people was that they would be uncaring parents. One student talked about her initial negative expectation of the single mothers she planned to work with: "My crudest impression would have been, 'Why didn't you use birth control?' I expected them to have a negative attitude toward their children, to blame them for the position in life that they now hold. They can't do anything 'cause they have this responsibility, and life has been dealing them a bad hand." But these expectations quickly gave way to the realization that these mothers cared deeply for their youngsters: "It was the opposite. . . . They actually wanted to do everything with their children. The children encouraged them to get on their feet."

A student who participated in a policy class engaged in community service with AIDS outreach organizations was surprised to find that the first person she worked with conformed to none of her previous stereotypes about this disease: "I guess, I just thought, 'I'm going to be seeing someone who's maybe like a poor, gay man who is real skinny, someone who didn't have too much family.' Instead I saw a lady who was thirty-five years old. . . . Her husband had given it to her, and he was dead. He had been an IV drug user, and she was her parents' only child. She lived with them, and they were taking care of her, and they were about seventy years old. . . . You could tell it had just completely taken over their lives." Others in the same class worked with volunteers providing housekeeping assistance for people with AIDS; they assisted for several weeks before realizing that the people they were working alongside who were so much like themselves were gay. Finding our common humanity as well as our differences happens through these personal connections.

Finding That Others Are "Like Me"

Students commonly move from developing a more positive view of people they work with to a sense that these others "are like me." For example, in summing up what she has learned from service, a student said, "Knowing that people are people! Like when you read, 'oh, the Latino community, or the low-income community,' you're really setting yourself apart. When you're there, they're normal, just like you and me. . . . People are people, I think that is just the most fundamental thing that we just can't forget." In interview after interview, students shared their delight in the personal relationships they formed and their realization that "when I worked with these girls, I realized that they were just like me." Students in the survey agreed with this insight; when asked to identify important things they had learned from their service, 23 percent indicated that the realization that people they work with in the community "are like me" was among the most important, and 52 percent placed this as most or very important.

Appreciating Other Cultures

Greater appreciation of other cultures was also something many students felt they learned, with 33 percent indicating it was among the most important learning outcome and 68 percent either most or very important.

Developing Tolerance

We measured students' assessment of their tolerance at the beginning and end of the semester and compared changes in students who did and did not participate in service-learning. In each of the analyses in this book that predict change over the course of the semester, we controlled for such factors as age, family income, gender, minority status, closeness to college faculty, and other community service participation so that our results could not be the result of differences between the groups on these factors rather than the effect of service-learning. (The regression tables are provided in Resource D.) When we compared students who did and did not participate, we found that participation in service-learning had a significant positive impact on tolerance over the course of the semester. One student commented, "I've learned not to judge people. I think that is the most important thing that I've learned. I can only say that I did before. And now, working with people who are not as fortunate as I am, makes me realize that they're just the same as I am."

Program Quality Has an Impact on Stereotyping

Community service adds value, and well-designed service-learning adds even more value. When we analyzed the impact of different program characteristics within service-learning, we used a regression technique that controlled for age, gender, family income, minority group status, and other participation in community service. We wanted to see if particular program characteristics add value above and beyond these other factors so that the changes are not explained because, for example, there are more young women in the programs with more discussion or proportionately more minority group members who participate in other community service options.

The program characteristic scales created through factor analysis are made up of items that are highly correlated with each other. These program characteristics are the quality of the service placement, measures of academic linkage such as application, oral and written reflection, and experiences of diversity and community voice. (These items are included in Resource C. A more extensive discussion of program quality is included in Chapter Eight. Regression tables showing the impact of program characteristics can be found in Resource E.)

Impact of Placement Quality on Tolerance

A consistently important factor in the effectiveness of service-learning is the quality of the actual service experience. *Placement quality* refers to the extent that students in their community placements are challenged, are active rather than observers, do a variety of tasks, feel that they are making a positive contribution, have important levels of responsibility, and receive input and appreciation from supervisors in the field. Placement quality was a significant predictor of tolerance over the course of the semester and of reduced stereotyping, with students believing that the people they worked with in the community were "like me." A student who chose to assist at a shelter where she helped develop activities for homeless teenagers noted, "I think I have a lot more compassion [than nonservice peers]. In class, they're just statistics. So many people are homeless, so many people are being killed by gang warfare, blah, blah, blah. But if you're actually out there, it's not so many people; it's lots of human beings that you know, and you know their names and you know who they are."

Impact of Application on Tolerance

Application characterizes the extent to which the academic study is related to the nature of the service experience. These academic connections between service and learning also made a difference. Classes where the community service was tightly linked to the material being studied were most likely to produce students who valued the impact of the service-learning on appreciation of other cultures and on the sense that the people they worked with were "like me." Application was a predictor of both of these outcomes.

Impact of Reflection on Tolerance

Although the degree of application is an important link between service and learning, reflection is the next step in the link where explicit attempts are made to consider subject matter in the light of experience. The reflective activity of writing, including journal writing, also helped students see their common link to others. Writing was a predictor of believing that the people in the community were "like me." Although the experience of service itself has an impact, reflection adds power to even the interpersonal dimensions of service. As a student who worked as a tutor with two small girls in an inner-city school noted about her journal, "I went back and read it over again—nine weeks of writing every week—and I saw how my ideas changed and how my sensitivities changed. And I saw how these two little girls had changed." The personal connection becomes vivid with reflection.

Impact of Community Voice and Diversity on Tolerance

When students thought that the projects they were working on met community-identified needs, they were more likely to feel that those in the community were "like me," and they showed increased tolerance over the course of the semester. Community voice was a predictor of both of these outcomes. When students had the opportunity to work with people of different ethnic backgrounds, they were more likely to report that appreciation of other cultures was something they learned from their service-learning; diversity was a predictor of cultural appreciation.

Service-Learning and Personal Development

Just as a fish has no consciousness of water, or fishness for that matter, students who work and study with people like those they have always known may have little cause to think about who they are and what kind of life they want to achieve; indeed we all take many things for granted unless we are challenged. Coming into contact with people whose life experiences and assumptions about the world are different calls one's own world into question. One student who worked in a mentorship program in a local high school expressed it like this: "It kind of stunned me that she and I both grew up in San Diego, and yet our cultures weren't the same at all. We had very different norms in our life and very different issues to deal with. We were both just incredibly different even though we had a lot of the same stuff—we both had strong family backgrounds, we both grew up in San Diego, and yet the issues we dealt with . . . were so completely opposite. And that just hit me right there." Confronting the fact that two girls from San Diego could still be from dramatically different cultures helped this student reflect on who she was: "It made me realize that my norm isn't the norm for everyone and that I need to be more tolerant of other ideas. And I have to think about when they're doing or saying things that aren't what I think is right or what I think is a good idea; I need to step back and realize that I might not know all their experiences . . . and not to judge people. It makes me want to find out more about people before I judge." Seeing oneself clearly within a broader social context is an early step in personal development.

There is more substantial evidence in the literature for an impact of service-learning on personal growth and development than for most other outcomes (Eyler and Giles, 1997; Waterman, 1997). Because there has been so much work done in this area, it was not our primary focus, nevertheless, we were interested in the impact of service-learning and the effects of particular program characteristics on personal growth.

Service-Learning Affects Personal Development

A number of outcome measures dealt with aspects of personal development.

Self-Knowledge

Students recognize the value of service-learning in their own personal understanding. In our survey, 38 percent felt that knowing themselves better was among the most important outcomes of their experience; 78 percent placed this as either very or most important. One student said, "I think it taught me where my buttons are—what things I can tolerate, what things I can't tolerate. I want to work in the community, but that doesn't mean I want to work directly with the kids. There are other avenues. And I think in trying that out, I realized, 'This is exactly what I wanted to do,' or,

'No, I don't like this part.'" So I think that was important on a reflective basis for me to figure out what I want to do."

Sometimes that self-awareness is gradual. One student felt that service-learning had made a big difference in her personal development: "It's given me an opportunity to develop in ways that I wouldn't have otherwise—like being more confident in myself and my abilities and being more articulate about issues and more responsive to the media portrayal of these issues, and being more of an advocate for these issues and just in conversations with friends and acquaintances." But she also noted that it had taken others to point these changes out to her: "I should get my husband in here to tell you. He turned to me about four months ago and said, 'You probably don't see it, but I see that you're really changing in great ways.' So, it's neat. It's the kind of thing that's so gradual that you don't notice it, but people around you see it."

Another student who was interviewed at the start and end of the service-learning semester challenged the interviewer with, "So, have I changed?" She did not think her responses had been different until she and the interviewer began to reflect. She had worked in a school, and the problem she had addressed was the failure of many children to make academic progress. In her initial problem analysis, she had focused on the families of the children, but in her follow-up analysis of the same problem, she had explored the politics of the local school board and the economic development of the community and how these factors affected school resources and policy. She was surprised to realize that her thinking had become more systemic over the course of her service-learning.

Spiritual Growth

Although fewer students chose spiritual growth as an important outcome of service-learning—20 percent selecting it as among the most important things they learned and 46 percent selecting it as very or most important—it was important to many students. For other students, discussion of a need to "give back" to the community because of the many benefits they had received in their own lives had a distinctly spiritual flavor. Some saw service as a definite opportunity to fulfill their religious commitment. One student who participated for several years in a buddy program, where she befriended and met regularly with a mentally disabled young adult living in the community, expressed it like this: "Like Jesus said, 'Serve each other.' I just want to follow that because I know there are a lot of needs and that I have lots and I'm really blessed. It's kind of like a commandment to me, even though there's a lot more I probably could do. It's just good to give back something."

Reward of Helping Others

Although not all students linked altruism with religious or spiritual values, finding reward in helping others was among the most often identified benefits of service-learning. Fifty-seven percent of the students indicated that this was among the most important things they learned from service; 85 percent indicated that it was most or very important. For many students it helped them feel good about themselves. "I like working and helping in the community," said one student. "I feel good about myself when I do it—helping other people. It's rewarding when I do something good for someone else." The thing that separates service-learning from other field-based and experiential forms of learning is the service, the giving to others, and students seem aware of this particular value.

For some students, this pleasure in helping others was closely linked to their growing sense of personal competence. One student talked about her work in organizing a community group and how proud she was that she had been able to be effective in a meaningful project. She noted, "It helps your self-esteem so much, and you feel like you're getting something accomplished and you feel like you're helping others, and it's the best feeling you can ever get." Personal reward is enhanced by community effectiveness.

Career Benefits and Careers in Service

Although career development was not a focus of our work, we did ask students if their service-learning provided skills and experience that will be valuable in their career. Forty-five percent indicated that this was among the most important things they gained from service-learning, and 78 percent agreed that it was most or very important. We also explored student values, including valuing a career in service, at the beginning and the end of the semester. Students who chose to participate in service-learning were significantly more likely than others to value a career helping others at the beginning of the semester, and this participation had a significant effect on positive change over the course of the semester. Service-learning strengthens the service orientation of students who are already interested in careers of service. For some students service-learning leads to a career of service. For one student it was a matter of needing to give back to the community for what she had received: "It really came down to my privilege again, of being able to do something for a few weeks and then pack up and go, and that is not okay for me. And that's when the idea of actually doing service for life came up—that I don't want to just go somewhere and drop it. . . . We have a lot of power to change things, and we can make a difference." She felt a need to give back, and she also felt that she had the competence to make a difference. This self-confidence or personal efficacy is one of the personal characteristics that we found was strengthened by service-learning.

Changes in Personal Efficacy

Feeling that what you do can make a difference has been well studied as political efficacy, personal agency, and self-efficacy. It has been a powerful predictor of active citizenship participation (Niemi and Associates, 1974) and of the ability to act effectively and sustain purposive action in the face of obstacles (Bandura, 1997), and is associated with identity development (Waterman, 1997). Service-learning, by providing the opportunity to act as well as an important context in which to act, would be expected to help students develop a personal sense of their competence.

Students who choose service-learning are already significantly higher in personal efficacy before they become involved in service-learning, and their participation was a significant predictor of increased personal efficacy over the course of the semester. Students have an opportunity to take leadership and see how their skills make a difference; this leads to increased self-confidence. One student who had helped organize a community action initiative was thrilled with his newfound sense of competence: "Just look at facilitating. I facilitated meetings. I *can* facilitate a meeting. I never thought I'd be able to say that. I know I need practice . . . , but I can see vibes, you know; I can try to get everyone involved, try to have everyone's voices heard."

Program Quality Has an Impact on Personal Development

Although participation alone in service-learning had an impact on personal awareness and development, most of the program characteristics we identified added value. Community service is useful for personal development, but well-designed service-learning is better.

Impact of Placement Quality on Personal Development

Placement quality was a fairly consistent predictor of outcomes throughout these studies. It makes sense that placements that challenge students, give them varied tasks to do, and involve them with important responsibilities will also be likely to create conditions for the authentic personal exchanges that make a difference. Placement quality was a significant predictor in students' reporting that their service-learning was important to their self-knowledge, their spiritual growth, their reward in giving to others, their belief that service-learning contributed to career skills and in promoting an interest in a career of service. It was also a predictor of growth in personal efficacy over the course of the semester. Students who are challenged to perform gain in their sense that they can be effective.

Impact of Application on Personal Development

Both spiritual growth and finding reward in helping others were strengthened in classes where the subject matter being studied and the work in the community applied to each other. Application had an impact on students' assessment of the impact of service-learning on their career skills.

Impact of Reflection on Personal Development

Self-awareness is part of reflection, and so we would expect such activities as journal writing and discussion to be related to personal development. Writing was in fact a consistent predictor of self-knowledge, spiritual growth, and finding reward in helping others. Discussion was a predictor of both self-knowledge and growth in personal efficacy over the course of the semester.

Impact of Diversity and Community Voice on Personal Growth

Just as diversity helps students break down stereotypes, we would expect interaction with people from different backgrounds to increase self-awareness and personal growth. And we did find that students who were in service-learning programs that offer greater opportunities for interacting with people from different ethnic backgrounds were more likely to report self-knowledge and spiritual growth. Diversity is a predictor of both of these outcomes.

Where the goal is to increase the reward that students feel in helping others, the program needs to be more than ethnically diverse; it also must be perceived to be genuinely helpful to the community. The best diversity predictor of feeling reward in helping others is for students to be engaged in service where the community itself has participated in identifying the needs addressed in the service project. Community voice is a significant predictor of students' finding reward in helping others. Students are more likely to grow in their desire to include helping others in their future careers if they are in service-learning programs with opportunities for ethnic diversity and community voice.

Service-Learning and Interpersonal Development

A common warm-up question for management training seminars is to ask managers to think about the last three people they had to fire on the job. The group is then asked how many of those employees had been fired due to inadequate technical skills and how many were fired because of interpersonal failings. For many managers this is a moment of insight that helps focus their further training. In most groups the overwhelming majority realize that they have more problems with employees who cannot work productively together than with employees who lack technical competence.

One of the great benefits of service-learning is that students have the opportunity to learn using arrangements that are more consistent with the learning they will be doing throughout their adulthood in the workplace and community. When students work in field settings, whether service-learning or internships, the nature of their work and the conditions of learning are different from what they experience in even fairly experiential classrooms. Among those differences are the nature of the tasks they perform; the nature of the feedback they receive; the role they play; their relationships with other students, faculty, and community members; and the way in which knowledge is sought and applied.

Most classroom assignments are synthetic; the work that is produced is designed to demonstrate competence to the instructor in order to allow evaluation of the student, but the work rarely has real use beyond that. Even in classes organized around problem solving or where students are engaged in complex simulations, the ultimate goal is to produce a product to be graded. These can be challenging and interesting assignments, but they create a different dynamic for students than work that has intrinsic worth, such as community service or internships. And the tasks completed in the field often require greater creativity and flexibility; students have to adapt their efforts to the complexities of a particular organization.

The emphasis on doing real work in the community while working alongside other students, faculty, and community partners creates an environment that some have characterized as moving students out of an "adolescent ghetto" and into collegial peer relationships with adults (Conrad and Hedin, 1980; Hamilton, 1981). The relationship between students and teachers in the classroom is hierarchical; instructors are the authoritative givers of information, and students are the receivers. Moving from the classroom, where they complete assignments for professors, to the field, where they complete real and meaningful work for the community, changes this subordinate role for students; part of the essence of adult citizenship is having important responsibilities. And students develop greater confidence in working with adults (Moore, 1981). Of course, the quality of the interpersonal relationships developed during service-learning depends on how that experience is organized, but the opportunities to work alongside faculty and community members as peers is often part of that arrangement.

When students combine work in the community with classroom study, the context for learning is also markedly different from traditional college classes. Lauren Resnick (1987b) described some of these differences in her presidential address for the American Educational Research Association, pointing out that programs that do the best job of achieving traditional learning goals, as well as a good job of teaching skills necessary for lifelong learning, tend to be modeled on principles of "out-of-school learning": "they involve socially shared intellectual work, and are organized around joint accomplishment of tasks so that elements of the skill take on meaning in the context of the whole" (Resnick, 1987b, p. 18). They also provide for reflection on the process of learning and continuous acquisition of skills, as well as focus on particular bodies of subject matter rather than general abilities.

High-quality service-learning experiences provide this context for learning, and more intensive experiences provide higher levels of such characteristics as challenge, task variety, active work, interesting work, important responsibilities, and collegial work with others (Owens and Owen, 1979; Eyler, 1992). Indeed when we looked at how the eleven hundred service-learning students in our survey rated the components of their experience, these characteristics did cluster together in a scale that we call placement quality. Placement quality did have an impact on student outcomes.

Although many types of field-based learning can provide the opportunity for teamwork in a real-world context, service-learning provides an additional quality that may influence personal and interpersonal development: the sense of making a worthy contribution to the community. Field-based experiences facilitate many forms of learning and development, service adds the dimension of giving back to the community—of making giving a part of how students define themselves. Service-learning is a form of field-based experiential learning with the added dimension of social contribution.

Service-Learning Has an Impact on Interpersonal Development

Given the multiple opportunities to work as peers with a variety of college and community participants, it is not surprising that students gain in interpersonal development when they participate in service-learning.

Working with Others

Many of the students we interviewed talked about the value of their service-learning experience on developing interpersonal skills. One student simply stated, "I have learned to work with people . . . an important skill." Another commented, "I learned personal interaction. You can read theories in a classroom, but you can't understand that until you hear a story and put a person's face to it and see their emotions." The students in our survey agreed with this assessment; 40 percent reported that learning to "work with others" was among the most important things they learned from service-learning, and 81 percent indicated that it was most or very important.

Change in Leadership Skills

An important aspect of working with others is developing the capacity to lead. The leadership scale included such elements as leading groups, knowing whom to contact for information, developing the ability to take action, and being effective in accomplishing goals. Participation in service-learning did have a significant impact on leadership skill over the course of the semester. Many students noted that the tasks they were called on to perform during their service-learning helped them to become more competent as leaders. This student summed it up: "It makes you more responsible because in some situations you have to take control of what you're doing. I've learned as much leadership in the past two semesters than I did in all of my high school. Now I'm not afraid to go and talk in front of thirty [people] or something. I'm not afraid to take control and be sure of what I'm saying, because I've become an expert in certain areas, and I know about that."

Program Quality Has an Impact on Interpersonal Skill Development

The characteristic that made a difference for interpersonal development was placement quality. Students in community placements where they had important responsibilities, and thus a chance to offer leadership, were more likely to show growth in leadership skills than those in less demanding placements. Students also completed a communication skill assessment that included such components as communicating ideas, compromise, listening skills, and speaking in public. Service-learning alone was not a significant predictor of increased communication skills, but placement quality was a significant predictor of improved communication skills over the course of the semester. A high-quality placement provides opportunities for students to present their ideas and engage in decision making with others; just as it hones leadership skills, it also provides a context for practicing and developing better communication.

Placement quality was also a predictor of students' endorsement of learning to work with others as an important outcome of their service-learning. And the quantity and quality of reflective discussion also predicted skill working with others as an outcome of service-learning. Other reflection variables and diversity were less central to this outcome than the challenge and interest of the activities that the students participated in in the community.

Developing Connections with Others: Community and College

One of the more powerful predictors that students will complete and benefit from the college experience is the degree to which they are engaged or involved in social and academic life on their campuses (Astin, 1992; Pascarella and Terenzini, 1991). College administrators devote considerable energy to devising programs and activities to encourage the active involvement that they hope will attract and retain students. The power of service-learning to forge strong links between students, students and community members, and students and faculty makes it a valuable resource for these efforts. Attention to the quality of the service-learning program adds to the likelihood that students will form these connections.

Community Connections

Most students have some involvement in community service in their home communities, but when they go to college, these connections are often broken, leaving them to form new ties to new communities. It may be this uprooting that contributes to the dramatic decline in volunteer service that has been noted between high school and college (Astin, 1991).

Connecting or Reconnecting to the Community

We explored these connections in a small preliminary study by trying to assess the impact of a community service lab in Vanderbilt's
human and organizational development major, which introduced
students to a variety of community service opportunities and
required them to choose one and provide a few hours of service a
week. Although students did engage in discussion of their experiences and received some course credit, this was neither service
intensive nor well integrated into academic study.

The fifty-seven students in our study had chosen an interdisciplinary major that values community participation and 81 percent
had been active in community service during their senior year of
high school, yet only 39 percent had been active in service during
the semester preceding their community service lab. One of the
results of the lab experience was that students felt a commitment
to continue their service in the future; 71 percent indicated they
would return to the same placement, and 78 percent were willing
to commit to a specific number of hours they would devote to service in the same site or another site. Thus even in a relatively low-
intensity service-learning experience with limited opportunities for
reflection and integration with study, students were helped to recon-
nect with community service. Just as much community service in
high school is incidental to other activities, such as church groups,
scouts, or school clubs, college students may need a nudge to
include service as an integral part of their college experience. Even
fairly modest efforts may have this effect (Giles and Eyler, 1994a).

The results of our survey supported this view that service-learning could help students become more involved in their communities. We found that service-learning was a predictor of increased
community connectedness over the course of the semester. As one
of the students we interviewed noted, "After I started college here,
[service] was kind of missing, like I didn't have those connections
anymore. I could have still done it, but I got wrapped up in all the
stuff going on here, and I noticed that was missing." When this stu-

dent tried to become reconnected through joining volunteer groups, he felt put off by those organizations, commenting that "they focused on the social, and the service part sort of got lost." Eventually he found satisfaction by involvement in a specialized academic program that combined intensive engagement in community action along with study.

Impact of Community Voice on Community Connectedness

Only one program quality stood out as significant in predicting increased community connectedness over the course of the semester. Community voice, where students felt that the work they did was shaped by input from the community, did predict that students would feel more connected to the community. About 31 percent of our eleven hundred surveyed service-learning participants felt that their service was very often responsive to needs identified by the community; 66 percent felt that this quality characterized their service at least fairly often. Some of these students may assume that their service meets community need without any actual involvement in community decision making, but some told us about more active involvement.

When students have the opportunity to work with community members in planning service, they can move beyond the rather patronizing role of charity giver to the role of partner. And working together in planning increases respect for community partners. A student who worked on an adult literacy project that involved new readers in their planning commented, "It was very interesting to hear what they thought. And they came up with things that the students hadn't thought of, such as choosing reading materials and why these materials are inaccessible but these aren't and things like that." He found, not surprisingly, that the new adult readers had some expertise about materials that would be interesting and usable for adults learning to read and came to see that "these are the people who are leading the lives that we're trying to help, and it doesn't make sense to me to exclude them from the decision making." Students who come to see the community members who need these services as partners feel a stronger sense that they are connected to the community.

Appreciation of the importance of partnership was something that students with more extensive service experience developed as they matured in their community involvement. One student characterized the change in how he viewed service like this: "In the past, growing up in my own community, I just sort of assumed—an unchecked assumption—that I knew what was best for people in my community, that I could be in the community role. I never put it in those words, but I could see that was what I was doing. . . . How absurd of us, how rude of us, to assume that we know. . . . Community voice is really what it is all about. This is absurd that we think we can know what's best for the community." He also noted that community voice itself is a complex concept; it is not always clear what or who is community and who speaks for community: "How absurd to think that there is just one voice in the community. If there was just one voice in the community, the problems would be solved."

Service-Learning and Connection to the College Experience

When students are socially and academically connected to their colleges, they are more likely to do well academically, graduate, and show evidence of personal and intellectual development. When the social and academic links are combined, the experience has particular power (Pascarella and Terenzini, 1991). For some students, service-learning creates this chance to combine social interaction, academic work, and service in ways that strengthen the bonds to the college. One student recalled his first aimless times at college: "I didn't know why I was here at this university until I joined the two-year service-learning program. I felt like I was lost, and I was just a number, and I didn't really want this to be my life, and I had never really heard of service-learning. Then education really started to make sense for me. It enhanced what I learned in books, not just memorizing before a test, but it's made it stick and click for me."

Creating Connections Among Students

When asked why she became involved in community service, a student commented, "I was sort of lonely. It was my freshman year at college, and I thought it would be a nice way to meet people who were like me and interested in helping." Community service activities, like other college activities, provide an opportunity to socialize. Another student commented, "You have lots of student contact, and that gives you an opportunity to meet a lot of people. I tend to be pretty shy, and after joining Volunteer Clearing House and Night Walk, it sort of opened me up, and I talk a little more than I usually do. I guess that's what I like about it." For some students, volunteer service and service-learning are additional methods to connect with like-minded individuals and find friends. There is evidence that these interpersonal efforts are more powerful when academic and social involvement are combined (Pascarella and Terenzini, 1991). For some students, an allure of service-learning is the chance to do something that is important and interesting while also making friends.

Students sometimes find themselves at loose ends in large, impersonal institutions, and service-learning provides the context for reducing this sense of isolation in a way that gives meaning to the student's life. "This is a big school—there are twenty-five thousand students here, and in most of my classes I don't know my professor; he has no idea who I am. Service-learning has given me an opportunity to have a personal relationship with some people in my school that I wouldn't have had otherwise—like people who care about these issues and want to make a difference."

Program Quality Affects Student Connections

Although a majority of students who participated in service-learning felt that they formed close relationships with other students, some service-learning experiences were more powerful in establishing these relationships than others. Placement quality was a significant predictor of closeness to other students; when students take initiative and have varied tasks and responsibilities and opportunities for leadership, they also appear to have more chances to work closely with other students in ways that strengthen those bonds. As might be expected, the quantity and quality of reflective discussion were also linked to this outcome. When considerable discussion is devoted in class to linking service and course material, students are likely to work together and form closer personal ties. Many of the students we interviewed discussed reflective methods that involved students in presenting material or leading class discussions with the opportunity for intense interaction with other students.

Faculty Connections

Forming close personal connections to faculty members is one of the more powerful factors for positive college outcomes for students (Pascarella and Terenzini, 1991). One of the reasons that parents are willing to pay the premium to send their children to private colleges is the belief that they will have more opportunities for interaction with faculty in these colleges. In large state institutions, many college administrators attempt to create opportunities for student-faculty involvement through residential college programs, freshmen seminars, honors programs, and a variety of specialized get-acquainted programs to bring students and faculty together. Our own college offered to subsidize the cost of pizza for faculty who wished to entertain groups of student advisees. Service-learning is a process that offers unique opportunities for students and faculty to work closely together—sometimes as peers on genuinely engaging community projects—and this may account for some of its effectiveness.

Program Quality Affects Connections with Faculty

When we looked at the service-learning characteristics associated with creating close student-faculty relationships, we found strong links between most of our measures of service-learning quality and this outcome. Students are more likely to report close relationships with faculty members if the service is applied to the course work, and vice versa, if there is more and higher-quality reflective discussion in class, and if there is ample written work. These are all factors that suggest a high degree of faculty involvement in the link between service and learning and would seem to offer opportunities for lots of student-faculty interaction.

Placement quality was also associated with closeness to faculty; perhaps strong placement opportunities result from close supervision and involvement of faculty in the placement. Faculty who manage this part of the process may be more in touch with the service, more in touch with the students' experience, and more likely to integrate what goes on in the field into what happens during class. And in fact, students in programs where faculty make the service placement were significantly more likely to report close relationships with faculty during service-learning than those placed through campus volunteer offices or the students' individual efforts. These students also reported higher placement quality and more reflection, including discussion, writing, and application. In addition to faculty placement, participation in other community service during college was a strong predictor of closeness to faculty members; the more opportunities for service participation that the student takes advantage of, the more likely the student is to develop close ties to faculty.

Closeness to Faculty Affects Student Outcomes

Because we were aware of the power of student-faculty relationships to affect many of the outcomes of college experience, we decided to see if the impact of service-learning might be explained, or explained away, by the indirect effect of better faculty relationships. In other words, maybe it is not community service connected with course work that really makes the difference; maybe it is the fact that students in these programs form the tight personal connections with faculty that have been shown to be important predictors of student personal and academic development.

When we conducted the regression analyses with data from our survey of fifteen hundred college students to determine if participation in service-learning had an impact, we included a measure of closeness to faculty as a competing explanation. We found that close relationships with college faculty did indeed have an impact on many of our outcome variables, but that this effect was in addition to the impact of service-learning. Regression tables in Resource D show these results.

Service-Learning Affects Student-Faculty Relationships

Many of the students we surveyed indicated that their service-learning experience had given them the opportunity to get to know at least one faculty member well; 31 percent reported this was true during the semester measured. Forty-one percent felt that they had many opportunities for informal interaction with faculty during service-learning experiences. When we compared our eleven hundred service-learning students with the four hundred nonparticipants, we found that 30 percent more of the service-learning students reported a close personal relationship with a faculty member. This is consistent with recent findings (Astin and Sax, 1998) that service participants in their assessment of Learn and Serve America were more likely than their peers to spend at least an hour a week interacting with a faculty member.

Perhaps one of the values of service-learning is in creating these relationships, which have subsequent positive effects on student learning and cognitive development. One student we interviewed had worked with a refugee resettlement program as part of his service-learning experience; he was helping a family with immediate needs, like "learning how to order at Burger King or go shopping for clothes or food or do your laundry." The professor who facilitated the original placements met with teams of students frequently and incorporated their experience into the class. The student commented, "I got to know my professor really well personally. Every other class is pretty much the same: you go in and take notes and you leave. I could go out to dinner with my professor now because we have such a good understanding and knowledge of each other. We're almost like friends. That's what transpired through this: a better relationship with my professor."

College Connections: Service-Learning, Recruitment, and Retention

Among the reasons that college administrators are concerned with creating close connections between students and faculty and students and the college are recruitment and retention of students. We did not address these issues directly in our study, but a number of the students we interviewed had positive things to say about the attractions of service-learning in choosing a college and in their feelings of belonging once involved in these programs. One student directly attributed the college's reputation in this area for her choice: "One of the reasons I came to this college is because of the service-learning. And it's a wonderful college, but I got into better ones—but I wanted to go here because of the service-learning programs. And I love it because I love the service. It's one of the main reasons I came here; it's made a big difference." The students we quoted earlier who felt lost before connecting with like-minded people engaged in service were also bound more tightly to their institution through service-learning.

Tinto (1993) has advanced an interactionist theory of college retention: students who are more socially and academically engaged in their colleges are more likely to graduate. There is a good deal of empirical evidence to support the model (Braxton, Sullivan, and Johnson, 1997). Service-learning provides precisely the mix of conditions identified in interactionist theory as most likely to create this constructive engagement; it provides multiple meaningful connections between students, faculty, and community and does so in ways that allow for diversity, which is also linked to retention. There is some research to support this link between retention and service, and it is a fruitful area for further exploration (Roose and others, 1997; Astin and Sax, 1998).

Summary: Personal and Interpersonal Development

Among the most frequently reported values of service-learning from our focus groups, interviews, and survey was the opportunity to interact in meaningful ways with people from diverse backgrounds. All forms of community service and service-learning have the potential to provide students with this kind of experience, and this experience of working together with others has an impact on their personal and interpersonal development. Programs that incorporate well-designed, challenging placements, include frequent reflection, and maximize diversity are even more effective. Following are our general findings:

Stereotyping and Tolerance

- Service-learning students develop a more positive view of the people they work with over the course of a semester.

- Students report that their service-learning contributes to their sense that the people they work with are "like me" and demonstrate their growing appreciation for other cultures.

- Service-learning is a predictor of tolerance over the course of a semester when service-learning students are compared with those who do not participate.

- Program characteristics such as placement quality, reflection activities such as discussion and writing, application of service and subject matter, and diversity have an impact on stereotyping and tolerance outcomes.

Personal Development

- Students report that service-learning contributes to greater self-knowledge, spiritual growth, and finding reward in helping others.

- Service-learning is a predictor of an increased sense of personal efficacy, increased desire to include service to others in one's career plans, and increased belief in the usefulness of service-learning in developing career skills over the course of a semester.

- Program characteristics such as placement quality, reflection activities such as discussion and writing, application of service and subject matter, and diversity have an impact on personal development outcomes.

Interpersonal Development

- Students report that service-learning contributes to their ability to work well with others.

- Service-learning is a predictor of increased leadership skill over the course of a semester when service-learning students are compared with those who do not participate.

- Placement quality—service situations where students are challenged and have opportunities to take responsibility for important and varied work—is a predictor of increased leadership and communication skill over the course of the semester.

Community and College Connections

- Service-learning is a predictor of feeling connected to the community over the course of a semester when service-learning students are compared with those who do not participate.

- Community voice—service that was responsive to needs identified by the community—is a predictor of community connectedness over the course of the semester.

- Service-learning creates opportunities for developing close personal relationships among students.

- Placement quality and the quantity and quality of reflective discussion during service-learning are associated with the development of close student relationships.

- Placement quality and all three measures of reflection—application, writing, and discussion—are associated with the development of close student-faculty relationships during service-learning.

- Close student-faculty relationships are an independent predictor of many positive outcomes during the service-learning semester.

Although service-learning begins with personal connections, it does not stop there. Linking community service with subject matter through action and reflection also has an impact on academic learning. In the next two chapters we focus first on exploring what and how service-learning contributes to subject matter understanding and then in Chapters Five and Six on how highly reflective service-learning contributes to critical thinking and opportunities to develop transformed social perspectives.

3

Understanding and Applying Knowledge

My analogy is that the class is like a piece of paper,
and then being able to do the community service ani-
mates that picture. So you have a piece of paper with
maybe a cartoon on it, and you can read the cartoon
and understand the cartoon, but when you do the
community service, it animates the cartoon and turns
the cartoon piece of paper into an actual movie, and
then you can experience the movie and maybe you're
even a part of the movie. So it's like the class is the
piece of paper, and the community service brings it to
life and makes sense of why you're even there.

"Community service is a wonderful thing for students to do, but they should do it on their own time, not as part of class." When a faculty member made this point in a heated discussion of the merits of service-learning, we were struck by the oddness of the notion that the academic life of a college student was somehow not "their own time." But it was also clear that his was a significant voice in the resistance to implementing service-learning. Although faculty might agree that community service

Susan Root and Julianne Price worked with us during the development and scoring of the problem-solving interviews. We are grateful for their insights.

contributes to students' personal and social development and that it makes them better citizens, many are dubious about its value in the academic program, where the most important goal is learning subject matter. We could argue about whether students' lives should be divided between "their own time" and their academic studies, as if academic studies were not important to students, but this does not resolve this pressing question for faculty. When faculty contemplate the extensive time and effort required to implement service-learning, they want to know if their students will learn more as a result. Few would deny that academic learning is a central goal of a college education.

Some faculty may be dubious about the academic value of service-learning, but students are generally enthusiastic. The student who told us, "I have learned more in my service-learning than in all my four years of college," expressed the view of many of the other students that we interviewed. And like the student whose quotation opened this chapter, they believe that the service-learning experience added something unique to their understanding of what they were learning in the classroom. Students who participate in service-learning believe not only that they learn more but that the quality of what they learn is different from what they learn from books and lectures alone. Thus, the answer to the question, "Where is the learning in service-learning?" may depend to some extent on what it means to "learn more." Is the "learning" celebrated by service-learning students important to adequate mastery of the academic goals of a liberal education?

In this chapter, the first of four that focus on the intellectual outcomes of service-learning, we will explore the unique value added to learning by the incorporation of service into the curriculum. We will try to identify the particular contributions that service can make to academic learning and present what we found out about achieving these outcomes. We will present the conflict between student perceptions that they learn more and the evidence from the literature that offers mixed support for this view. We will identify the particular things that students in our large survey believed they learned from service-learning. We will explore what it means to "know" academic material and how service-learning outcomes support deeper understanding and application of knowledge. Then, using extensive problem-solving interviews conducted at the beginning and end of the semester, we will explore what students in highly reflective service-learning classes have demonstrated that they have learned.

This chapter focuses on the increased understanding and application of what students have learned. The next chapter explores why this might be so, and the two following chapters address related intellectual outcomes—increases in critical thinking and problem-solving ability and perspective transformation.

Finding the Learning in Service-Learning

Students who participate in service-learning are frequently enthusiastic about what they learn, yet studies that have attempted to document learning have been mixed. It is useful to explore the contrast between students' perceptions of what they learn and previous studies of learning, which have focused on grade-point average (GPA) and course grades in order to try to make sense of the unique contributions of service-learning and to point to how we might assess academic service-learning more effectively.

Students Report Learning More in Service-Learning

Students like service-learning. Eighty percent of the eleven hundred service-learning students in our survey reported that they had a good or excellent experience; only 20 percent felt that their experience was poor or fair. These same positive responses occurred when we then asked the students to compare their service-learning experience with other classes they had taken and followed up with questions about the specific things they learned from their participation.

When the students were asked to compare their service-learning experience with other classes, 58 percent felt that they had learned more, 20 percent felt that they learned less, and 24 percent reported they had learned the same amount. Those who had positive service experiences were, not surprisingly, somewhat more positive about what they learned; 65 percent of them reported that they learned more than in regular classes, while only 12 percent reported they had learned less. Responses to a question about motivation were similar; 55 percent of the students felt motivated to work harder in service-learning classes, while only 14 percent felt that they worked less and 34 percent were motivated to the same degree of effort. For those with a positive service-learning experience, 61 percent were more motivated and 7 percent less motivated to work hard. These figures are consistent with previous smaller studies, which generally report that students like and claim to learn more from service-learning and also suggest that part of the reason might be that involvement in the community is motivating for students. Students are likely to work harder on courses they find interesting, and 68 percent of our service-learning students found the work they did in the community to be interesting at least fairly often.

The issue of intellectual stimulation was a bit trickier. About a third of the students found their service-learning course to be either more, equal to, or less intellectually stimulating than their regular classes. Those with more positive service experience were somewhat more positive, with 46 percent finding the experience intellectually stimulating compared to other classes and 26 percent finding it less so. Possibly a larger number of students reported that they learned more in service-learning than that they were intellectually stimulated because of the definitions that some students give these categories; "intellectual" may connote traditional classroom activities for some students, so that although they feel they learn more in service-learning, they recognize that this learning may not be expressed in traditional academic forms, such as research papers or final exams. We found some evidence for this inference in a focus group of service-learning students who tended to see some academic learning as sterile or unconnected to their lives and labeled this "intellectual."

Previous Research on Academic Learning Has Been Mixed

Our results are consistent with other studies that show that students like service-learning and feel that they learn more in these classes than they do in the more typical classroom-bound curriculum. However, these students' sense of accomplishment is not entirely consistent with the evidence for academic achievement in the literature, which is mixed at best. This may well be because studies of academic achievement generally have been limited to class grades or GPA, which may not capture the value added to the quality of learning by service.

Although students who perform volunteer service during college do somewhat better on their graduating GPA than those who do not, this service is not necessarily linked to the classroom or particular academic subjects (Astin and Sax, 1998; Astin, Sax, and Avalos, forthcoming). It is quite possible that the relationship between service and grades occurs because better students are more likely to involve themselves in service; in fact previous studies have found this to be true (Fitch, 1991; Serow and Dreyden, 1990). We also found significant differences between students who chose service-learning and those who did not on most of our pretest measures at the beginning of the semester (Eyler, Giles, and Braxton, 1997). Since service-learning remains a choice in most colleges, students who choose to involve themselves may already be more serious students and more engaged community members.

Good students choose service, but does service make good students? There is a long tradition of work in field-based education in secondary schools, which has found that traditional and field-based instruction usually result in equivalent gains in factual knowledge (Hamilton and Zeldin, 1987; Braza and Kreuter, 1975).

One exception to this pattern has been peer tutoring programs; students who tutor have often shown modestly improved math and reading scores (Hedin, 1987; Alt and Medrich, 1994). It is not surprising that students learn what they teach; most faculty know how much they learn about a subject as they prepare to teach it. It is not clear that other forms of service participation would be such close analogues of the traditional academic experience.

There have been a few attempts to study academic learning in college service-learning classes, with mixed results. Markus, Howard, and King (1994) found that students randomly assigned to service-learning sections of a political science class received significantly better grades than those assigned to nonservice sections. Sugar and Livosky (1988) found that the students in a child psychology course who elected the service option had higher course grades. In similar studies with a psychology and sociology class, respectively, Miller (1994) and Kendrick (1996) failed to find an impact on class grades. In a study of college political internships, when the same test of facts about the legislative process was used for interns and those who completed a traditional advanced course on the legislative process, there was no difference in knowledge acquisition (Eyler and Halteman, 1981). Although service-learning students do not fare worse, they often do not do better when grades are the measure.

In addition to the fact that better students tend to select the service option when it is offered, studies comparing service and nonservice options also have to contend with difficulties in grading standards between different assignments. One of the students we interviewed spoke of choosing a community service project because "I thought the service would be more fun. If we took the other option, you have to take all the midterms and all the tests. And if you took the service-learning, you didn't have to do that." It would be difficult to compare his academic performance with those of peers who took the other option in this course arrangement. There is some evidence that this difficulty has affected some of the research on academic performance and service-learning. For example, the major cause of better grades for students who added a service component to their child psychology class was the extra credit these students received for their service in a preschool, not improved test performance (Sugar and Livosky, 1988). Markus, Howard, and King dealt with the tendency of better students to select the service option by randomizing assignment to service and nonservice sections of the course, but since the library research paper assigned to students who did not complete service was different from the assignments completed by the service-learning students, the extent to which course grades reflected different standards for these different assignments is unclear.

Thus although service-learning students certainly do as well academically as those who are in more traditional instructional settings, it is not clear that they learn more as measured by course grades. If, as students believe, they do learn more from service learning than from regular classes, then a more careful analysis of the value added to traditional learning by service-learning is called for.

Broadening the Definition of Academic Learning

Acquiring factual information and demonstrating it on final exams is only one way to look at academic learning, and there is no particular reason that service would increase information acquisition over well-designed didactic instruction. If students can acquire information equally well in the classroom or through field-based experience, what makes the considerable extra effort of arranging and using service experience in the classroom worthwhile intellectually? The answer to this question involves a better understanding of what it means to learn academic material. Our service-learning students have identified deeper understanding and application as two of the most important ways that their service-learning differs from traditional course work; this student insight is consistent with the way that many current scholars of education view the nature of learning.

The notion that the acquisition of factual information is a weak definition of academic learning is neither new nor a unique insight of service-learning practitioners. In 1929 Alfred North Whitehead described the tendency of students to acquire "inert knowledge"— knowledge that was memorized but went unused when the learner confronted real-life problems. Like modern cognitive scientists, he explored ways in which traditional educational processes often led to this outcome. A tendency to compartmentalize knowledge and the failure to apply material that has been learned to new situations where it would be relevant are among the failures recognized by Whitehead and by modern advocates of higher education reform.

Service-learning practitioners have long viewed knowledge as something actively constructed by the learner, not simply given to the learner to master. And like Dewey, Whitehead, and other experiential learning theorists, they believe that if knowledge is to be accessible to solve a new problem, it is best learned in a context where it is used as a problem-solving tool. To understand academic material is to be able to see its relevance to new situations; without that capacity, the student's knowledge is useless. Dewey called such knowledge "static knowledge" and distinguished between information that has been stored in memory and that which has actually been understood. Understanding is distinct from the ability to recall information when prompted by a test; it is the ability to call it up when it is relevant to a new situation and the ability to use it in that situation. Material that is understood has meaning for the learner.

Richard Feynman (1985), a Nobel laureate physicist, is not a learning theorist; nevertheless he gave a particularly vivid description of the inert quality of learning that may be the consequence of even high levels of decontextualized knowledge acquisition. He was working with university students in another country and discovered that although they had an exceptional ability to recall highly detailed information about physics, they had almost no ability to use this knowledge when it was presented in ways novel to them. He tried various ways of getting them to think experimentally but could get a "correct response" only when he phrased the question as it was phrased in their text. These students had been trained to memorize information presented in texts and lectures, and they were well prepared to answer questions that demanded highly detailed recall but not to be scientists. Because their instruction involved the transmission of complex, abstract text but virtually no anchors in concrete experience, they could reproduce this information with no hint of understanding. As Feynman observed with some dismay, "They could pass examinations and 'learn' all this stuff, and not *know* anything at all" (Feynman, 1985, p. 213). Unless the right cue word was given, they could not even access what they knew. Inert knowledge prepares students for tests, but is not likely to be available as a tool for lifelong learning, problem solving, or action.

A similar phenomenon occurs when students are able to marshal a body of knowledge to solve problems presented in class but fail even to see a problem, much less the relevance of what has been learned, in a different setting. The new situation does not provide the cues associated with what has been learned; the "key words" from the classroom are not present in the wider environment. A service-learning student will have more ways to access this understanding. The student we interviewed who read about school ability group tracking in *Lives on the Boundary* (Rose, 1989), observed the process when working with children in a tutoring program, and spoke with a homeless person about his experiences with schooling and tracking has a rich set of images and experiences that are evoked when tracking is mentioned. When information is acquired in rich problem-solving and experiential contexts, students construct and refine an elaborate structure of knowledge. Knowledge is not organized in discrete bits, but is connected to a complex network of principles, concepts, and other facts. There are many cues to help retrieve information, since one can arrive at the information sought through many paths. The concept evokes a series of memories and images.

The fact that knowledge involves an interaction between the learner and the context in which it is learned is a major barrier to transferring that understanding to new settings. In order to overcome that barrier to using knowledge, students need to learn in rich contexts, such as complex simulations or community settings, and they need to be guided in their reflection about the meaning and use of what they are learning. Just as we found that our interns did not apply the material from their interdisciplinary curriculum to new problems unless they had practiced this process through repeated reflective activities (Eyler, 1993), Bransford and his colleagues have found that students typically cannot solve novel problems even when they involve principles they have recently learned. Repeated application opportunities coupled with coaching and reflection are necessary to increase the ability of students to use what they have learned. Without this repeated practice and explicit coaching, students do not develop the ability to see the nature of a problem and its relevance to what they are learning, and they often operate from previous misconceptions. Building a more adequate structure of knowledge does not happen automatically with exposure to new information; it is the product of continuous challenge to old conceptions and use of the new material (Bransford and Vye, 1989).

The purpose of learning is to use what is learned. Understanding cannot be severed from active use of information and instruction that allows students to question preconceptions and adjust the way they think about the subject. As Whitehead noted, "We cannot think first and act afterwards. From the moment of birth we are immersed in action, and can only fitfully guide it by taking thought" (Whitehead, 1994, p. 223). Acting and thinking cannot be severed; knowledge is always embedded in context, and understanding is in the connections. For science students work in the laboratory provides some of this application practice that allows them to anchor their understanding in experience; service-learning allows them to test what they learn by applying it to environmental problems in the community or sharing it with younger science students. For students in the social sciences and humanities and for students preparing for professional roles, community service may be the best way of providing some of these same anchors.

Much of the work that cognitive scientists are doing involves creating simulated learning environments where students can be assessed and coached while struggling with complex information and problems (Bransford, 1993). This has the advantage of matching challenges to the students' needs but loses the motivating effect of doing worthwhile work. Service-learning offers students this opportunity to become engaged in authentic efforts in a complex community context; service-learning practitioners have the challenge of providing appropriate levels of challenge, support, and reflective activity to make the most of the experience.

There is some limited precedent in service-learning for expanding the definition of academic learning beyond end-of-course grades or GPA. In the study comparing political interns with students studying the legislative process in advanced political science classes, students were asked to define a current state problem and create a strategic plan for a legislative solution. Although both groups showed equal mastery on a test of a set of facts about the legislative process, those with hands-on experience in the legislature were significantly more likely to write strategic plans that showed a realistic, nuanced understanding of the political process. They discussed the importance of power structure, informal processes and communication, and organizing support, while those whose study had been limited to the classroom tended to rely on mechanistic textbook solutions that emphasized "how a bill becomes a law" and individual rather than cooperative effort (Eyler and Halteman, 1981). In a study comparing problem analysis essays written before and after a semester of study in which some students had performed course-linked community service, Batchelder and Root (1994) found some significant differences in the quality of analysis between service-learning students and others. Both of these efforts suggest that it is fruitful to think about the possible contribution that service-learning may make to qualitative differences in understanding of academic material. Service-learning students may not always perform better on tests of information recall at the end of a semester—although there is no evidence that they perform worse—but they may gain a greater depth of understanding and greater ability to apply what they learn. This is what students repeatedly told us.

Student Views of the Value Added by Service to Learning

We began to explore how we might come to a sounder definition of learning through service-learning by talking with focus groups of students active in community service and service-learning. They agreed with the student whose quotation opened the chapter that their learning from service is richer and more three-dimensional and that they felt part of the subject matter. For these students service-learning helped bring theory to life and helped them to understand "why you're even here" in school. These students frequently stressed that what they learned was more than facts. They agreed with Dewey (1933) that "it is assumed too frequently that subject matter is understood when it has been stored in memory and can be reproduced on demand. Nothing is really known until it has been understood." And this understanding was multidimensional, moving students from what Anderson (1982) has called "knowing what" to "knowing how." Learning helps students make sense of the world and to act in the world.

We followed up on the focus groups by asking our survey sample of eleven hundred service-learning students to assess the impact of their experience on twelve learning outcomes. These choices were created by analyzing open-ended responses of students who responded to an earlier instrument. We discussed the personal and interpersonal development outcomes in Chapter Two. Here are the items that relate to the learning discussed in this chapter:

- "Deeper understanding of things I have already learned about in my classes"

- "Understanding how complex the problems faced by the people I work with are"

- "Apply things I have learned in class to real problems"

- "Specific skills such as carpentry, food preparation, computers, etc."

- "Knowledge about agencies which help people in the community"

Students Report Better Understanding

When we asked our reflection interview subjects what they learned from service, they agreed that it was easier for them to make sense of material because "hands-on experience is definitely a lot better than hearing it, because it doesn't click in your mind until you experience it or relate to it." They found that the understanding attained through service-learning enhanced what they learned from books and lectures. "We learn these theories and ideas in school, but until we really apply them or see them in action, they're not real. And we come out of school—if we haven't done something like this—come out of school not understanding." Students recognize that understanding is more than acquisition of information or memorization of theories.

Repeatedly service-learning students talked about this qualitative difference in their understanding: "It's enabled me to see poverty on a more personal level, to see the humanness—to see it more three-dimensional rather than just a picture or something that is 'over there.' I see how it affects the human being, and I see the complexities of people's lives and how it's not black and white."

This sense of the complex dimensions of the real world compared to the textbook world was a continuing theme. The edge that students felt they had obtained from their service-learning was qualitative; they had a deeper, more complex understanding of issues and felt more confident about using what they were learning. Service made the subject matter come to life and put them inside the subject matter rather than outside, as abstract, disinterested observers.

The results of our survey were consistent with the views of the reflection interview students. Most of the eleven hundred service-learning students felt that service-learning contributed to their understanding of subject matter. Thirty percent of the students agreed that "a deeper understanding of things I have already learned about in my classes" was among the most important outcomes of their service-learning, and 62 percent agreed that is was either very or most important. Forty-three percent agreed that "understanding how complex the problems faced by the people I work with are" was most important, and 77 percent cited it as most or very important. We also asked about the acquisition of specific skills such as "carpentry, food preparation, computers, etc." and about acquisition of specific knowledge about "agencies which help people in the community." Twelve percent of the students felt that the service-learning contributed most to skill acquisition, with 31 percent including it as the most or a very important outcome. Twenty-nine percent felt that one of the most important outcomes was learning about service agencies, and 57 percent thought that it was the most or a very important outcome. Thus service-learning contributes to practical skills and knowledge in addition to deepening understanding of course material. These practical skills may contribute to the sense that many interviewed students report of being better able to use what they learned during service-learning.

Students Report Better Application

Some students saw the link between understanding complexity and applying that understanding to effective action. A student assisting in an inner-city classroom explained how her approach had changed; she had become more thoughtful and effective in her work with the students as a result of her experience. Initially she was "hitting a brick wall" in her service and was frustrated. Her views about how to approach the students changed, partly as a result of "seeing what real situations are like, what real life is. It's not just you do your midterm and your final and throw in a paper. And you get so used to that pattern, that routine, in every class. In the service site, they're always throwing you for a loop. And you can't just go at it by rote memory or anything like that. You have to stop and think and evaluate, and then prepare for a plan of attack." Like the students in the internship study who recognized the complexities of political influence, these students understood in a way that prepared them to take action, and sometimes they had a chance to act within their service setting.

When we asked specifically about application in the survey, students endorsed the idea that part of understanding is the ability to apply what is learned. Thirty-one percent of the students indicated that one of the most important things they learned was "to apply things I have learned in class to real problems," and 61 percent said that it was most or very important. Deeper understanding and application are central to the goals of service-learning and echo what the student focus groups and interview participants had to say about learning in service-learning.

Program Quality Affects Student Learning

We also gathered information from students and faculty about the particular characteristics of the service-learning experience. These descriptive items yielded the six scales described in Chapter Two: placement quality, which included such factors as variety of work, interesting work, challenge, and responsibility; application of course material to the service and vice versa; reflection, including scales for both writing and the amount and challenge level of discussion; community voice, which describes the relationship of the service to needs identified by the community; and diversity, whereby students interact with people from ethnic groups different from their own. As one might expect students who participated in programs with challenging, high-quality placements that were applied to the material studied in the classroom and where higher levels of classroom discussion took place were significantly more likely to report that they learned more, were motivated to work harder, and were more intellectually stimulated than they were in their regular classes. Service-learning classes vary in the quality of both their service opportunities and their discourse; quality does make a difference in how students perceive their impact. Regression tables that include these and other data linking program characteristics to learning outcomes are contained in Resources E and F.

Program characteristics were also predictors of student endorsement of specific learning outcomes. Characteristics that predicted that students would identify understanding and application as important outcomes of their service-learning were those in which service was applied to course material and where reflection activities such as discussion and writing about the experience were more complex or frequent. This was also true for specific skill development, although, as might be expected, the quality of the service experience itself was also important; students who had more responsibility, more varied tasks, and so forth were more likely to have developed specific skills.

Diversity variables, including community voice and diversity, had a more complex relationship with perceptions of learning. Although we found that community voice was a positive predictor of such important outcomes as tolerance and community connectedness, both it and diversity were actually negative predictors of students' perception that their service-learning experience was more intellectually stimulating than their regular classes. There may be some tension between doing what is needed in the community and doing intellectually stimulating work; when students are not actively engaged in partnership in developing a project, they may feel less engaged in work identified by the community while acknowledging that it is work that the community needs to get done. The fact that diversity was also a negative predictor that students will learn to apply material they are learning to the community suggests that this disconnect between service and learning may be a casualty of some community-driven projects. Practitioners need to give particular thought to the balance between student opportunities for responsibility and leadership and the needs of the community to direct service efforts.

Students Demonstrate Understanding and Application

Students in our survey reported that they learn more, understand more, and are more motivated through service-learning, and students in highly reflective service-learning classes and those with high-quality, challenging placements are even more likely to claim this effect. This finding is consistent with what students in focus groups told us about what they learned from service-learning.

To find out if we were on the right track, we interviewed a handful of very experienced service-oriented students and those who were either novices to service or were not involved at all. We wanted to go beyond student reports of learning and see if experienced service-learning students really did have a qualitatively different understanding of complex social issues. We first asked the students to discuss how they would define a particular issue as a community problem and then asked them to analyze the causes and potential solutions and suggest strategies for change. Results of the exploratory interviews suggested that this was a fruitful direction for further work; the benchmark students who were experienced with community service and service-learning had an easier time identifying a community problem to address, produced more elaborate analyses of the issue, and had more convincing practical suggestions for community action (Eyler, Root, and Giles, 1998). Encouraged by these preliminary results, we devised an interview that would help us trace changes in students' understanding of the social problem they were studying. We wanted to see if service-learning would change how students analyzed the issues over the course of a semester and if the quality of the service-learning experience would make a difference. Would students in more intensively reflective courses where service and learning were fully integrated show greater learning than non-service controls or students in classes where the service was less central to study?

We interviewed fifty-seven students in six colleges or universities at the beginning and end of the semester. The interviews, which took about fifty minutes each time, were audiotaped and transcribed and then scored by someone who was not involved in the planning or data collection process and did not know the categories to which student protocols were assigned, and there were independent reliability checks. We examined the complexity of the analysis of both causes and solutions to the problem, amount of subject matter information applied in the analysis, and the personal political strategy.

We controlled for age, previous service, gender, and the pretest scores and found that involvement in what we called integrated service-learning—courses where the service experience was integral to the day-to-day activities of the course and where there was frequent reflection linking the two—was a significant predictor of the quality of problem analyses at the end of the semester compared with service that was more loosely connected to the class or with the analyses of students not engaged in service-learning.

A comparison of mean scores before and after the service semester are presented in Table 3.1. Regression tables showing the impact of integration of service-learning with understanding are in Resource F.

Increased Causal and Solution Complexity

One of our expectations was that as students worked with people in the community who were involved in or affected by the social issues they were studying, their analyses of these issues would become more elaborate and complex. This is one of the claims students often made about service-learning in both the surveys and the interviews. One student said, "I kept hearing things like, 'People are poor

Table 3.1. Mean Issue Understanding and Application Scores Before and After Service-Learning: Problem-Solving Interviews.

	Causal Complexity		Solution Complexity		Knowledge Application		Personal Political Strategy	
	Before	After	Before	After	Before	After	Before	After
Control group (no service)	1.75	2.00	1.82	1.83	1.92	2.08	2.08	1.75
Low-integration service-learning	2.00	2.37	1.94	2.13	2.00	2.13	2.19	2.19
High-integration service-learning	2.15	2.52	1.96	2.63	2.19	2.70	2.12	2.96

Note: Scale scores run from 0 to 4. Based on interviews of fifty-seven students before and after service.

because they don't try' or 'People are on welfare because they don't want to work.' I hear things like that, and it's definitely made me aware of how complex people's problems really are. You can't answer it by saying, 'Here's the answer, and if you would just do what I say you should do, then your life would be better.' It's just not like that." Another student who was working with an environmental action group discussed the difficulty of devising a plan because "after you do a lot of investigation, you realize that changing something on this end of the line might actually hurt people at the other end of the line." She described a situation she had observed in a Native American community where coal mining was damaging the environment and the traditional culture, but at the same time was providing paying jobs for residents who had few economic opportunities.

Participation in well-integrated and highly reflective service-learning classes was a predictor of increased complexity in analysis of both causes and solutions to social problems. Students with complex responses to these interview questions identified more causes or potential solutions and also showed interconnections among causes and solutions. These were lengthy analyses and difficult to excerpt, but this student's remarks about the causes of poverty give the flavor of the responses: "I can't narrow it down to one or two things, but some of the major problems that we have in our town are that we have a lot of migrant workers . . . with seasonal working patterns. In the winter they're left without money. We have people who simply lose their jobs. We have people who fall through the social net, . . . people who were receiving welfare but decided to go and try to work harder, and their welfare is cut, which leaves them without enough money to get by. If you have two parents working, welfare won't cover things, whereas with one parent it would. So it leaves you with breaking up the family. . . . Illness is a big one. We have people who had to deal with medical debt they weren't expecting. . . . Lots of teenage mothers come in with their kids and have no place to go."

When pushed about her confidence in her analysis of the causes of poverty, she replied, "I think everything is interconnected, and that you can't just pinpoint a few things and say that works for everyone. It's more complicated than that."

Increased Application of Issue Knowledge

If one of the benefits of service-learning is that students are able to use the information they acquire in the classroom, then we would expect to see them refer to facts, authorities, and perhaps even specific readings or assignments as they analyzed the social issue in our interviews. In an earlier study with interns in our own college, we had asked students to write a letter of advice to a friend who has just taken a new job. Students who participated in a highly reflective internship experience used material from their human and organizational development curriculum. Student who had had the field experience but limited reflection fell back on glib clichés. What was particularly interesting about that study was that both groups had considerable field experience and some reflection, but only the group with extensive reflection that was well integrated into the internship experience used their academic knowledge in the task. Experience combined with extensive reflection contributed to the transfer of knowledge (Eyler, 1993). The same patterns were found in the FIPSE interview study, with the amount and quality of reflection being central to increased understanding and application.

Students in highly integrated service-learning classes were significantly more likely to increase their application of information and resources to their analysis of the social problem over the course of a semester than those in less reflective service-learning classes or with no service. This is not a measure of what they know but of whether they draw on what they know when they are not completing a class assignment, and thus it addresses the "inert knowledge" problem.

By the end of the semester most students showed some limited concrete grasp of the issue and some mention of supporting information. Over the course of the semester, there was only a modest increase in using information for most students, those who participated in service that was well integrated into the course were more likely to refer to issue information and resources in the postsemester interview. In the analysis of the impact of well-integrated and highly reflective service-learning on application of information, service-learning alone was not enough to differentiate the participants from the control group; well-developed integration of service and learning was necessary. Students do not draw on what they have learned without considerable practice linking what they are studying in the classroom and what they are observing in the field through structured reflection.

Developing Strategic Knowledge

Students who participated in highly integrated service-learning were also more likely to develop a realistic personal strategy for community problem solving. When we asked them how they would proceed if they were in charge of organizing a community group to solve the problem, three things jumped out. They tended to talk about the need to gather information and define the issue before proceeding. They often discussed the difficulties inherent in organizing a group and involving those with disparate points of view. And they talked about specific agencies or activities already present in the community or about the need to identify and hook up with those ongoing efforts. Students who included these types of considerations in their personal strategy scored near the top on our four-point scale. For example, one student who had participated in a variety of community activities, including helping to write a grant proposal for Habitat for Humanity, and whose class helped students apply community change concepts to their work discussed the importance of identifying different points of view among community participants and collecting information about the issues. As she noted, this information-gathering process would give the group an idea of "what is possible and what is not possible." By gathering information from "legislators or commissioners or talking to them about what's been done before, . . . you don't reinvent the wheel. . . . You want to lay out a plan before you actually act, and maybe have a plan B just in case something fails."

Another student was concerned about creating consensus in the group before acting because actions that solve some problems can create problems for others; she stressed the importance of gathering information for political as well as issue understanding: "I think you need to investigate who the players are—like, if you are concerned with poverty, [you need to learn] what's out there to help people, what prevents people from being helped, rules and regulations within the government, rules and regulations within organizations, and understanding where would be effective places to change." She noted that these data will help in selecting sensible courses of action: "It would be good to start with smaller targets so that you could work on getting some change done, and then go from there." It would also be critical to work on leadership development—"training people to have their own skills and utilize their own qualities. I think that is really important because . . . I think that if I was to do something and then I left and it just didn't happen or it fell apart, then I'm not really doing anything." The critical issue became "How are we going to get it institutionalized and keep going? . . . I think you really want to build up the leadership, build up the people's skills and abilities and confidence in what they're doing so that they can continue after you leave."

Students who scored less well on this task produced vague, unrealistic plans that seemed to bear no link to the political realities in the community or failed to show clear awareness of how to overcome gaps in knowledge of those realities. They wanted to start a program without an awareness of programs that already existed or they wanted to "just tell them" how to solve their problems. Higher-scoring students were not always extremely detailed and knowledgeable in their plans, but they were acutely aware of the difficulties of implementing strategy and had some plan for overcoming gaps in their knowledge and experience. Lower-scoring students seemed somewhat oblivious to the difficulties inherent in trying to bring about change in the community.

This "just tell them" strategy, using those words, appeared several times in interviews of less sophisticated students. In a typical example, a student explained what she would do to prevent youngsters from dropping out of school. Her plan was to organize a meeting of parents and teachers: "I would mainly sit down with them and go through, you know, when your child is trying to do homework, you can't tell them 'no, you're wrong, you're stupid' or whatever. . . . I mean, I would mainly just start out with a meeting of parents and teachers and really tell them to stop being negative. And then I'd probably start up a program for those who are doing poorly in school . . . and have a counselor there, or whatever, to talk with the kids and hopefully evolve and cancel out this problem." She was aware that such an approach might make people defensive: "Oh, I think I would get a lot of people mad at me. 'Oh, I'm not negative to my child.' I think I would have a fight the first meeting." But she seemed confident that telling would solve that problem. "I'd hope to calm them down and to really seriously say, 'Well, it may not be you personally, but I'm sure you've seen it; this really shouldn't be going on.' Just mainly talk it out with them and hopefully get them to listen and stay focused." Certainly no one can fault the idea that parents and teachers need to be positive and supportive of students, but this response reflects considerable naiveté about group dynamics and shows no practical grasp of how communities are organized to deal with issues like this or how one might organize an effort to have an impact.

Summary: Service-Learning and Academic Learning

Service-learning—particularly service—learning that is highly reflective and where course and community service are well integrated—has a powerful impact on student understanding. Although studies that compared grades between students completing service and nonservice options in courses have been mixed, with some studies showing no difference and others giving the edge to service-learning, when we expand our view of learning to include more complex understanding of issues and greater ability to analyze and apply information, service-learning came out ahead. In our surveys and interviews with students participating in service-learning we found these outcomes:

- A majority of service-learning students report that they learn more and are motivated to work harder in service-learning classes than in regular classes.

- A majority report that a deeper understanding of subject matter, understanding the complexity of social issues, and being able to apply material they learn in class to real problems are among the important benefits of service-learning.

- Application of subject matter and experience, as well as opportunities for structured reflection through writing and discussion, is associated with reports of more learning.

- High-quality community placements where students have real responsibilities and interesting and challenging work resulted in student reports of more learning and the learning of specific skills.

- Students in classes where service and learning are well integrated through classroom focus and reflection are more likely to demonstrate greater issue knowledge, have a more realistic and detailed personal political strategy, and give a more complex analysis of causes of and solutions to the problem at the conclusion of their experience than those in classes where the service was less well integrated into the course or no service was done.

- Quality of the service-learning experience is a predictor of most of the learning outcomes that we explored.

In this chapter, we have identified some of the learning outcomes of service-learning; in the next chapter, we will use intensive interviews in which students reflect on their service-learning experiences to explore some of the ways in which service-learning has an impact on increasing understanding and application.

4

Engagement, Curiosity, and Reflective Practice

To hear the professor talk about a theory and then for
her to say, "Now here's a project; go do it," and then,
after the project's done, to say, "Okay, what theory is
applicable to this project?" The light bulb comes
on. . . . I understood it more by first having the
assignment and then going out and doing it and then
coming back and reflecting on it.

Students think they learn more from service-learning, and they believe that that learning is qualitatively different from what they get from traditional classes. In Chapter Three, we saw that this belief is affected by the quality of their service-learning experience. When they are engaged in highly reflective classes that integrate service with learning, they demonstrate greater understanding of the complexities of social issues and have a clearer sense of how to apply this knowledge in their community. Here, relying on extensive reflection interviews, we explore how students see the unique value added by service to learning. These student voices give us insight into the dynamics of how service-learning contributes to academic learning.

Understanding Through Service-Learning

When students reflected on how and what they learned during service-learning, it soon became apparent that many such programs created what Dewey called an educative experience for students. Students were engaged in intrinsically worthwhile activities that generated their interest and presented them with problems that awaken curiosity and the need to know more and extended over a considerable time span to foster student development (Dewey, 1938). Dewey was aware that the intellect cannot be separated from the heart; just as true understanding is linked to action, learning needs to be "wholehearted," tying feeling to intellect. The personal connections discussed in Chapter Two are valuable in the personal development of the student, but they are also pathways to learning. Caring leads to the need to know. As one of our students noted, "I think great service, great learning, and just good being happens only when you are entirely engaged. The whole person needs to be engaged. When you just talk about what you thought, you miss part of it. You miss the feeling part. . . . I think people will do more thinking once they have felt."

This combination of high interest, emotional ties, and rich experiential contexts may be what led our students in well-integrated service-learning classes to their more complex understanding of issues as well as their greater practical knowledge. People and situations engaged them so that they wanted to know more, and the combination of real community settings and structured reflection helped them construct rich and complex pictures of issues and processes. Service-learning, when it is well designed, can include precisely those elements that both experiential learning theorists like Dewey and cognitive scientists have linked to effective learning. When students talked about their experiences with service-learning, they stressed the engaging character of service and the importance of work in the real world in building their understanding. Service-learning stimulates curiosity—a need to know more—

and provides context and experience that enable students to acquire knowledge they can use.

Service-Learning and Curiosity: The Need to Know

Learning begins with curiosity, with wanting to know. As we saw in our survey students' responses to the question about motivation to work harder, students often find the link between learning and doing to be a powerful source of motivation, and they recognize the role of service in producing a passion to learn more. "I can honestly say that I've learned more in this last year in community service than I probably have learned in all four years of college. I have learned so much—maybe because I have found something that I'm really passionate about, and it makes me care more to learn about it—and to get involved and do more." When this learning supports action, it is qualitatively different from how students often perceive classroom learning. As another student noted, "You're not just studying to take a test and forget about it. . . . I know when I take a test, I just want to get it over with. This doesn't happen with community service. It stays with you."

This passion for the experience also spills over into the classroom, producing higher levels of engagement in the subject. A student in a class in which some students produced research papers and some engaged in service had this to say: "I felt like we—the people who did the service—were a little more able to discuss in the classroom. . . . We were all doing basically the same kind of subject matter. When we had discussions that pertained to that [subject], it was very personal to us, and we felt a lot about it and said a lot about it too." When students have this personal stake in the subject matter of the class, they feel a genuine need to know.

One of the frustrations many faculty members feel is the lack of intellectual interest that students bring to their study. One of the pleasures of working with students doing service-learning is that experience in the field often brings students back to class surprised or bemused or outraged—but brimming with curiosity. Students engaged in service-learning are engaged in authentic situations; they get to know real people whose lives are affected by these issues, and they are often engaged in real work to address these problems in the community. As a result they have lots of questions—real questions that they want to have answered.

Authentic Situations Generate Questions

Material that might have seemed cut and dried when presented as an abstraction in the classroom seems more problematic when students are immersed in complex situations. A student who had been studying medical care policy knew about the problem of gaming the system to obtain unintended benefits and saw it as an evil—a flaw in the system. The problem was defined as cheating that increased medical cost; the solution was better regulation and enforcement. She spent time working alongside an AIDS patient preparing materials for a fundraiser. As they chatted, he told her about the difficulties of obtaining expensive medications and how he coped by having his doctor prescribe twice the dose he really needed since the state would pay 50 percent of the cost of the medication. She came back to the classroom with fundamental questions about health care access; seeing "cheating" in action made the issue more complex. It raised new questions about how our society is organized to provide health care and convinced her that she needed to know a lot more.

Another student met a mother and her child who both were HIV positive while providing transportation for patients to an AIDS clinic. The woman had a bit too much income from social security to obtain Medicaid support for their medication but too little to afford it herself. The student reported that this woman was resentful because she felt that "she was underserved because she was not part of the homosexual population who have comparatively a lot of services." This was a point of view that had never occurred to this student before, and soon the class was grappling with a new series of questions about the role of political organizing in obtaining services.

A student who began his work with the juvenile court watching a hearing for a twelve-year-old boy came back stunned and full of questions: "Questions I wanted to ask were, 'Why in the world would a twelve year old be involved in a situation like this? What kind of family does he come from? What kind of neighborhood? Why, if it is bad, is it like that in the first place? What could happen to improve the situation? Why is it that everyone in the courtroom is so mechanical and without feeling? Was it because they had seen this a million times or that they didn't care?'"

For another student, this need to know was also a need to act. He contrasted his own class experience with those in his class who had not chosen to take the service option: "I think there is a lot less perspective on their part. When you're in class, . . . it's all kinds of theory and ideas. It really interests you, but you don't feel it. And once you are in a situation where you're actually working with those people you're talking about in class, it makes it seem much more real and much more urgent to do something about."

Caring About Others Generates Questions

For many students, much of the power of a service experience comes because they get to know and like people they meet in the community, and this sympathy leads the students to want to learn more about them and their situation. It is easy to have opinions about homeless policy in the abstract; the need to find out how this policy works becomes more compelling when the policies affect someone you know.

A young woman told us about helping to feed a homeless man with palsy: "No one else felt comfortable, and so I said I would do it. And it took me a long time to do it, and almost everyone was gone when I left. I took about an hour to feed the gentleman. It was a great experience for me. It totally changed me. I wanted to know why these people were on the street, and I wanted to know who was helping them. . . . Right there, that one incident changed me." This student had never met a homeless person before; she was a little bit afraid and shy about sitting down with him. But even this brief introductory experience kindled her need to know more about the issues that affected her new acquaintance. Because she knew him, suddenly it became important to know more about his world. The barrier between an abstract issue and a three-dimensional, authentic situation that the student is part of had been broken by human contact.

While a brief encounter with another can have an effect, we were also struck by the power of more intensive relationships to generate a long-lived questioning approach to social issues. A student who was involved in a week-long immersion experience where he lived in a homeless shelter said that "just getting to know some real people who were in this situation had a profound effect on me. I started to think about the issues in terms of individuals, hearing legislation, and wondering, how does that apply to this woman and her kids, or how does this apply to that man and his problems—or that doesn't address the issue." This student went on to explain that the experience led him to question what he read in class and saw in media reports about homelessness.

Another student spoke of the ways in which the sustained relationships service students had with community members affected their academic approach throughout the semester. She contrasted the kinds of questions she and her fellow service-learning students had with the questions raised by their classroom peers who were doing a library research paper instead of service. In her classroom discussion group, her research paper teammates raised few substantive questions about the issues facing people in the Latino community that they were studying: "Very few questions came up. They were more concerned . . . about how to get their paper done in a short period of time and how much material there was out there." She noted that because "the service-learning people got involved with the people they were with—they listened to their concerns—

they could see what was happening to those people." They became more engaged in wanting to explore issues like crime and poverty that were affecting the community. They wanted to know "what caused . . . the people to get in the situation in the first place—and then why hasn't anything been done? Or why are things so slow in getting done? Those kinds of issues." Their questions did not focus just on getting an assignment done but on the substantive issues they were studying; these issues were real because they affected the lives of people they knew personally. And this need to go beyond the particular issue first assigned to other social problems that affected these people is testimony to the power of service-learning to help students avoid compartmentalizing their learning.

These discussions were not always smooth. Sometimes they generated more anger than understanding as the students involved in the service found themselves accused of lack of objectivity and of "being on their side," that is, on the side of the people in the community with whom they were working. The real world is a messy place and cannot be easily split into discrete issues or problems; nor can emotion be separated from intellect easily. These connections of problem to problem, of one set of individual needs to another set of circumstances, become clear to students who participate in community service projects. This process may be what led to the results reported in Chapter Three where students in well-integrated and reflective service-learning were more likely to define problem causes and effects in more complex and systemic ways rather than in neat categories or compartments.

Important Work Generates Questions

Beyond seeing real events and situations and knowing people affected by community issues, students also often had genuine work to do and found this work strongly motivating. One of the differences between rich simulated exercises and service-learning is that students know that the work they are doing makes a difference in someone's life besides their own. In an earlier study with our own

internship program, we compared the journals that fifteen students kept in a policy class where they did a number of team projects with the journals that these same students kept during a later full-time internship. Although both classes analyzed important issues, the difference in the way that the students characterized their work was dramatic. In the classroom, students talked about completing projects in order to get good grades and do what the teacher wanted; in their work at internship sites, they focused on their pride in making a contribution and doing work that made a real difference. One student noted, "I come back to the dorm, and my roommate is happy because her eleven o'clock class was canceled, and I am happy because my press release was used" (Eyler, 1992). When students do real work, achievement is its own reward; when the work involves community service, there is the additional reward of having done good in addition to having done well.

Our service-learning students talked of these same rewards. One student talked about watching little girls who were shy and fearful at the beginning of the year develop personal confidence and begin to learn to read. She was thrilled to see "how these two little girls had changed."

The students were particularly excited when they were able to learn complex material while engaged in a community project. One student talked of his class's concern about homeless people who were mentally ill and "chose" to live on the street and not seek shelter, even in dangerous weather. His class provided legal research for a team trying to create a law that would allow intervention in such cases. He noted, "We wrote a proposal and worked with a counselor in Boston. It didn't pass or anything, and they keep working on it. But our teacher was really excited about it too. Here we were taking real-life stuff and trying to make a law . . . and all of us working on it had worked with homeless people for two years, and we were really into it. And we understood that there are people out there who can't make those kinds of decisions."

Once the students became heavily involved in trying to formulate policy, they became even more aware of how complex the issues are. This struggle with complexity proved enlightening rather than discouraging. This same student working on the issue of intervention with the homeless said, "We had to do research on it, and we found that Chicago had tried it and New York had tried it. And New York actually took a person off the street, and the person sued them and won. So that's an example of trying to do the right thing but not getting results." Although the project did not succeed in making new policy, it was nevertheless a powerful learning experience for the students: "It's another thing that didn't work out in our favor, but it was something good, because here we are in a law class, but we're making it pertain to stuff that we're really interested in, and we had a say and helped out a counselor a lot with our opinions and our experiences. Instead of just doing a basic research project on a topic in law, we were actually trying to make something happen."

A key element of an educative experience is engagement in worthwhile activity. The student who is trying to solve a real problem with real consequences sees the need to look up one more case, to understand just how a similar policy failed elsewhere, to learn a new technique for dealing with a child's reading problem. Genuine problems provide the most powerful need to know and are thus motivating for many students.

Anchoring Understanding in Rich Experiential Contexts

Curiosity is important, but so is the process through which students answer their questions. Cognitive scientists agree with experiential learning theorists like Dewey that the most powerful learning takes place when situated in complex contexts. One avoids the inert knowledge problem by involving students with real problems in the real world. Concepts become tools for action rather than words to memorize, and memories are anchored in emotionally powerful experiences. Students can move from "memory to action" when knowledge and skills are acquired through repeated use (Schön, 1983; Bransford and Vye, 1989; Resnick, 1987a). Our students gave us many examples of these processes at work.

Concrete Referents

A colleague approached us at a service-learning workshop to share his frustration. He had spent a semester teaching about the intricacies of the American system of health care. He felt that he had done a good job of covering the issues and was stunned at the simplistic answers he received on his final exam. How could students who had been exposed to multiple perspectives and lots of information still write that health care costs are rising because patients demand too many tests and other services? His frustration had him wondering if adding a service component to his classes might help students learn and apply more complex ideas to this issue.

We did not find it surprising that students fell back on a simplistic analysis when asked to apply what they had learned. These college students were young and healthy, most were covered by their parents' insurance policies, and their primary experience with the medical care system was as a patient. It was easy for them to visualize the role of patient demand, but they had no way to visualize some of the other complex elements of health care policy. When challenged by the instructor's test question, they fell back on the knowledge that made the most sense to them because it was rooted in their own experience.

When people think about an issue, they tend to anchor their thinking in their own experience. In our pretest interviews, students often used examples from their own high school days when analyzing issues related to school success. For example, one student addressed the dropout problem by remarking, "Maybe students are just bored with the school curriculum; it's pretty boring. I don't have any friends who have dropped out, but I know people who have, and the students just say the classes are boring; the teachers don't care about them personally. . . . I'm talking here about when I was in high school." And another student suggested that high school students were disaffected because schools offer little beyond classes; if more was offered, the school would be a more positive place for students. "It's like when I was in junior high school, they used to have noontime activities. That's when everyone joined in, but they were there, and there were a lot of people doing that." These students make sense of the world by fitting what they know about a social problem into their own structure of understanding about schooling, an understanding based on their own extensive experience with schooling.

When another student talked about juvenile justice issues, she remarked that "a lot of times people who have committed a crime are regarded as hopeless," but she did not because of the positive experiences her fiancé had had when he became involved in crime as a youngster but went to boot camp and "turned his life around." She then discussed the need for second chances, illustrating with her fiancé's experience and her own: "I think people deserve a second chance usually, because I messed up a lot and if I didn't have my parents there or I didn't have money, I would have been up a creek, so I think they need help; otherwise they're going to be in prison, and they're going to be frustrated, and they're going to commit a crime again."

We are all familiar with this phenomenon. People visualize issues and abstract ideas in terms of their own personal experience. It is easier to understand a $100 haircut than a complicated bureaucratic regulation that costs taxpayers millions; it is easier to think in terms of the family budget than a trillion-dollar national budget. When reading about an international conflict, students are likely to assume that foreign leaders can be dealt with in the same way that recalcitrant family members might be, although the cultural differences may make the analogy useless. In trying to sort out issues, people use what they know and know what they experience. Part of the function of higher education is to broaden that experience.

Students with extensive service experience can call on that experience when asked to think about an issue. One student noted that "the personal experience is like a case example." Working in the community gives students concrete examples to work with as they try to understand new concepts. A student explained how his service experience helped him understand the material that he was studying in a sociology class. The class had read *Lives on the Boundary* (Rose, 1989) and were discussing the effects of tracking in school. "Then I'd jump in and say, 'I can see how the tracking does affect people because my homeless person was tracked at a very young age and put in a low track. He never considered college because he wasn't in college classes where he could have been.' So right away we were seeing how tracking does affect people, where if we had just read it in a book that week, it wouldn't have mattered to us. We wouldn't have had proof."

Once they have had the experience of anchoring their learning in experience, students come to value this process: "I have learned to respect experience and to picture things. I really am more interested in working on the political level—the macrolevel. It's just that every issue and every policy has very personal implications and hits the particular homeless mother that I had pictured in my mind. It really just relates things to reality." Examples from the real world make issues more vivid and real to students; they also give them an opportunity to understand theories that often are abstract and difficult.

Using Theory

In college classrooms simply acquiring information is not enough; students are also learning to analyze this information using varied theoretical perspectives. These theories are often difficult for students to grasp when the learning process is what Resnick (1987b) termed "pure mentation," or manipulation of symbols rather than use of theories as tools to understand the world. Until students can use the theories to evaluate experience, they have trouble making sense of them.

Students talked about the usefulness of theory in helping them "organize what you see," but perhaps the most vivid example in our interviews was from a student whose service project had been a failure in his eyes. What could have been a poor learning experience was transformed when he was able to see how what he was learning might help him understand the failure.

The student was participating in a class on communication theory, and teams of students in the class developed service projects and applied communication theories they were studying to their experiences of developing and implementing these projects with community partners. His project was to involve assisting residents of a group home for people living with AIDS. Planning meetings were scheduled and then canceled at the last moment by residents of the home, and meeting times convenient for residents were not convenient for students. On one occasion students showed up, but the resident who was to meet with them was not there. Although there were a number of interactions with members of the community group, the project never got off the ground, and students were frustrated. When it came time to analyze their experience, they were forced to analyze their failure to communicate. The student explained it in this way: "The two theories that we chose were reasons communication doesn't work. And it sounds so hokey—like I'm just doing it for this interview— but really it was kind of enlightening. We didn't know why communication didn't occur between the two of us and why we weren't able to meet." But the theory application project that his team completed for the class helped him to sort out what happened. "These were just theories, but it was so neat to say, 'It could have been this,' and who knows what actually happened, but it was so neat to say, 'This is the reason why,' and it all made sense. And it was, wow, this is perfect! Both of them were just these really applicable theories to reasons why communication doesn't work. With the other students in the class, they used communication theories why it does work, and it was obvious from their oral presentations that they put a lot of thought into it. The theories they came up with really came close to hitting exactly what was going on with them."

Thus the "failed group" was able to observe how communication theory accounted for some of the success of the other groups and also understand what went wrong in their case. And they were able to look at what could have been a very negative situation and understand how their own behavior, as well as the situation of the group they were attempting to work with, might have contributed to the impasse. They might have rationalized their failure by blaming the community group; instead they used their negative experience to understand the situation better: "It was so neat . . . just to sit there reading these [theories] and say, 'My God, this might really be what happened.' This is so neat to have a real understanding for once, instead of saying, 'Oh, he was a flake.' This was the reason why this would happen."

Learning in Context

As cognitive scientists have demonstrated, learning occurs within a context. Much of the failure to transfer what is learned in the classroom to use in the world occurs because students have not learned the material in a way that makes sense to them in new contexts. People apply information that they have learned in similar situations to new situations. If we want students to use what they are learning about complex social problems, then we must have them explore these issues and use this information in multiple settings. Service-learning is an ideal way to experience the messiness and complexity of these issues and actions in the community. Students acknowledge the importance of the service component to their learning by their frequent references to the real-world importance of what they are learning.

Students studying public policy learn about the importance of evaluating programs and holding agencies accountable for results. But those who struggle to implement policy learn that this is far from a cut-and-dried process. A student who had worked with the homeless told us about her frustrations in dealing with a funding agency that wanted to help the homeless find employment by providing a voice-mail service so that people looking for a job without a home address would have a way to provide a telephone number to employers and receive messages from them. The program addressed a significant problem for the homeless, and the funder was very concerned with measuring results. A student who had been asked to assist with the evaluation of the program remarked, "I think that with any social issue, no matter who you're working with—problems like AIDS or battered women—the results are kind of deceiving. If people want results, they are not going to get them right away. . . . If you're trying to get a person a job, it takes a long time to get them the confidence to go in and talk to a person. They've lost a lot of pride and self-esteem." She contrasted her experience in the business community with her lengthy experience working with the homeless: "I don't think the results are there like in a lot of other things. Like in business, you can always see how you are doing. The voice-mail people want results. I don't think that's the way you can go with social issues."

This student contrasted her earlier experience working with a lumber company ("You always have to perform there. You did or you didn't") with the struggles of the homeless. While "it was clear" if you were performing well at the lumber company, "when you work with a homeless person, you may not always get through to them. And that doesn't mean you have failed. I think the funders look at those issues, and if they don't see progress, they are out of there. They don't realize that actually it did work, but you aren't going to see success for awhile." She spent the semester trying to convince those sponsoring the voice-mail program not to cut homeless people off immediately if they did not actively look for work. She noted that "they asked me to come in and be a homeless expert on this board; the people behind the scenes didn't work directly with the people. . . . And I gave them my view and told them why you can't take people off for these reasons. They still didn't go with it; they were still very much into their agenda and their paperwork." Although she was frustrated that even when people agreed with her input, they would not modify the system, she also understood: "I'm not the boss. Sometimes you have to listen to people. Sometimes you don't agree with them. . . . You've got to understand where they are coming from too. You've got to be able to swallow things and move on."

Summary: How Service-Learning Contributes to Understanding and Application

Students believe that the learning that results from their service-learning experiences is richer and more applicable to real-world contexts than material they learn in traditional classes:

- Students suggest that this greater learning results because they are more engaged and curious about issues they experience in the community.

- Students find that they remember and can use material that they learn from the rich and complex community context.

- Students report that service-learning is powerful because it is rooted in personal relationships and in doing work that makes a difference in people's lives, which helps them connect their learning to personal experience.

High-quality service-learning enhances understanding of subject matter, but students' limited capacity to think critically may hamper the usefulness of this knowledge. In the next chapter, we explore the relationship of cognitive development to problem solving and discuss our attempts to discover a link between service-learning and critical thinking.

5

Critical Thinking

*Prior to being exposed to a lot of different information
and different experiences, I was so much more sure
my opinions were the end-all, and that my perspective
was the only perspective, that I had to be right about
certain things, and I think the more educated I
became, the more I know I don't know, and the more
I'm able to see that as a valuable point of view, actually, and that I can get more from life saying, "I'm
not sure, let me find out," rather than saying, "No,
this is the way it is because that's what I think."*

We recently observed a lively discussion among faculty about
their frustrations with students who lose heart in community service. Some faculty members thought that students become
discouraged because they come to feel that the community problems they are studying cannot be solved. Some of their students
seemed to think that action was pointless because problems like

We are grateful for the insights about postformal reasoning provided by Cindy
Lynch, who helped us develop questions and the scoring protocol for the critical
thinking component of our problem-solving interview and supervised its scoring,
and for the help of Charlene Gray in evaluating these interviews.

poverty are always with us and that their efforts would make no real difference. Some faculty viewed this discouragement as an attitudinal problem, something that needed to be addressed through a focus on student emotion and motivation. But we suspect that the issue may be cognitive as well as affective. Feeling committed in spite of the intractability of social problems requires the ability to accept the complexity of and think critically about the social problems related to community service.

Students who begin service confident that social problems are like those puzzles in the back of the *Times*—hard but with right answers—may feel helpless when the right answers are hard to come by. Many students push past this initial frustration and acknowledge, as this student did, that "I am more hopeful, but still pretty pessimistic—but more hopeful and more accepting of the fact that maybe I'm not going to change everything, but I can do something—maybe." And like the student in our opening quotation, they come to accept uncertainty and complexity as the way of the world; they understand that their awareness that the more they know, the less certainty they have is a positive insight rather than a defect in themselves or society.

This insight often comes as they reflect on their community experience. A student who worked in a domestic violence shelter while studying sociology was intensely interested in new policies being considered by the state legislature. She recognized the paradox between the easy answers that come with superficial knowledge and the confusion that results from more knowledge and experience: "I guess the more I learn about any social issue, the more I realize how complex they are. It never gets any easier. It's like the less you know about an issue, the easier it is to say, 'Oh, we'll just put a Band-Aid on it and send it away.' The more you learn about it, the more you realize that it's just not going to work, and the more you realize that our whole society is tied up in every issue. So it gets more and more complex."

Whether students see this paradox as a revelation that enhances their service or as a barrier that discourages them may depend to some extent on their intellectual development. Critical thinking, which allows students to identify, frame, resolve, and readdress social issues, is dependent on both knowledge and the students' level of cognitive development. As Pat King (1992) observed in her analysis of the Association of American Colleges' goals for the liberal arts, many of the goals for students, such as the ability to analyze controversial issues, evaluate competing claims, and justify their positions, require a level of cognitive development greater than college students typically reach. Students seriously disheartened when they discover that they cannot save the world may be operating from a limited view of the world and with a limited capacity for understanding. One task for all of us as citizens is to figure out how to act in spite of the fact that no one can ever know for sure. Students who expect to find simple truth about social issues in the classroom and are confronted with the fact that even experts do not know precisely what to do may be simply unable to address the issues effectively. But this experience of frustration may place students in the position to develop the skills and abilities, and service combined with the challenge and support that can come with well-structured reflection may facilitate this process. Effective service-learning can help students reach this important educational goal.

In this chapter, we will explore the nature of the social issues that students face in their service settings and the reasons why they are particularly difficult to understand and resolve, the importance of cognitive development to critical thinking about these issues, and how the experiences students have in service-learning may contribute to the development of critical thinking. And we will present evidence from our studies that provide support for the idea that highly reflective service-learning programs may contribute to improved critical thinking.

Community Problems Are Difficult for Students to Understand and Resolve

When students take a test in the classroom, they usually have a pretty good idea of what theories, concepts, and knowledge will be needed to solve problems presented on the exam. Sometimes it is quite straightforward. The previous weeks have been devoted to studying social class theory; the exam asks them to complete multiple choice questions about social class theory. A unit on analysis of variance has just been completed; the exam gives them some data and asks them to perform an analysis of variance. Even when students are presented with a more open-ended task such as a case study to analyze, the syllabus, the chapters read, and the class lectures have framed the content and perspective. Tasks that on their surface seem to call for sophisticated levels of analysis often involve more recall of material laid out in lecture or text than genuine higher-order thinking by the students.

But life does not come with a syllabus. In the real world, problems are not neatly arranged by discipline, and no one can look back at the chapter to guess what kind of problem they are facing. Before we can even begin to solve social problems, we have to be able to recognize that a problem exists and frame the nature of the problem. This task is difficult not only because the problem is embedded in a complicated real-world context, but partly because of the ill-structured nature of most social problems (Voss, Greene, Post, and Penner, 1984).

Community Problems as "Ill-Structured" Problems

Most of the problems we face in our communities are not what social scientists call well structured, with clearly defined goals, with the information and processes necessary to solve the problem known, and general consensus among experts about how to proceed. Our service-learning students were studying problems like homelessness, poverty, crime, the HIV epidemic, and school achievement of poor children. Problems in the social sciences, and certainly the issues faced by most of these service-learning participants, are ill-structured problems. They have vaguely defined goals and few givens. The information needed to solve them and constraints on problem solving are not obvious at the start and emerge only as the problem is explored. Experts rarely are in full agreement on either the definition of the problem or what should be done to resolve it (Voss, Greene, Post, and Penner, 1984).

When service-learning students are confused and discouraged by the difficulty of solving social problems, they are discovering something essential about the nature of these issues. For Dewey problem solving was about doubt that, when resolved, leads to new forms of doubt. The doubt results from the nature of the situation, not just our poor understanding of it (Schön, 1995). Citizens in a democracy must be able to tolerate uncertainty and make decisions in spite of the doubt inherent in the process. Hannah Arendt made a similar distinction when she cautioned about the dangers of confusing work with political action (Clohsey, 1998). Work involves the creation of enduring objects and can be finished; political action is taken by a group who have come to a decision as a result of the convergence of numerous perspectives and minds on a problem. Attempts to solve a social or political problem are attempts to create a new world—a new arrangement of things and a new way of acting—and the process is full of surprises and unexpected, perhaps unintended, outcomes. Such actions naturally give rise to new decisions and attempts to modify mistakes if the course we have set does not please us. Arendt cautioned people not to become frustrated with political action out of the assumption that creating policy is like creating a watch or some other object that can be finished once and for all. Political action such as service or advocacy or policy-making will never be done; it is a continuous activity. Uncertainty and change are central to its nature.

The ability to recognize that the social problem they were dealing with was ill structured was expressed in several of our student interviews, as students struggled to frame the questions they were dealing with. For example, one student we interviewed suggested a plan for training teachers to deal with cultural conflict in their class-rooms. When asked how sure she was that this was the right solu-tion, she clearly articulated her understanding that this issue is an ill-structured problem. She could not be completely sure "because it is not a black and white issue. There's no right and wrong answer, so everyone is not able to say, '2 plus 2 may equal 4,' but when you say, 'So, tell us what you think the problems are,' everyone's com-ing from different positions. . . . It is not a black-and-white issue."

Another student acknowledged the cyclic nature of the policy process and its relevance to attempts to define the problem. "The first step to solving the problem is to acknowledge that there *is* a solution but that there is *no* solution. There is no way we can do something or implement a plan that's going to totally, from now on 'til kingdom come, solve the issues and the problem that the AIDS epidemic has created. With that step, I think the next part is, given that there is no apparent one solution, to see that given the entire spectrum, what can we do best to not solve but go toward the way of maybe alleviating. And I think that's where a lot of policymak-ers are stuck; they're doing things, trying stuff to solve the problem, but something happened or something does not happen, and it causes them to go back toward square one. It's just an endless cycle." This student has come to terms with the fact that solutions are ten-tative and temporary, but this cycle need not necessarily discourage action.

Effectively addressing ill-structured problems requires both con-siderable expertise about the particular subject at hand and advanced abilities to evaluate competing claims. Before exploring the cognitive developmental underpinnings of critical thinking, it is useful to acknowledge the importance of acquiring specific infor-mation and skills about an issue if one wants to make effective judg-ments about it.

Information and Critical Thinking Skills

It is no wonder that students become daunted by the complexity of social problems. For those who expect right answers and definitive solutions, the ambiguity inherent in ill-structured problems is unnerving. Although information may help students understand and address these complex issues, the critical thinking skills they need to identify and frame an ill-structured problem also depend on how they understand and use this information (Lynch, 1996). There is considerable evidence to support the idea that levels of knowledge and experience with a particular subject affect the way that people structure their thinking about it. Expertise is about acquiring extensive knowledge and skills and about the way that knowledge is organized (Voss, Greene, Post, and Penner, 1984).

In Chapter Three we saw evidence that students could do a more complex job of analyzing a social problem when they had both experience in the community with the issue and also a class where the issue and experience was well integrated through reflection about the subject matter. When people who have studied expertise look at how experts approach a problem, they find a qualitatively different understanding of the subject in people with a great deal of experience. Experts have more elaborate mental models of the issue than novices do. Experts seem to pay much more attention to understanding and describing a problem before trying to fix it; novices tend to jump quickly to assumptions about what the issues are and offer immediate solutions. Experts forge clear connections between their analysis of the causes of a problem and their array of potential solutions, which makes it easier for them to come to a sound decision about how to proceed (Voss, Greene, Post, and Penner, 1984).

Experience, knowledge, and reflection build this expertise. And with experience comes a greater tendency to pay attention to one's own problem-solving progress. Those with greater expertise are more likely to plan, monitor, and revise their problem-solving strategies; familiarity with the information and skills necessary to deal with an issue frees up resources for self-awareness of the learning and problem-solving process (Brown, Bransford, Ferrara, and Campione, 1983). When students are not struggling to meet the minimal requirements of functioning in a situation, they are better able to reflect on their effectiveness and modify their behavior.

A student who had spent a good deal of time in an inner-city school as part of her education program illustrates this transition from action based on preconceptions to greater self-awareness and monitoring of problem-solving strategies. Like the students quoted earlier, she found that "the less you know about an issue, the easier it is," at least until you actually have to act on your decisions. She began her work with children in the school brimming with ideas about what she wanted to do and tremendous enthusiasm, but she found working with the students very difficult and had tried and failed with a number of her efforts. As a result of this service-learning experience, she felt that she was "a lot more analytical about problems as they arise. I'm not quite so reactive as I was in the beginning. I don't get as frustrated. I tend to be more of a problem solver than I was and look for solutions more." She spoke about how her class had offered different approaches and helped her place the small things that happened in her service setting into a larger context: "I think a methodical approach that I didn't have before is something that I learned to apply. It's a little more restraint in my approach rather than just jumping into something and then finding out it's wrong or it doesn't work. I'll tend to look at a situation more and evaluate it, and then step back and think about it." Reflecting on knowledge tested with experience changed the way she approached the complexities of working with students. Although she was not perhaps an "expert," she certainly had greater expertise than she had when she began her service-learning assignment and had moved toward a more thoughtful approach to action than her early naive efforts, where she "jumped right in" and often "hit a brick wall" of frustration and failure.

This ability to self-monitor and the problem analysis principles acquired in a particular service setting do not necessarily transfer to a new situation. To the extent that the issues of homelessness or welfare reform are different from what the student faced in learning to work with children with achievement problems, there will likely be poor transfer of problem-solving strategies. Just as doctors who show great expertise in diagnosing and treating illness may show poor analysis and judgment when faced with investment decisions, or plumbers who are able to assess a problem in their field quickly and accurately may fall back on untested assumptions when they face a social issue in their community, students who have explored one ill-structured social problem in great detail in their service-learning class may not necessarily respond with great sophistication to a different situation. To increase the likelihood that students will be able to apply critical thinking principles to future situations they face as citizens, multiple opportunities to deal with a variety of ill-structured problems should be created. These skills develop within specific contexts, and transferable skills develop with extensive well-structured application (Bransford and Vye, 1989; Fischer and Bidell, 1997).

Although critical thinking as a consequence of service-learning has not been well studied, there is some evidence that students do better when the problem they are addressing is similar to the issues confronted in their community service (Conrad and Hedin, 1980; Batchelder and Root, 1994). Familiarity with information about an issue frees them up to think more reflectively about it. The Batchelder and Root (1994) study is particularly interesting because it asked students to write two essays analyzing social issues, at the beginning and the end of social science classes. For students who participated in service, one of the problems they were asked to write about was related to their service experience; the other was not. In comparison to students who did not perform community service as part of their classwork, students who engaged in this service wrote more complex essays; they also did more complex analyses of problems related to their community service than on the topics that were not related.

This link between the particular subject and sophistication of critical thinking suggests that if we want students to apply critical thinking skills to problems they face as citizens, we need to expose them to many issues and experiences; expertise is specific to a particular subject and may not generalize easily to new subjects. There is also reason to believe that the ability to think critically about social issues is constrained by the level of cognitive development the student has reached.

Cognitive Development as a Prerequisite to Critical Thinking

For Piaget and the theorists who have built on his work, understanding and using experience is not simply a matter of knowing more and having lots of practice so that one becomes automatic and expert. Understanding is also constrained by the capacity to interpret experience. The process is developmental and proceeds through a hierarchical sequence of stages, with each stage corresponding to a cognitive structure—a way of organizing and understanding reality. Each successive cognitive advance creates a structure that is a bit more powerful for understanding experience. As we are confronted with problems at each stage that cannot be adequately resolved, we are pushed to reflect on this difficulty and develop increasingly complex and adequate ways to know and understand.

While Piaget focused primarily on the development of thinking in children, many of his followers have directed attention to the cognitive abilities of adults. Where Piaget defined mature adult thinking in terms of formal operational thinking, that is, the ability to handle abstraction, theorists like Perry (1970) and King and Kitchener (1994) have looked at the nuances of adult intellectual development, or what has come to be known as "postformal reasoning." Even among those who are capable of thinking in abstract terms, we see a wide range of abilities to think critically about ill-structured problems. It is not enough to think abstractly; adults also need to be able to draw well-reasoned inferences from complex material, and this depends to some extent on their understanding of the nature of knowledge and authority.

Perry (1970) studied the changes in the way that college students view the nature of knowledge, authority, and responsibility over the four years of their college experience. He found that younger students tended to view the nature of the world simplistically as being divided between right and wrong or black and white and that they assumed that truth was likely to be derived from authority. This dualistic view gives way to a series of stages that Perry characterizes as relativistic. The student begins to accept the presence and legitimacy of multiple points of view and of the indeterminacy of truth and in fact may come to believe that all positions are equally valid. Perry's final stages involve an ability to make judgments and commitments within the context of relativism. In Perry's model these higher stages tend to shift from a focus on intellectual development to concern with identity formation (Pascarella and Terenzini, 1991). Service-learning practitioners are concerned with the ability to act as effective citizens and thus recognize the importance of identifying development and making commitments.

Our interest in the critical thinking component of this process might be better served by applying King and Kitchener's (1994) reflective judgment model. This model, which tracks Perry's earlier stages closely, retains the focus on critical analysis through its upper stages. The ability to make and justify a decision is also an element of effective action and a central intellectual component of citizenship. The reflective judgment model has particular strengths in understanding how students learn to succeed at each step of the problem-solving process (Lynch and Wolcott, 1998; Lynch and Huber, 1998). And it is in evaluating open-ended or ill-structured problems that this model is particularly helpful.

In King and Kitchener's model (1994), those at the highest stages are able to identify an ill-structured problem, frame it in complex ways, and justify their choices for resolution of the problem;

they are also open to adjustments to their resolution and readdress the issue as new dimensions of the problem emerge. They are comfortable with the reality that social problem solving is not something that can be accomplished once and for all and that human decisions are always subject to error and revision. The relationships among King and Kitchener's reflective judgment model, Perry's model of student development, and core problem-solving skills are shown in Table 5.1.

Students at the lowest stages of King and Kitchener's theory of reflective judgment are not even able to recognize that a problem is ill structured. These first two stages are characterized as prereflective, and indeed there seems to be little evidence of insight or analysis. At stage one, the individual is oblivious to the idea that truths are problematic; at stage two while lack of consensus might be recognized, there is an assumption that there is a correct solution and that correct authorities know what it is. The idea that there is no "right" definition of the problem or a "right" solution is

Table 5.1. Relationships of Perry's Model of Student Development, King and Kitchener's Reflective Judgment Model, and Core Problem-Solving Skills.

Perry's Model of Student Development	Reflective Judgment Stage	Core Problem-Solving Skills
Dualism	*Stage 1*: What a person believes is true.	Person is unable to distinguish between well-structured and open-ended or ill-structured problems.
	Stage 2: A person can know with certainty either directly or based on authority.	
	Stage 3: In some areas knowledge is uncertain and justification is based on what feels right at the moment.	

Table 5.1. (continued)

Perry's Model of Student Development	Reflective Judgment Stage	Core Problem-Solving Skills
Multiplicity	*Stage 4*: Knowledge is uncertain because of situational variables. How we justify beliefs is idiosyncratic.	*Identifying*: Person distinguishes well-structured problems with "right" answers from open-ended problems fraught with uncertainty.
	Stage 5: Knowledge is contextual; people know via individual contextual filters. Justification is context-specific.	*Framing*: Person looks beyond the personal perspective; articulates the larger context; makes legitimate qualitative interpretations from different perspectives.
Relativism	*Stage 6*: Knowledge is constructed by comparing evidence on different sides of an issue or across contexts. Justification involves explaining comparisons.	*Resolving*: Person uses relevant principles for making sound judgments across perspectives; provides well-founded justification.
Commitment within relativism	*Stage 7*: Knowledge is an outcome of an inquiry process generalizable across issues. Justification is probabilistic; evidence and argument are used to present the most complete understanding of an issue.	*Readdressing*: Person coordinates identifying, framing, and resolving skills into a process that moves toward better solutions or more confidence in a solution as the problem is addressed over time.

Sources: Adapted from Kitchener and Fischer (1990) and Lynch and Wolcott (1998).

incomprehensible. Few college students function at this level. In our problem-solving interviews, no students appeared to be reasoning at stages one and two as they struggled to identify and suggest solutions for a problem related to their service-learning assignment.

At stage three, students recognize conflict but still are unable to distinguish clearly between well-structured and ill-structured problems and tend to act as if they assume social problems are well structured and with right answers, if only we could discover what they are. A student who worked on a service project in a public school and was discussing solutions to the problem of poor student achievement commented, "Well, I think it is good that people have different opinions, but I wish there were ways that people could come to a solid answer. Some of the time they do, but most of the time they don't, and that's why it takes a long time for progress to happen." This student started by acknowledging what is perhaps a cliché in education—the virtue of multiple points of view—but quickly fell back on an assumption that there is a solid answer, that is, a truth to be found if everyone just looks hard enough for it. He was also persuaded that the stubborn inability of people to find this right answer is what blocked progress. This became clear as he responded to a question asking if one position can be right and the other wrong when disagreements occur: "At the time, yes. And . . . there are some arguments one can get into where you just know you're right. I mean, you know, give me a break!" And like many other people reasoning at this stage, he relied partly on a hunch: "First of all, it's a feeling. Second, you can prove you're right, and they're extremely wrong, if you have more knowledge about what you're talking about." The hints of relativism are there in this student's response, but he was uncomfortable with this and did not know how to resolve the conflict brought about by complexity and so repeatedly fell back on the idea that there is a truth even if that truth is out of reach: "As far as the world goes, I don't think the world will ever find the real cause. There can be lots of causes. I don't think there's just one cause. But I think maybe that with all these different causes the world probably sees, I would say it's funneled down to one cause." Another clue to this student's insecurity with the ambiguity inherent in the problem he was discussing was his repeated attempts to gain reassurance in the interview that he was on the right track with comments like, "I'll bet you're probably wanting to hear things like there was a drop in the crime rate" and "Is this what you want?" although the interviewers repeatedly told students that they were interested in how they thought about the issues and that repeated probes were "not designed to get you to change your answer, but just to describe a bit more how you came to hold that view."

Students who view social problems as if they were well structured and the task is uncovering a right answer may be prone to jumping quickly to a simple solution like "just telling" the parents to pay more attention to their children or "providing education" on AIDS. They may also be quite impatient with reflective techniques in the classroom that focus on surfacing and analyzing multiple perspectives. For a student seeking a right answer that presumably authorities like the teacher know, spending time sharing views with peers and completing reflective assignments may seem like busywork.

The transition to stage four of King and Kitchener's model is important for social problem solving because it is at this point that students clearly understand the ambiguity inherent in an ill-structured problem. By accepting uncertainties as a legitimate part of problem solving, these students are in a position to begin to try to identify the complexities of the problem and attempt to resolve it. They will still have a good deal of difficulty with the more advanced tasks at this stage. Students may tend to view the problem holistically and have trouble breaking it into multiple components. When they have identified multiple perspectives, they have a great deal of difficulty deciding how to judge among different points of view. This student's frankly relativistic response when asked about her confidence in her assessment of her AIDS policy solution was typical: "I don't think there is really a right or wrong answer. It's your opinion, and what you believe is right or wrong, but I think everyone is entitled to their opinion, and some people may feel more strongly about it. It's such a complex issue with so many facets that it is really hard to get to know each side of it."

When there is conflict among experts, there may be a tendency to attribute bias or ulterior motives to some experts as a way of dismissing some perspectives. This makes judgment easier for students reasoning at this level who have difficulty coming up with standards for judging among perspectives. One student, when asked why experts might disagree, immediately jumped to his observation of expert witnesses during the O. J. Simpson trial and commented, "One of the reasons that they disagree is that they're paid to be experts. If they didn't disagree, what is the point of them being there?" If experts have ulterior motives and are not genuinely presenting perspectives as their view of truth, then they can be discounted and other methods used to make decisions.

Another common way to deal with conflict among perspectives is to fall back on personal experience as the arbiter. A student discussing the problem of homelessness gave this process for making up her mind about the issue: "It would be better if I, as opposed to someone else, had actually been there and talked to . . . numerous people in the homeless shelter, and realized that the majority of the people didn't just get homeless by being real lazy or on alcohol as the stereotype of many of the homeless people in America. I would say my opinion would be better if I had actually been there, experienced it, and they hadn't. That's the only way I would see it as better." A student working in a tutoring program in a school had a similar view: "Part of it is personal experience. I'm not an expert, but I have gone to school with people in a lot of these situations, through high school and middle school. And just knowing people, and then knowing teachers who have worked with teens. I hear stories . . . ; they just tell me things." The things she observed herself or heard from people she knew were central to understanding the issue.

While students who reason at this stage have difficulties judging among multiple perspectives and dealing with conflicting expertise, they clearly grasp that these conflicts are inherent in the problematic situation. With this understanding, they are likely to be interested in and open to reflective practices that lead them to explore alternatives sources of information. For some the difficulties in moving beyond the view that it is all a matter of opinion may make reflective activities seem pointless, but for others the importance of sharing opinion and exploring the issue fully becomes more legitimate. With practice at framing and analyzing perspectives, they may develop the ability to interpret evidence from competing perspectives with greater skill and confidence.

Students who are reasoning at stage four or five have some difficulty forming a well-integrated big picture of a complex issue. At stage four the student has trouble forming a well-reasoned or warranted judgment and tends to fall back on personal experience or discounts the credibility of experts on one side of an issue. At stage five students are more inclined to want to keep the issue open and avoid closure; if pressed, they will often fall back on similar strategies as those at stage four. Although students reasoning at stage five do have difficulty arriving at warranted judgments, they are able to identify ill-structured problems and recognize multiple perspectives. Although they have difficulty sorting out and integrating multiple perspectives, they can begin to frame in a balanced way multiple ways of looking at the issue. They note that experts may disagree because of different disciplinary perspectives and are likely to place heavy emphasis on diversity in perspective, legitimacy of different views, and the importance of trying to develop a more objective view. Like those reasoning at stage four, they have difficulty coming to a well-reasoned decision that integrates information across multiple perspectives, but they may be able to find closure within perspectives.

A student who was assisting with an AIDS education program for high school students discussed why experts disagree about the AIDS epidemic: "Experts, when they consider the AIDS epidemic, may be seeing just a side of it while integrating that into a collective whole, but though they present various opinions, I think what causes a lot of experts to disagree with each other is that they're coming from different areas, different intellectual levels, different experiences, and have expounded on that, maybe leaving out some other aspects." This student went on to discuss selecting a viewpoint based on the aspect of the problem to be solved; she decomposed a problem into elements and focused on one at a time: "My initial inclination would be to go with the person who has done the most research, is most knowledgeable on the issue I specifically address." She did not discount expertise or denigrate experts as the student reasoning at stage four did, but rather tried to make a choice among them. What she could not do was integrate their differing perspectives into some larger picture of the issue.

Students who are moving to the highest stages—six and seven— tend to be reflective about their response, asserting and defending a position but acknowledging that it is tentative and subject to revision. Like Dewey, they see answers in terms of the new questions they raise. A student working with the local emergency management agency talked about how he makes decisions about disasters involving chemicals or environmental hazards: "I don't think that you can ever be 100 percent sure on a situation like that, that I'm 100 percent sure that I'm right. The chances are I could be wrong, but looking at it and looking at the information that I have available, I think, 'Okay, this is what I have to go with right here, right now. Now tomorrow, I'm going to learn something new, and that might change my decision.' I think that that has to be your outlook and that you have to look at it . . . [as if] you're always looking for the right answer, or a better answer, or a better way to do it, almost reforming what you're thinking, because if you stop and say, 'Okay, this is it, I figured it out,' what if you didn't? I think the trick is you don't stop; you continue pursuing what the right answer is." This student clearly sees that when experts disagree, "You can't stop disagreeing, and one can't give in. They both have to go on. . . . I think ultimately you have to keep searching for the next clue; you have to keep searching for the next piece of evidence, the next piece of proof." Students at this stage are confident though tentative, because they recognize that we are always acting in the face of uncertainty; uncertainty is inherent to all knowing.

Development of Critical Thinking Abilities

Students need high levels of critical thinking ability to address social issues effectively, and the processes that lead to cognitive development are very similar to those associated with well-designed service-learning experience. Although there is not a lot of previous research linking service-learning and cognitive development, our surveys and in-depth problem interviews provide some tentative support for the proposition that highly reflective service-learning can contribute to increased critical thinking capacity.

Service-Learning and Processes of Cognitive Development

The process of struggling to identify, frame, resolve, and perhaps readdress unstructured problems is made possible by both more advanced cognitive development and the process by which development occurs. People develop more complex structures for dealing with information when the approaches they commonly use are challenged and prove inadequate. When our student remarked that "it never gets any easier. It's like the less you know about an issue the easier it is," she is acknowledging the challenge posed by more experience with an issue. Some students talked about hearing one viewpoint and embracing it, only to be confronted with another perspective that seemed just as plausible. As one student observed, it was difficult to settle on one viewpoint: "Each time, each new assignment [convinced me], "Well, this is the way I think," and then another assignment is assigned and it's like maybe it should be *that* way." Others clearly recognized that they had made a transition from dualism to relativism in their thinking: "Service was enlightening, but at the same time it was more confusing because I learned that nothing is black and white, and it's very gray. Does that make sense?"

Coming to terms with conflicting perspectives and taking a position, no matter how tentative, is intellectually engaging work. Students who function at different stages of development are likely to react differently to attempts to engage them in the process of understanding issues and justifying their positions. This process requires a balance of challenge and support so that students are neither discouraged by facing difficult issues nor complacent because answers are neatly provided for them in the classroom (Knefelkamp, Widick, and Parker, 1978).

The principles of effective service-learning (Honnet and Poulsen, 1989) are strikingly similar to the elements associated with cognitive development during the college years. Pascarella and Terenzini (1991) have noted that development of critical thinking ability is associated with instruction that places an emphasis on engaging students in problem solving, focuses on problem-solving procedures, and involves students in discussions at relatively high levels of cognitive activity. Course work that is interdisciplinary and asks students to apply themes across the curriculum also promotes critical thinking. These authors also observed the importance of engaging students in intellectual and cultural activities. Working closely with faculty and other students on intellectual matters rather than purely social ones is associated with higher levels of cognitive development.

Service-learning can provide precisely this set of conditions for growth. Students may be engaged in interesting and meaningful work where they have a chance to work closely with other students around substantive intellectual issues. As we report in Chapter Eight, in service-learning classes with high levels of discussion, writing, and application of subject matter to the service situation, students are most likely to build the close connections with faculty associated with development. The reflective link between community service and classroom learning in well-designed service-learning classes also allows both challenge and support, which Pascarella and Terenzini (1991) identified as central to progress in critical thinking using Perry's scale. Because students engaged in social problem solving are encouraged to come to closure—to create solutions—they have to reconcile conflicting points of view and sources of information. For some this process will help them apply their most advanced abilities; for others it will be the factor that helps them move to the next stage in their ability to evaluate and use complex information.

The fact that service-learning takes learning out of the classroom and into the community may also be central to its power in facilitating cognitive development. As Resnick (1987b, p. 19) wrote, "When we begin to focus attention on thinking and learning abilities as goals of education, the distinctions between learning in school and out seem less sharp." She notes that many of the qualities of learning outside school, such as sharing in the learning process with others, and direct engagement with real people, issues, and problems, rather than knowledge in the abstract, are central to learning how to think. Schooling can provide the opportunity to engage in structured reasoning and reflection about the real world; experience in that world anchors the process. Her suggestions are a fair description of well-integrated service-learning where formal reflection is tied to community service.

Service-learning provides the conditions that experiential educators, cognitive developmentalists, and cognitive scientists link to increased ability to solve ill-structured or open-ended problems.

Service-Learning Contributes to Critical Thinking

Astin and Sax (1998) asked seniors whether they developed critical thinking skills over the course of their college education. They found that performing community service during college is linked significantly with this measure of critical thinking. Of course, this is a link with service, not service-learning, and may well reflect a selectivity bias: students who are more serious about their studies and have a higher regard for themselves intellectually may choose service over other available activities. And, of course, we are dealing with a self-assessment of critical thinking at one point in time rather than over the course of the college years or with a demonstration of critical thinking skill. But this link does suggest that the issue is worth exploration, which we have done in both our survey and intensive problem-solving interviews with college students.

In our survey, students assessed their ability to "identify social issues," which is related to the first stage of the problem-solving process, and their ability to "see consequences of actions," which is part of sorting out competing solutions in resolving issues. They also responded to an item that asked about their ability to "think critically," which is similar to the measure Astin used. Students also responded to a four-item scale that sought to capture their openness to new points of view, which is central to the process of continuously evaluating new evidence and perspectives when students try to make and justify well-reasoned judgments about issues. We found over the course of the semester that participating in service-learning positively affected students' perceptions of their "ability to identify social issues," as well as their openness to new ideas; it did not, however, have an impact on their assessment of their ability to "think critically." Regression tables showing these relationships are in Resource D.

Program Quality Affects Critical Thinking and Problem Solving

When we looked only at the eleven hundred survey students who participated in service-learning over the course of the semester, we found that all four survey measures of critical thinking were affected by the quality of their service-learning. Service-learning with a high level of discussion—a measure combining both more discussion and discussion that focused on higher levels of intellectual activity— had a positive impact on students' assessment of their critical thinking ability, and this, as well as the application of course material to

the service experience, were both positive predictors of issue identification ability; application, writing, and being involved in service
that met the needs of the community and brought students into
contact with people from diverse ethnic groups were associated with
the ability to see the consequences of actions.

The openness scale showed an interesting pattern. Placement in
a high-quality service situation, which included such elements as
having varied tasks, challenging responsibilities, and interesting
work, and completing more writing assignments were both predictors of openness over the course of the semester. Thus exposure to
the need to act and reflection in the form of writing reduced the students' conviction that they "knew for sure" and should stand pat on
their particular opinion. At the same time, application of the course
work to the service experience, and vice versa, was associated with
reduced openness and greater confidence in one's position. Perhaps
their perception that they had gained expertise on the topic reduced
their openness to new information. Indeed one student noted, "I'm
sure I'd have to listen to what everyone else is saying. I listen to
what everyone is saying up to the point I make my decision. Once
I make my decision, I just think that's it, and I shouldn't listen any
more." Since skill at readdressing problems already resolved falls at
the highest levels of critical thinking ability, it is not surprising to
have mixed results on this openness measure.

The findings relating program characteristics to these outcomes
is consistent with theory about how service-learning might promote critical thinking abilities. Discussion, writing, and application are all forms of reflection and engagement that one would
expect to promote development. But survey measures ask us to
rely on students' assessment of their abilities rather than a measurement of those abilities. Although these findings are encouraging, it would be more convincing to be able to examine how
students think about complex social problems and about how they
justify their positions in order to see the effects of service-learning
on critical thinking. That is what we did with the problem-solving

interviews. Regression tables pertaining to these outcomes are in Resource E.

Measuring Critical Thinking

In the problem-solving interviews students discussed causes of and solutions for a problem closely related to their service-learning placement and studies. In the analysis of the social problem interviews discussed in Chapter Three, we focused on the substance of the students' problem analysis: what they saw as the causes of such problems as homelessness, poor school performance, or racial conflict. In order to assess the cognitive developmental level of their critical thinking, we also had them discuss a number of questions that focused on how they arrived at their understanding of these issues.

Students not only discussed causes of the social problem, but how sure they were about their judgments of those causes, how they might become more certain, how they would judge among conflicting sources of information, and how they would justify their own position. These questions are based on reflective judgment theory, but we did not use the standardized interview developed by King and Kitchener to assess reasoning. The Reflective Judgment Interview (RJI) focuses on standardized problems, such as the theory of evolution and the question of who built the pyramids. We wanted to have students respond specifically to the problems they faced in their service-learning, and so we integrated questions about how they justified their positions into a more comprehensive interview that assessed their substantive thinking about the social issue, as well as their reactions to their service-learning experience. Their responses were rated using a system developed by Cindy Lynch, who has worked extensively with reflective judgment measurement. Although it does not produce formal RJI scores, the process rests on the same theoretical constructs and the scores on the resulting critical thinking and problem solving scale are roughly analogous to the seven-stage reflective judgment model described in Table 5.1.

We decided on an interview approach in order to measure critical thinking in the context of the actual issues that students were dealing with in service-learning. Because this is a developmental construct that generally changes slowly over time, it was not clear that we should expect a lot of change over the course of a single semester. Some preliminary study using the paper-and-pencil Reflective Judgment Scoring Instrument did show upward shifts in score that approached significance with a small sample of interns in our undergraduate program. This suggested to us that intensively reflective programs might have an impact on a cognitive developmental measure of critical thinking. By using our problem-solving interview, we were able to combine interest in the substantive analysis of these problems with our interest in the students' cognitive development.

Critical Thinking and Understanding Social Problems

Our measures of critical thinking and the measures of causal and solution complexity, personal strategy, and application of knowledge reported in Chapter Three were developed separately, scored by different raters, and applied to different parts of the problem-solving interviews, but there were fairly high correlations between the students' critical thinking score and these other measures on the posttest. These correlations, which ranged from .36 for the relationship between critical thinking and solution complexity to .58 for the relationship with issue knowledge, were all significant. The processes that help students develop a richer understanding of the social issue may also encourage cognitive development, or perhaps students with greater critical thinking ability reach higher levels of understanding and application.

Since it is easier to assess a student's essay for level of knowledge used in support of a position and for the complexity of both causal and solution analysis than it is to assess the stage of critical thinking evidenced in their writing, it may also be possible for faculty interested in helping students develop to use these complexity elements as rough markers of progress rather than attempting to master reflective judgment models.

Integrated Service-Learning Affects Critical Thinking

The average pretest critical thinking and problem-solving score for all sixty-five of the interviewed students was 4.08, which is close to the similar reflective judgment scores for college students reported in the literature (King and Kitchener, 1994). No one scored below 3, and very few were at 5 or above. As might be expected with a developmental construct for students in a similar college environment, age was the only significant predictor for this initial critical thinking score. Neither gender nor previous service was a predictor. Students reasoning at this level have the ability to recognize the ill-structured nature of a social problem but will have some difficulty in identifying the complexities of alternative perspectives and considerable difficulty forming well-founded resolutions for these conflicts and confidently justifying their choices.

Most students remained relatively stable on their critical thinking score over the course of the semester. When we compared service-learning and control students, service-learning in and of itself was not a predictor of change in critical thinking.

Although most students did not show growth in their critical thinking scores over the semester, about a third did show some upward movement. A significant predictor of this change was participation in a class where community service was central to the day-to-day focus of the course. On average, the students in the high-integration group were also at a slightly higher stage at the beginning of the semester; some of them may have been especially ready to move to or perform at a more advanced level. The means are presented in Table 5.2. The regression table that shows these relationships is in Resource F (see Table F.2).

Some might argue that the change captured here may have been more a matter of students being better able to function at their already attained levels than of stage change; as with other cogni-

Table 5.2. Mean Critical Thinking Scores, Before and After Service-Learning Semester.

	Control Group	Low-Integration Service-Learning	High-Integration Service-Learning
Pretest	3.96	4.07	4.16
Posttest	3.94	4.08	4.41

Note: Analysis of sixty-six pre- and posttest problem-solving and critical thinking interviews. Scores are based on a scale from 1 to 7, roughly analogous to reflective judgment levels.

tive developmental measures, students tend to do better on subjects they know a lot about and in environments where their efforts at analysis are well supported. This has been reported in other studies of postformal reasoning (King and Kitchener, 1994; Lynch, 1996; Kitchener, Lynch, Fischer, and Wood, 1993). Certainly the reflective activities in these interdisciplinary courses may have provided that support, and the students' familiarity with the issues through study and experience might have also allowed them to apply their critical thinking skills at a level closer to their optimal level. Whether a semester of well-integrated, highly reflective service-learning helps students consolidate or exhibit previous gains or helps them develop to a higher level, the findings support the value of service-learning in intellectual development. The fact that cognitive development is a slow process supports the idea that multiple experiences combining community service with academic courses may be valuable.

In one example of a highly integrated class, students worked in teams studying issues related to public policy and AIDS and met for training and service activities with local community groups. They then spent an intensive spring break week working full time in AIDS outreach activities and attending reflective seminars. After the intensive experience, the teams completed policy recommendations and continued service with local agencies. In another example, students participating in a multisemester service-learning program were engaged in community service combined with a class on social change that provided theoretical input as well as organizing skills and used the students' work as a discussion focus.

In the less integrated service-learning classes, service was either an option taken by only some students or less central to the day-to-day work of the class. For example, when asked about how the service was used in the class, a student described a day when some of the children who were being tutored came and made a presentation to the college class as a whole: "That was kind of the only time it was really brought in." When asked what else she would have liked to have seen done, the lack of integration became obvious. She agreed that more in-class activities would have been good "for me but not for the rest of the class that wasn't doing it. I mean, it was definitely a very small minority of the class that was participating in the volunteer thing that we were doing, so the rest of the class wouldn't have really had any interest in it. I would really have liked to sit around and discuss it with the other students working with other grade levels and see what they thought, but having the whole class do it would have been kind of silly." Not only did the student report little link between the academic focus of the class and her service, but she did not see how that link could be achieved in this case. She could not imagine that her experiences and those of her fellow volunteers would have anything to contribute to the learning of students who were not participating. Not surprisingly this student did not think that her service had changed the way she thought about the issues.

Students in this and other classes where service was an option or was not central to class discourse liked this option and felt that they gained a lot from their service. Including a service option in a course can make many contributions to student development. As Astin and Sax (1998) have shown, service even without the link to the academic program can be linked to positive gains during the college years. But where the goal is increased critical thinking ability, frequent opportunities for challenging reflection are important in theory, and this appears to be supported in practice. Students in our study who showed change over the course of a semester were in classes where reflection was intense and frequent and tightly linked to the service experience.

Summary: Critical Thinking and Problem Solving

Service-learning, particularly service-learning that is highly reflective and where course and community service are well integrated, has an impact on the quality of student thinking and problem solving. In our surveys and interviews with students participating in service-learning, we found the following:

- Service-learning did not have an impact on student reports of their critical thinking skill over the course of a semester, but did affect their reported ability to identify social issues and changes in their openness to new ideas.

- The quality of service-learning, including application, opportunities for structured reflection, and diversity and community voice, was a predictor of reports of critical thinking, ability to see consequences of actions, issue identification, and openness to new ideas.

- Students who are in service-learning classes where service and learning are well integrated through classroom focus and reflection are more likely to show an increase in their level of critical thinking demonstrated in problem analysis than those in classes where the service was less well integrated into the course or where no service was done.

- The reflective judgment theory that King and Kitchener developed provides a useful frame of reference for

viewing the development of problem-solving and critical thinking abilities in college students.

Changes in critical thinking ability represent a transformation
in the way students see and use knowledge. In the next chapter we
explore how service-learning may contribute to transformations in
the way students view society and social problems.

6

Perspective Transformation

*It kind of brought me to a situation where I would
stop, rewind, and replay a lot of the happenings as
I've processed and digested how it has affected me.
It's as if I just put on a new pair of glasses. I see
things totally differently.*

Some people leave service-learning with a new set of lenses for
seeing the world. For this student who spent spring break working in an AIDS outreach program as part of her policy class, it is not
about accumulating more knowledge but about seeing the world in
a profoundly different way, one that calls for personal commitment
and action. Her frame of reference has shifted. Another student,
who worked for several months at a local food pantry, illustrates
how such a shift occurs. As she described the agency with which
she worked, she noted that "it was supposed to be a relief organization for people in an emergency, but it doesn't really. It's working
on a problem that's never really going to go away if they don't do
anything about it. If they don't start changing . . . the institutional
structure, the problems are going to exist forever." Her realization
of the limited impact of her efforts grew slowly: "It was kind of a
cumulative thing for me instead of being an instantaneous thing.
Because when you see the same people coming in month after
month in the same exact situation they were in the month before,"

she realized that this was a continuing problem, not an emergency. She added that in the classroom, "we did some reading on the theories of change—like you can have change within the existing structure, or you can change the existing structure itself. And that was one thing that I thought about and kind of related the two together. So it was also the classroom that helped me make that decision to change focus in my service." Subsequently she began to look for service where she could put her new desire to "work with people rather than work for them." She felt uncomfortable with the charitable role: "In the family emergency assistance agency, I was in a position of authority. People would come to me, and I wouldn't be able to work with them to find the best alternative, but I was working always within these guidelines that forced me to treat them a certain way. . . . So I thought it would be better and our efforts would be more focused and make a bigger change if we worked on something that could have a long-lasting impact by changing the structure of something rather than just giving someone a can of food."

This student's perspective about poverty was transformed in the course of her service. The shift in her frame of reference began when she was exposed to a situation and a program that did not make sense to her. She could not see how something could be serving an emergency, by definition a short-term crisis, when families who used the system returned month after month for aid. The situation bothered her, as did her own role as charity giver. She was able to share these feelings with others in her classroom, many of whom were working in different service settings, and in that classroom setting she also had the opportunity to explore theories of social change. She was helped to reflect on the nature of the problem and solution that she was involved with and to explore the assumptions that underlay the work of her agency. Out of this framework of reflection and service she was able to join with others to commit to working with efforts more closely aligned with the need to bring about social change rather than accommodate to current palliative approaches to poverty.

This chapter focuses on the role of service-learning in helping some students critically examine what they know and "put on new glasses" as they reframed their understanding of social issues and social change. In this chapter, we will explore the meaning of "transformational learning," discuss evidence for the impact of service-learning on perspective transformation, and identify some ways in which service-learning facilitates this process.

Perspective Transformation as a Goal of Service-Learning

For many people, the ultimate goal for service-learning is social change, or at the very least educating students who will be agents of social change (Lempert, 1995). There is some tension around this goal because social action is a process that involves advancing some interests over others or changing arrangements that are already quite congenial to some people in the community. In other words it is political, and politics is about competing interests and controversy. Some educators shy away from activities where students take a political stand, wary of being accused of using students to advance their own personal social agendas. Some are concerned that advocacy may get in the way of objectivity. Others have learned firsthand that encouraging students to question fundamental arrangements of their society is not welcomed by some parents, administrators, boards, or alumni. This is a risk that is very apparent to those working with high school students, but college programs are not immune. Others worry that government funding agencies will not support activities that have a political flavor, and indeed there is considerable nervousness among funders about anything that might be construed as partisan politics or advocacy. In a previous project, we were asked not to include even the mildest and most abstract criticisms of politicians made by the students because it might offend those needed to support funding for service-learning.

Some fear that bringing politics into education will somehow undercut support or deflect education from its mission of enlightenment, but for many others education itself is ultimately a political act. Paolo Freire (1970), one of the better-known leaders of this movement internationally, saw the development of political consciousness as central to instructing adults in literacy. Education was not just about learning to read, but learning to question the conditions that left many without access to education, economic opportunity, or political power.

Service-learning practitioners tend to come down on the side of transformational learning, supporting education that raises fundamental questions and empowers students to do something about them. Many believe that the essence of effective service-learning is in moving students beyond charity to active, committed citizenship. They hope that students will move beyond handing out cans of food to becoming actively engaged in long-term community problem solving. Students who work with community partners to make real changes happen in the community are political actors; this commitment to finding the roots of a community problem and making changes that address those root causes is likely to involve the student in questioning the status quo. It is this questioning of assumptions about how society is organized and how these assumptions underlie social problems that is at the heart of transformational learning. The process by which this transformation occurs is critical reflection—first recognizing what is and then stepping back and asking more fundamentally, "Why is it this way?" and "What needs to change to solve this problem?" Service-learning provides an ideal opportunity for students to confront situations that raise questions, be encouraged to question assumptions, acquire additional information and experience, and be pushed to rethink their view of the world and their future role in it. While genuine perspective transformation is probably a rare educational outcome (Shumer and Cady, 1997), service-learning is a process ideally suited to setting students on a path to bring this change about.

Transformational Learning as a
Theory of Adult Development

Among theorists concerned with transformational learning, Mezirow's approach is useful for educators because it is "directed at the intersection of the individual and social" (Tennant, 1993, p. 36). As educators our first commitment is to development of our students, and yet for many of us, social transformation is also central to our lives. Mezirow (1991, 1994) places perspective transformation into a broader context of learning; he views transformational learning as a comprehensive theory of adult development. Like Dewey, Kolb, Schön, and others who have contributed to our understanding of service-learning, Mezirow is a constructivist who views learning as "the social process of construing and appropriating a new or revised interpretation of the meaning of one's experience as a guide to action" (Mezirow, 1994, p. 223).

Not all learning is transformative. Learning can involve simply acquiring new information or elaborating on information that we already have. Service-learning students who become aware of the role of deinstitutionalization in homelessness or begin to understand the complexity of an environmental problem exhibit this type of learning. Transformational learning occurs as we struggle to solve a problem where our usual ways of doing or seeing do not work, and we are called to question the validity of what we think we know or critically examine the very premises of our perception of the problem. So while students who acquire more complex information on the many factors that contribute to homelessness are merely deepening their understanding of the issue, the student who begins to question government budgetary priorities or zoning regulations or the way in which access to medical care is linked to employment is starting to question some assumptions about the way society operates. This process of questioning may lead to a transformation of perspective.

Mezirow sees two types of meaning structures: meaning perspectives, which consist of the basic psychocultural assumptions on which our view of the world rests, and meaning schemes, the more specific manifestations of our meaning perspectives—that is, the content of our concepts, beliefs, judgments, and feelings that shape our particular views. Perspective transformation involves changing fundamental assumptions; meaning transformation addresses a specific issue. Students in our study who realized that "AIDS is not just a gay disease" ("I met women and their children with AIDS") or who had believed that homeless people "just don't want to work" and then met people who are struggling to find jobs without a phone or address were transforming their meaning schemes. They had more information about the subject and a richer context in which to comprehend this new material. The focus of this chapter, perspective transformation, concerns confronting not just new or discrepant information but situations that bring the very definition of the problem into question. The student who became impatient with defining poverty needs as "emergencies" and wanted to address structural inequities was questioning these premises. It is not just that she knew that people in poverty lived in a constant state of emergency, but that she questioned the usefulness of defining a continuing structural problem in society as an emergency.

Mezirow categorizes meaning perspectives into several subcategories. One is the structural way that people process knowledge; the changes in problem-solving skill discussed in Chapter Five fit this category, so that one can argue that cognitive development of postformal reasoning associated with critical thinking skill is in fact transformative learning. The fact that well-integrated service-learning changes the way knowledge is constructed and tested is an example of the link between service-learning and perspective transformation. In this chapter the focus is on the impact of service-learning on the social norms, ideologies, and theories of the way society works. Although Mezirow has often been criticized for emphasizing personal development rather than collective social action (Newman, 1994), transformation in perspective about these social arrangements is central to education for social action. When we looked at how the students we interviewed conceptualized the problems they were trying to solve—at whether they emphasized the systemic context of the problem or possible political solutions—we were attempting to explore this aspect of transformational learning.

Service-Learning Affects Perspective Transformation

One of the things that struck us in our initial focus groups and interviews with benchmark service-oriented students—those who were very active as participants and organizers of service and service-learning—was how powerfully they felt that their lives had been transformed by their service. One student was adamant that "service is an integral part of who I am. It really is the basis for how I live my life, and so to ask me to stop would be to ask me to stop living." We particularly found students talking about political action when they were in service-learning programs with a long-term commitment to integrating service-learning into the curriculum and the curriculum was specifically directed at social change.

A student need not raise fundamental questions to feel changed by service-learning, however. Students who meet homeless people for the first time and learn about some of the many factors that contribute to homelessness feel that they see the issue in a new way, perhaps because they had seen it hardly at all before. Although many of the changes we were able to capture through survey and interview are probably closer to what Mezirow calls meaning transformation than perspective transformation, we did find that involvement in service-learning, particularly in highly reflective programs, moved students toward a more systemic view of social problems and a greater sense of the importance of political action to obtain social justice.

Service-Learning Changes Students' Views of Social Problems

Perspective transformation—questioning and overturning one's fundamental assumptions about society—is not something that happens often in a lifetime. Nor is it something that we would expect to occur for most students in most service-learning courses. There is evidence that it is indeed a relatively rare outcome; Shumer and Cady (1997) found that only 8 percent of the participants in their evaluation study of Americorps reported that their service had a profound, life-changing effect.

Based on the feedback from the students we interviewed, we did expect to see some mention of more limited changes in students' views of the world. In our survey, we found that 34 percent of those who participated in service-learning indicated that one of the most important things that they learned was "to see social problems in a new way." Another measure of perspective transformation was the change over the course of the service-learning experience in how students explain social problems and what approach they believe needs to be taken to solve them. We looked at the extent to which students came to see social problems from a systemic rather than individually focused perspective. Would locus of social problems shift over the course of a semester of community service experience? We also measured changes in their sense that a pressing need in our society is to "achieve greater social justice," that "the most important community service is to change public policy," and that it is "important to me personally to influence the political structure." Each of these outcomes shows an emphasis on fundamental structural aspects of social problems and on political action for social change. Service-learning had a significant impact on all four of these outcomes in spite of the fact that those who participated in service-learning began the semester already higher on each measure. Students do experience some changes in their perspective on social issues as a result of service-learning. These results are presented in Resource D.

Program Quality Affects Perspective Transformation

All of our categories of program characteristics—placement quality, application, reflection, and diversity—increased the impact of service-learning on perspective transformation. (See Tables E.3 and E.6 in Resource E for regression statistics using the survey data.)

Impact of Placement Quality

Students in programs where they had varied tasks, important responsibilities, interesting work, and challenge were more likely to report that service-learning had led them to a new perspective on social issues. Perhaps the challenge component of this measure was the key since challenge to students' current opinions is central to the process of critical reflection that is at the heart of perspective transformation, and program characteristics related to reflection were consistently the most closely linked to changes in how students view social issues.

Impact of Reflection and Application

We would expect service-learning programs that spend a good deal of time challenging students to think about their service and reflect on their assumptions to have the greatest impact on perspective transformation. This appeared to be the case. Reflection characteristics of service were consistently linked to these outcomes. Application, amount of writing, and the quantity and quality of class discussion related to the service were all predictors of "learning to see social issues in a new way." (See Table E.3 in Resource E.)

Application was also a good predictor of change in personal commitment to influencing the political structure, belief in the importance of social justice, and the importance of changing social policy. Academic study related to the service provides an avenue for questioning assumptions and gathering more extensive information to address questions that emerge when students are surprised or puzzled by what they experience in the community. When there is not a strong academic link, students may fail to follow through when confronted with a puzzling situation. We talked with students who expressed curiosity about issues but then noted, "I never did anything more about it." Discussion predicted that students would be more committed to influencing the political structure, and both writing and discussion produced students who believe in the importance of social justice. Reflection appears to shift students in the direction of heightened social concern. (See Table E.6 in Resource E.)

Impact of Diversity and Community Voice

The opportunity to work with people from different ethnic backgrounds should create opportunities both for challenge to old stereotypes and to expose students to points of view with which they might not be familiar. We described some of the impact of diversity on stereotyping and personal connections in Chapter Two and as a catalyst to learning in Chapters Three and Four. We would expect these experiences to be useful in helping students attain new perspectives on social issues. Diversity was a predictor that students would report that they "learned to think about social issues in new ways" and that students would be increasingly concerned with social justice. A greater tendency over the course of the service-learning semester to attribute social problems to more systemic causes resulted from programs where students had the opportunity to work on service projects that met needs identified by the community; community voice was a predictor of a more systemic locus for social problems. Both diversity and community voice are characteristics of a program that would seem to offer opportunities to break down stereotypes and create disorienting perceptions of issues.

Well-Integrated Service-Learning Affects Systemic Orientation to Social Problems

Students who were intensively interviewed before and after service showed the impact of reflection on changes in their analysis of the causes and solutions of social problems and on the degree to which their solution strategy is systemic and political. In Chapter Three we discussed the impact of a well-integrated and reflective service-learning experience on increased causal and solution complexity, application, and personal strategic knowledge, and in Chapter Five we linked it to increased critical thinking and problem solving. In those same interviews we examined the causal and solution locus implicit in the students' analysis of their social problem and the nature of their general strategy for solving the problem. Average scores for interviewed students with no service, service not well integrated into the class, and highly integrated service-learning are presented in Table 6.1.

Locus refers to the source of the problem and the central thrust of the solution: whether the problem is centered in individuals and their behavior that is best solved by attention to changing individuals or whether it is a problem that has systemic roots and solutions. For example, one student accounted for poverty by focusing on the personal characteristics of poor people: "I'd say maybe education. They can't find a job because they don't have certain skills. They don't know how to manage their money, or they spend it on things that really don't help them get out of poverty." Students with a strong systemic view of these issues tended to identify both individually oriented and systemic problems and place individuals and community groups within a larger context. A student working with a program designed to assist people in crisis identified half a dozen specific local factors that contribute to poverty in his town and then went on to talk about the social safety net and policies that affect the poor: "I think it is really important to look at the actual effects of how the system works now, not necessarily look at the regulations themselves, but how the regulations play out in people's lives. . . . Also [important is] realizing that things are very interconnected and that some small change over here is going to affect some other change and realizing that you can't just adjust one area of a system. . . . And I think you also need to consider long-term outcomes rather than short-term fixes."

Students with this systemic view of causes and solutions also tended to create practical solution strategies with an increased emphasis on political change. The student who realized that an "emergency" that lasts for a very long time may suggest a need for fundamental social change rather than a food pantry was thinking

Table 6.1. Mean Perspective on Social Problems Before and After Service-Learning: Problem-Solving Interviews.

	Locus of Problem		Locus of Solution		Solution Strategy	
	Before	After	Before	After	Before	After
Control group, no service	1.83	2.00	1.90	1.92	2.72	2.67
Low-integration service-learning	1.94	2.19	2.25	2.56	2.81	3.19
High-integration service-learning	2.26	2.85	2.37	3.15	2.78	3.51

Note: Scales run from 0 to 4. Based on interviews with fifty-five students before and after service.

about political strategies for change. Part of the process of perspective transformation is seeing the way current understanding is embedded in a system of assumptions about reality. We expected students engaged in critical reflection to begin to think in more complex and systemic ways about social issues and about the organized political action that might bring about change. As we can see in Table 6.1, students who participated in well-integrated service-learning experiences had higher average scores on both the locus and strategy dimensions of their problem-solving interviews at the end of the semester.

In these interviews, participation in more integrated and reflective programs was a predictor over the course of the semester of a more systemic analysis of both the causes and the solution of the target problem and of a shift toward a more policy-oriented solution. These students saw problems embedded in complex social structures not as simply evidence of personal failings or immediate program failure. Regression results for the interviews are summarized in Table F.2 in Resource F.

How Service-Learning Encourages Perspective Transformation

Service-learning offers students an opportunity to involve themselves in issues. They are also likely to interact with people whose experiences are different from their own and to come into contact with situations or ideas that challenge their previous assumptions. In a well-designed program, they will have the ability to confront these conflicts and sort out ideas and experience through continuous reflective discourse. For some, these experiences will help them critically assess some of their fundamental orientations to society and their role as citizens and will forever change how they involve themselves in their community.

Creating Disorienting Dilemmas

Transformational learning occurs when individuals confront disorienting dilemmas; transformation becomes possible when this dilemma raises questions about fundamental assumptions. Although there is a tendency for people to avoid information that disrupts their worldview, the powerful emotional component of community involvement in service-learning may make dissonance harder to ignore. There are a variety of ways in which service leads to disorientation; personal attachments develop that challenge stereotypes, students have the chance to step into another person's shoes, personal values are challenged, and students confront situations that surprise them.

Challenge to Stereotypes

Perhaps the most striking example of dissonance is the impact of community service on students' stereotypes of others. Even in service experiences of limited duration and without much opportunity for reflection, students report, often with surprise, that the people they worked with were very different from their expectations (Giles and Eyler, 1994a). As we saw in Chapter Two, survey and interview students showed reductions in stereotyping, greater appreciation for diverse cultures, increased tolerance, and the sense that the people they met through community service were "just like me."

This sense of fellow feeling is certainly something of a transformation of perspective, and it may serve as a platform for future growth, but many of these students did not seem to move beyond this epiphany to a deeper questioning of the social structure. For some, however, the realization that people who seem quite different are in fact a lot like themselves causes them to begin to reflect on why people like themselves have such different resources and opportunities. A student who spent a week living in a homeless shelter commented on his shift from providing charity to wanting to become involved in community change: "There was a lot of talking with them and with their kids and realizing they are exactly the same. When you see someone that has the same intellectual capabilities and the same capacity for work and everything else as you but their situation is different—at that point I just lost my desire to 'help' them. I guess it grew into a desire to work with people rather than to work for them."

Another student noted, "Before service-learning I didn't really think a whole lot. I thought of myself as a pretty smart person, but at the same time I hadn't developed the awareness of how interconnected the social structures are and how people are affected. I was really in a tunnel vision of me and where I came from, and I really hadn't broadened my horizons." When he began to work with homeless people, he fell back on old assumptions: "In the back of my head I had one of those old tapes that were like, 'Well, people are in their positions in life and everyone needs to be in this hierarchy' . . . not that people deserved what happened, but that it happened for a reason." He noted that when he became involved in a well-integrated service-learning program, "those stereotypes were just destroyed." He had moved beyond friendship or identification with the homeless people he worked with to reflection on the nature of the social structure. And unlike the experience of many of our other interviewees, this reflection was built into his service-learning course.

Challenge to Personal Values

Service-learning frequently puts students in situations where they work with people whose values and behaviors are very different from their own. As long as they view these people as different and their role as providing charity, this situation may not produce internal conflict. But when they get to know these people well and begin to see them as "like me," the differences create dissonance, and they are challenged to develop a worldview that can accommodate these discordant elements. A young woman with very deeply held religious values participated in a class that worked intensively with an AIDS outreach organization. Although she felt that homosexuality was sinful, she also worked closely with many gay men and women whom she liked and respected and spent a good deal of time grappling with her dilemma of accepting and yet not accepting homosexuality. She spent a good deal of time in her journal and in group reflection puzzling over her contradictory feelings. For her the defining moment came when she spent a day working alongside a man living with HIV who shared with her his experiences in his own church. She was particularly struck by his story of rejection by a fellow parishioner: "He told me that AIDS was God's punishment for my sins, but I asked him if perhaps AIDS hadn't been sent into the world to test his Christian compassion." This story provided an insight that allowed her to restructure the way she thought about AIDS and her own faith; suddenly there was no conflict between her own moral values and her friendship and compassion for the people she was working with. Her new perspective on Christian compassion had room for both.

Walking in Another's Shoes

A number of service-learning programs immerse students in situations designed to allow them to live the life—if only for a short time—of the people whom they are planning to serve. They live with and work alongside residents of shelters, reservations, or third world communities. A student who worked with women whose husbands were in prison talked about working intensively with one woman to help her find a job and obtain services for her children and how very difficult the burdens were that this woman faced in struggling to hold her family together: "I just learned a different perspective on life, I guess. I would try to imagine myself maybe poor or uneducated and my husband locked up for armed robbery. . . . I guess you could learn it in class, but I never did. You need to look from these women's point of view and just imagine yourself in their shoes."

A white student who worked with members of minority groups found her awareness of racial preference heightened: "This is something that really shocked me—how much I felt like people treated me preferentially because I was white. . . . Other folks who were Latino told me that would happen: 'Yeah, they will treat you that way.' I was just surprised at how much that sort of racism is ingrained in things that I totally take for granted a lot." But she also experienced feeling like a member of a minority group when she accompanied black children to a beach and her group was stared at: "It made me forever feel more comfortable being in the minority. And it also made me feel how so many people must feel in the dominant culture every day. I'd never thought about it when I was in a room full of people with only one person of color—how that person must feel. Even though the people in the room are welcoming them, it's still just odd to be the only one. I felt like I was onstage sometimes, like everyone was watching us."

Surprising Information

There were countless examples of students' finding themselves in situations that surprised them and challenged their view of the world. The phrase, "I had just never seen anything like this before," occurred in several interviews. Two students worked with children who were seriously injured by violence. One discovered that a third grader participating in a play she was producing would not be in the performance because he had been shot. Another student learned that the child she was tutoring was in the hospital with a stab wound:

> One of my favorite students was having the worst time trying to learn fractions. And I stayed after one day, and we worked and we worked, and he was saying . . . , "I don't care! I don't want to learn!" And he finally picked it up. It was Friday afternoon and he got it! And his face lit up—like you can imagine—and he said, "It'll be so great. On Monday we'll do all the rest of this book, and then I'll be caught up with my classmates when I get back to school." . . . But on Monday he didn't come to school. Over the weekend his sister stabbed him with a butcher knife and beat him over the head with a two-by-four, so he's in the hospital. . . . I thought, why would he even care about school if [his] home environment is such that [he] can't focus on school? I think what struck me most about that was the environment they were living in. . . . I'm from a very middle-class upbringing, and at the school that I was in, we never confronted any of those problems.
>
> We had to evacuate our service site one day because we had word that there was going to be a gang drive-by shooting. It was terrible but amazing—a part of America that I didn't even know existed at the time.

Transforming the Disorienting Dilemma into New Understanding

Critical reflection—systematic examination of one's fundamental assumption—is central to the process of perspective transformation. Without this struggle to explore the roots of the disorientation they experience, students are unlikely to restructure the way they view the world or be motivated to try to bring about structural change.

We found in our interviews that students who formed bonds with the people they worked with and found old stereotypes breaking down often did not take the next step to ask why, if these people are "like me," this problem exists. Students who did question assumptions were those who were continuously challenged to do so and in some cases were provided with the analytic tools to accomplish the task. Structured reflection was central to creating a habit of questioning and integrating experience and subject matter.

Challenge

One student discussed a detailed analysis of the service site that was conducted in his class: "Anything that's a challenge, I think, makes you think things differently. Everybody goes through their mindless mentality, and it's kind of the norm. When somebody's challenging you, I think they deviate from the norm; I think they get off-track, and it really makes them think of something differently. And I think that's what this reflection does; it really challenges people to do something they're not used to doing. They see things in a different way and are able to analyze it or get something out of it that they normally wouldn't have." When students are challenged, this reflective process can become a habit. As one student noted, she learned that "just getting that second perspective and probably learning to question things too—not to just absorb what you're reading in the textbook and take it at face value but to think about where the author is coming from: Why are they writing that? What's their background and perspective on this?" This critical reflection on the text extends to the field, where students ask, "Is this woman's life changing?" "Is this really working?" "Is this policy actually having the effect that this guy says it is, or is there some other side to it?"

Continuity of Experience

Another student stressed the importance of continuity in both experience and reflection: "An important part of any experience is that you question continually. It is easy when you go in once or twice to go the first time with preconceived ideas and look for information that affirms those ideas. Only when you go through it and study a thing for every week or every other week for a semester will you really have your experiences challenged." He stressed that continuous service alone is not enough: "If you don't reflect on it, it's easy to just keep going there for the same assumptions and operate on those. Only when you reflect and other people say, 'What about this?' or your professor writes in your journal, 'What about this?' Then you go back and say, 'Well, she asked about this. Maybe I can look for this information.' So it's important to have this experience on an ongoing basis."

Conceptual Tools

Students found that in attempting to reframe their understanding of issues it was also helpful to have class instruction that provided them with the intellectual tools to challenge fundamental assumptions. One student described how her class approached this: "We did some very tedious diagnostic analysis: take a problem and break it down, step by step by step, and get to the root structure of why. What's supporting the problem? Who are your adversaries? Which ways are we not seeing? And the whole idea of reframing is important. How can we reframe our problem? What are some creative solutions to this problem? Those are the most helpful for me." They weren't just learning information about the problem but learning how to question their perspectives. Another student said that she had been "given the vocabulary to critically look at the situation." She noted that "a lot of the things we've read this year, like we've even had stuff on reframing, being able to look at situations and to interpret them differently than your consciousness takes them to be. And that's part of ingesting information that's so different—like we read lots of different feminist perspectives—books that definitely bring in a whole lot of changes in the way you are thinking." Students who said their fundamental assumptions were challenged were most often involved in courses that gave explicit attention to critical reflection.

Reintegration and Commitment to Action

For some the reframing of perspective leads not to more service but to a change in the way they view service. As a student said, "When I was younger I wasn't really aware of the whys behind everything. I thought of it as, here I am in this social class and it was sort of an us-and-them sort of thing with people in the other class; that's kind of how my parents taught the social structure. You belong here, and they belong there. You can help them if you want to, but you're not a part of their world, and you stay separate." Over the course of her service-learning experience she became aware that "this sounds really condescending. . . . Now I think of it more as working with [people], . . . as a thing where everyone is part of everyone else in a society, and it's just as much your responsibility as everyone else's to do what you can. . . . I see it more as a give-and-take sort of thing now than just sort of a give-and-help."

Students who have spent lots of time in service—developing leadership roles and studying the issues in the classroom—may challenge their assumptions and move in the direction not just of action but of political action, as this student said: "I think I've become more politicized in my service. Growing up, I didn't have the questions, the structural questions. I didn't see the inequities on a day-to-day basis that exist in our society that I see now or that I'm now connecting my service with."

Summary: Service-Learning and Perspective Transformation

Dramatic transformations of perspective are rare, and we would not expect service-learning to lead to this outcome routinely. However, sufficiently engaging and intense experiences may facilitate such changes in some students. We found that service-learning, particularly service-learning that is highly reflective and where course and community service are well integrated, can have an impact on perspective transformation. In our surveys and interviews with students participating in service-learning, we found the following:

- About a third of participants in service-learning claimed that it gave them a new perspective on social issues.

- Service-learning had an impact on student perceptions of the locus of social problems and on their belief in the importance of social justice, the need to change public policy, and the need to influence the political structure personally.

- Application of subject matter and experience as well as opportunities for structured reflection are associated with these measures of perspective transformation.

- High quality community placements where students have real responsibilities and interesting and challenging work led students to report seeing issues in new ways.

- Students who are in service-learning classes where service and learning are well integrated through classroom focus and reflection are more likely to demonstrate a more systemic locus for causes and solutions of problems in their problem-solving interviews than those in classes where the service was less well integrated into the course or no service was done.

- Students who spoke most clearly in transformational terms, mentioning the importance of fundamental social change in our interviews, were those in intensive long-term service-learning programs where social transformation was an explicit part of the curriculum.

In the preceding five chapters we have explored some of the learning outcomes associated modestly but consistently with service-learning, in particular with service-learning that involves strong placements, opportunities for reflection, and experiences with diversity. In Chapter Seven we explore how these outcomes contribute to preparing students to be effective citizens.

7

Citizenship

The Government of the United States was developed
under the idea that nobody knew how to make a gov-
ernment or how to govern. The result is to invent a
system to govern when you don't know how. And the
way to arrange it is to permit a system, like we have,
wherein new ideas can be developed and tried out and
thrown away. The writers of the Constitution knew
of the value of doubt. In the age that they lived, for
instance, science had already developed far enough to
show the possibilities and potentialities that are the
result of having uncertainty, the value of having the
openness of possibility. The fact that you are not sure
means that it is possible that there is another way
someday. That openness of possibility is an opportu-
nity. Doubt and discussion are essential to progress.
                                              Richard Feynman

This quotation from Richard Feynman's 1963 lectures on science
and democracy illustrates the tentativeness of democracy from
a cognitive perspective (Feynman, 1998, p. 49). In keeping with Jef-
ferson's idea that each generation of informed citizens had to invent
its own forms of democracy, this characterization views democracy
as constantly constructed and inherently problematic, as well as full

of possibility. Reinhold Niebuhr put forth the theological variation of this view; he saw that the human capacity for good is what made democracy possible and that the human capacity for evil made democracy necessary. Whether you are reading *The Federalist Papers*, written over two centuries ago, or a current debate in a local newspaper about a petition drive to change the form of city government, this understanding of democracy seems inescapable. In the language of the cognitive science perspectives used in our earlier chapters, democracy is an ill-structured problem. Solving this problem requires citizens who have developed positive attitudes about community involvement, the intellectual abilities to think and plan, and the understanding to live with uncertainty.

Forms of Civic Participation

Depending on whether one's view of democracy is a Jeffersonian direct participation model or a more representative republican democracy, different forms of civic participation are relevant in different combinations. Nevertheless, it seems that some key forms of participation are relevant and necessary for a democratic society. As we will show in this chapter, each of these forms of participation has implications for the knowledge and skills required to be effective citizens.

Political Participation

Voting is the most commonly mentioned behavior of this type of participation and is the one that political scientists and trend watchers have been concerned about because of its decline. Informed and responsible voting is a necessary but not sufficient basis of democracy. The traditional notion of political leadership and public service at all levels is a more demanding form of political involvement, including dealing with tough issues of public policy and the fundamental issues of inventing and reinventing government itself.

Participation in Voluntary Associations

The American tendency for private citizens to talk about problems and form associations to address them surprised Alexis de Tocqueville during his visit to America in the mid-nineteenth century. This approach shocked his French sense of how to organize public life and was the focus of much of his writing about democracy in America. One of us had an experience recently that reminded us that this was not just a contrast between the established European ways and the social patterns of a new frontier democracy. While visiting a local fire brigade in England and during a discussion of the similarities and differences between the two countries, the brigade captain commented on the American phenomenon of volunteer fire departments. He said that firefighting was too important to leave to volunteers. We replied that the latest statistics we had at that point indicated that 80 percent of U.S. firefighters are volunteers.

Generation of Social Capital

The two dimensions of social capital are direct helping or service and social problem solving. Social capital exists in addition to market capital and infrastructure or government capital (Rifkin, 1996) and is created throughout the ongoing associations in a community or neighborhood. This capital is mobilized in times of need. (See Putnam, 1995, and Sirianni and Friedland, 1997, for a discussion of whether social capital has declined or increased.) The helping dimension initially involves neighbors' and residents' helping an individual or group of individuals in need. This is the fabled bucket brigade approach founded by Benjamin Franklin in Philadelphia and usually predates a formal voluntary association or becomes part of the work of one. This helping dimension is seen in our contemporary society as both a local phenomenon and the provision of help to fellow citizens hundreds of miles away in times of floods, hurricanes, tornadoes, and other natural disasters.

Social problem solving draws on the civic capacity to recognize, frame, and address a problem. This is often a local effort or a coordinated series of local efforts, such as the first Earth Day in 1970, that then develop into formal associational, political, and even governmental approaches. This is one of the key reasons that social capital for problem solving is crucial and involves a whole range of knowledge and skills.

Democracy, Education, and Citizenship

Dewey's dictum—"Democracy has to be born anew every generation and education is its midwife" (1933)—is hard to dispute at the general level. What remains problematic is to specify that relationship and then to translate it into educational practice. What is clear, if anything can be clear from Dewey's extraordinary large and complex body of writing, is that democracy, education, and citizenship are inseparable. Although the phrase "education for citizenship" is not uncommon, for Dewey it was education as citizenship and citizenship as education (Giles and Eyler, 1994b). Related to this linkage is the idea that educational philosophy and social philosophy about democracy and citizenship are inseparable. This linkage seems to run deep in service-learning practice, even though there are differences in emphasis (see Pollack, 1999).

Creation of Expert Citizens

One of the most intellectually challenging and exciting parts of this project has been to grapple with the relationship between learning in college and behavior as citizens after college. Earlier we used the term "expert citizens" to link the problem-solving literature on novices and experts in cognitive science and the problem-solving demands of citizenship (Eyler, Root, and Giles, 1998). This synthesis has led us to see the role of a citizen in a democracy as a solver of open-ended social problems. As we noted in the beginning of this chapter, democracy is an ill-structured problem.

This view has some special implications for service-learning and the data we present here on service-learning outcomes. Benjamin Barber has been the national proponent of a required civics curriculum that includes service in order to develop citizenship knowledge learned in the context of actual community engagement (1990; Barber and Battistoni, 1994). This view that service is for citizenship and not for charity raises one of the key issues in understanding the goals of service-learning. The idea that service-learning moves students from charity to justice is a pervasive one, although little is known about how it occurs or what programmatic elements may facilitate it (Morton, 1995). Recently we were given T-shirts at a national conference on service, sponsored by one of the national organizations that promotes service in higher education. On the front of these shirts is the slogan, "The path of service leads from charity to justice." Although we would not devalue individual helping as part of the development of social capital, we would argue that service-learning and higher education in general need to pay attention to the problem-solving capacities of college graduates in order to sustain lifelong constructive involvement in the community.

Curricula for Citizenship

In Chapter One we cited Boyer's notion of the move from competence to commitment. Robert Bellah and others have argued that the fundamental tension in American life is between individualism and commitment (Bellah and others, 1985). It is not surprising that the literature that looks at specific knowledge and skills for citizenship focuses on social commitment as well as individual competencies. Acknowledging that service-learning is one of several relevant pedagogies for citizenship education, Thomas Ehrlich (1997) has proposed three approaches for civic learning: community service-learning, problem-based learning, and collaborative or cooperative learning. In the next chapter we present our data on program characteristics that are effective in fostering service-learning outcomes.

One way to look at our data there is to note that the three types of learning Ehrlich argues for civic learning are present in the most effective service-learning programs.

In a parallel set of recommendations, Suzanne Morse (1989) recommends six ways to prepare college students for citizenship. The second of the six is "community and public service and experiential education" (p. 34). From the perspective we have developed through this project and from our data, we find the conclusions of this report to be correct in prescribing a curricular approach for higher education to develop civic responsibility in its students. Morse writes, "This recreating of our civic life requires skills beyond knowledge or subjective evaluations. It is more attitude, personal efficacy, acceptance of new ideas, diversity, and opposing opinions. It is about using political talk, thinking, judgment, and imagination to create the capacity to act thoughtfully and prudently on critical public issues" (p. 79).

The Five Elements of Citizenship

We organize our data in this chapter according to the five dimensions of citizenship that we have come to see as crucial in linking the attitudes, knowledge, values, and cognitive skills that comprise citizenship. Three comments are necessary to understand these data. The first is to understand that many of these outcomes were presented in five previous chapters as learning outcomes or the ends of service-learning as a pedagogy. Here we move those data to a higher level and view them as means to the end of citizenship. We also need to caution that any full understanding of how service-learning promotes effective citizenship requires a longitudinal study that examines actual citizenship behaviors over a significant period of time and determines if they are related to participation in service-learning programs of various types. Our data trace change over a briefer period, but they do demonstrate an increased willingness to participate in service, which is one of the dimensions of citizenship.

Our data also show that students develop increased abilities to solve ill-structured problems, which we are convinced is the heart of citizenship. Our final comment is that when we gathered our data, we found that few programs specifically articulated citizenship goals (for an exception, see Cooper and Julier, 1995; Cooper 1998). This may be related to Marilyn Smith's earlier finding (1993) that although policymakers and service-learning advocates promoted citizenship as the main goal for service-learning, students rarely think in those terms.

The personal, interpersonal, and intellectual development outcomes we have examined in earlier chapters prepare students for active participatory citizenship. Service-learning provides an ideal environment for connecting these disparate elements of student development into effective citizenship development. Here we examine how these outcomes combine to provide the essential elements for social responsibility and effective participation (regression tables in Resources D, E, and F support the data presented):

Values	"I ought to do."
Knowledge	"I know what I ought to do and why."
Skills	"I know how to do."
Efficacy	"I can do, and it makes a difference."
Commitment	"I must and will do."

Values: "I Ought to Do"

Feeling a sense of social responsibility is the first step in participatory citizenship. Engagement, or feeling connected to the community, provides a powerful motivation for involvement. When coupled with a belief in the importance of social justice and political action, this connectedness may lead to active citizenship.

Community Connectedness

We found that service-learning led students to a stronger sense of community connectedness, and this was heightened if they felt that the community had a voice in shaping the service activities. It was common for students to say, "It's my responsibility as someone who lives in this community to be a member of the community and help." Many students talked about how their service broke the barriers between "us" and "them" and helped them to feel a part of their community. One student said, "I would never have really truly understood these issues like homelessness. . . . It is learning a larger scale of these issues. Instead of just seeing myself working with the shelter or a few kids, I guess I have a picture of myself as part of a larger community working with these issues. I don't feel isolated. I've learned the importance of community when you are working in the social arena."

Importance of Social Justice

The belief that one should be actively involved in community change also rests on a vision of the need for change. We found that service-learning affected students' valuing of social justice and the need for political change, as well as their belief that it is important to have an impact on the political system. Application and discussion also facilitated change in these values, and diversity affected commitment to social justice. For some students exposure to injustice during their service-learning made it hard for them to turn away. Here is what one student had to say: "It really came down to my privilege again, of being able to do something for a few weeks and then pack up and go, and that's not okay for me. And that's when the idea of actually doing something for life came up. I don't want to just go somewhere and drop it. . . . We have a lot of power to change things, and we can make a difference."

Commitment to Service

For many students, like the one just quoted, social justice and commitment are tightly joined. Service-learning had an impact on students' belief in the importance of volunteering, for both themselves and citizens in general, and the quality of that experience, including application, diversity, and community voice, increased its impact. Although requiring community service of students was controversial among the students we surveyed, as it is among educators generally, the majority endorsed the idea of requirements, and those with applied and reflective service-learning were more likely to see its value.

Knowledge: "I Know What I Ought to Do and Why"

It is not enough to feel committed to community. Students also need the expertise and cognitive capacity to make intelligent decisions about what needs to be done.

Understanding Social Problems

As we saw in Chapters Three and Four, students report that service-learning contributes to their understanding of social issues and their ability to apply this information. They were more likely to report such benefits of service-learning if they were in classes where material was applied and there was considerable written or oral reflection. Even more important, students who were involved in highly reflective and well-integrated service-learning demonstrated their increased ability to analyze problems and apply what they were learning in the classroom, and their solution strategies were more likely to include systemic change and political action. Students in service-learning have told us in the surveys and shown us by the quality of their problem analysis in the interviews that service-learning can contribute to knowledge that can be used in the community.

Cognitive Development

To function as a problem solver in the civic society requires advanced cognitive capacity. The capacity to entertain doubt and yet forge ahead, mentioned by Feynman in his lectures on science and democracy, rests on the qualities of critical thinking discussed in Chapter Five. The capacity for thoughtful citizenship participation rests on the capacity for dealing with ambiguity, understanding with Dewey that the proper test of inquiry is "not only 'Have I solved this problem?' but 'Do I like the new problem I have created?'" (Schön, 1995).

Although change in postformal reasoning capacity, like that described by King and Kitchener (1994) and Perry (1970), is a slow developmental process, we did find a modest but significant change among students in well-integrated service-learning experiences.

Skills: "I Know How to Do"

Even students with a sophisticated understanding of social issues and public policy options may be unaware of how to proceed to make a difference. One of the particular strengths of service-learning is in helping students acquire practical experience for community action, as well as the interpersonal skills that make people effective. A student who is oblivious of the agencies and organizations already present in the community or who naively thinks that "telling them" is an effective method of changing behavior will find having an impact difficult.

Strategic Knowledge

Service-learning students in our survey reported an increased understanding of social agencies in the community. The students we interviewed demonstrated that integrated service-learning programs can increase their competence in identifying practical strategies for community change. Students who had those experiences showed sensitivity to the importance of mapping the community to identify the individuals and groups with a stake in the problem and the organizations already actively addressing it. They were aware as well of the need to understand the unique dynamics of the problem in the particular community.

Interpersonal Skills

In addition to practical skills and knowledge of community organizing, generic interpersonal skills are essential for effective citizenship. Students reported that service-learning helped them work better with others, and over the course of a semester the quality of their community placements contributed to leadership and communication skill development. We were impressed with the quality of strategic thinking of many of the students we interviewed; they were aware of their increasing competence as leaders and able to articulate how difficult and rewarding that was.

One student talked about the particular difficulties of organizing volunteer groups, where people are free not to return and participate if they are not sufficiently engaged. This is a real leadership challenge for anyone, and one that this student felt he had mastered through his service: "Tactics! Learning a lot about tactics and things you need to do in different situations. For example, to get people to stay in a group is hard. . . . The hardest thing was to get kids to keep coming back. I would go to each person individually and try to find a connection so that they felt that they had a say, a stake in what we were doing, that they put themselves into it and so therefore they didn't want to leave. That's the kind of tactics that I used, and that is how it all applies." He described the difficulty of acquiring skills for organizing a group but expressed confidence in his ability to succeed. The challenges of organizing in a diverse community setting helped students build stronger skills and confidence in their ability to act.

Efficacy: "I Can Do, and It Makes a Difference"

Being effective requires knowledge and skills, and it depends on the willingness to take the risk of involvement, which depends on personal self-confidence. People who do not believe that their skills will make a difference are less likely to participate in community action. Eagerness to act and lead carries an implicit message of personal confidence. We can hear that confidence in the voice of a student anxious to organize an activity in his community: "I felt it would be a new opportunity to approach the issues that I'd been working with, and I was eager to take on leadership positions because I wanted to implement some of my own ideas and get other students involved. . . . To me that was a challenge to be able not just to see someone else's ideas through, but to create my own ideas about how to do things."

We looked at two types of efficacy: belief in personal efficacy and community efficacy (the community's ability to solve its problems) (Scheurich, 1994). Both were increased by service-learning and the quality of the service experience, as well as the application of the service to the learning. Reflection and diversity increased the likelihood that students would feel that the community was competent to solve its own problems. Sometimes the road to efficacy began with a single effort: "I always thought one person couldn't make a difference. Why am I going to go and help?" This student went on to describe a day at a homeless shelter where she provided assistance to a man who had trouble eating: "I think I realized that day that one person can make a difference because I made a difference for that guy that day. And if every time I go into the shelter I can make a difference for one person, then it's worth it."

Commitment: "I Must and Will Do"

The ultimate test for the impact of service-learning on citizenship is behavior—what college graduates do in their community. For some, their experience creates a real urgency to do something about social justice: "You can study policy in the classes and it sounds good, great, until you actually see how it doesn't work. My anger level goes up, and I want to run for president or something."

The closest we could get to action in the time frame of our studies was to measure intent. In our survey 75 percent of the eleven hundred service-learning participants indicated that they would continue community service during the next semester. These participants were more likely than nonparticipants to grow in commitment to a career involving service. Students in service-learning that included high-quality placements, reflection, and community voice were more likely to find personal reward in service.

Service-learning has the capacity to develop students who feel connected to community and have the capacity to make a difference; perhaps most important it helps students incorporate community involvement into their sense of self: "Service is an integral part of who I am. It really is the basis for how I live my life, and so to ask me to stop it would be to ask me to stop living. . . . In the face of how overwhelming the problems are and how it seems as though our contributions are so minuscule, just a drop in the bucket, I've really been inspired by my peers who serve alongside me and the fact that the two of us, or the three of us, or the twenty of us, or the hundred of us can serve together. It's really energizing to me and gives me more hope and optimism that we can make a difference."

Summary: Citizenship and Service-Learning

Active and effective citizenship requires the personal qualities and interpersonal skills and also the understanding and cognitive development that are strengthened by well-designed service-learning. All of the outcomes identified in previous chapters are means to this end of active, committed community participation. This chapter has summarized these outcomes in the context of citizenship goals.

As we have noted, service-learning—particularly, well-integrated service-learning—contributes to attainment of each element of our citizenship model:

- Values

- Knowledge

- Skills

- Efficacy

- Commitment

Participation in service-learning leads to the values, knowledge, skills, efficacy, and commitment that underlie effective citizenship.

In the next chapter, we shift from exploring outcomes of service-learning to a focus on the kinds of program characteristics that increase the likelihood that practitioners will attain their goals for students.

Program Characteristics of
Effective Service-Learning

*All those things that we had to do for the service-
learning, each one, successively helped me pull
together what I'd learned. As you're going along,
you're not really seeing what you're learning every
minute. But when you have to pull it all together and
really think about it, I think it helped me realize what
had taken place.*

I s a one-day service event during student orientation worth doing?
What about offering an extra hour of credit for a class for students
who choose to add a service option? Should we structure student
journals, or let students write whatever comes to mind? Do we need
to read and respond to these personal journals? Should I require service in my class or make it an option?

There are no simple answers to questions like these; the answers
will depend on our goals, as they do with most of what we do in
higher education. Certainly students may make friends during a ser-
vice-related orientation activity, and they may feel better about
their college. They may, if the program is well designed, become
acquainted with further service opportunities and thus be connected
to service throughout their college years. Similarly, although an add-
on extra-credit service project may not have much of an impact on
student learning or cognitive development, it may foster personal

growth and future interest in more demanding service-learning options.

Although the personal and the intellectual cannot be separated—Dewey's notion of the wholeheartedness of effective education is well taken—the studies reported in this book support the view that many of the intellectual goals of higher education, including learning and application of material, critical thinking and problem solving, and perspective transformation, depend not on service experience alone but on how well integrated theory and practice are through application and reflection. And many goals, including personal development and perspective transformation, are enhanced by attention to the quality of diversity and community voice in service-learning. The quality of service-learning makes a difference.

In previous chapters we have focused on student outcomes of service-learning and explored some of the service-learning experiences that led to those outcomes; in this chapter we reverse the process, with a focus on the characteristics of effective service-learning programs.

This chapter is designed to help practitioners planning service-learning. First we discuss these characteristics, describing what practitioners should do if they are interested in particular goals of service-learning. We include a table that summarizes the relationships between program characteristics and categories of student outcomes. Then we discuss how service-learning might be adapted to the individual needs of students with different learning styles, different levels of service experience, and differences in cognitive development. We also touch briefly on the issue of requiring service in the context of our findings regarding how students who choose service differ from students who do not.

Program Characteristics That Make a Difference

There is a consensus among practitioners about what constitutes good practice in service-learning, and students when surveyed have tended to concur (Honnet and Poulsen, 1989; Sigmon, 1979;

Owens and Owen, 1979). When we interviewed students about what made their service-learning effective, they offered lots of examples of particular assignments and approaches, but they consistently stressed the importance of what they did in the community; their relationships with others—community members, peers, and faculty; and the challenge of integrating their service and academic study through reflection. When we looked at the impact of these kinds of program characteristics on student outcomes in our survey and analysis of problem solving and critical thinking, there was consistent support for what had begun as practitioner wisdom. Program characteristics make a modest but significant and consistent difference, and for the most challenging outcomes, such as development of critical thinking ability and transformation of social perspective, programs have to be very thoughtfully designed to create opportunities for sustained community involvement and intellectual challenge.

Here we examine some key characteristics and link them to the outcomes to which they are most central. Table 8.1 summarizes those relationships. We categorized the many variables into such outcomes as personal development or learning/understanding and application and then examined the extent to which particular program characteristics were significant predictors of the variables included in each outcome category. Dark blocks represent very consistent relationships between the characteristic and the outcome measures; the medium-shaded block indicates that the characteristic was linked to some of the measures in the category. White blocks represent little or no relationship and striped blocks either mixed positive and negative or negative relationships as indicated. It is a quick way to get a sense for what is most important to different kinds of outcomes. Regression tables that show the links between program characteristics and student outcomes are in Resources E and F.

Placement Quality

Placement quality is about the service in service-learning. Before any other consideration, service-learning practitioners must pay attention to establishing community connections that will provide

Table 8.1. Program Characteristics That Are Predictors of Service-Learning Outcomes.

Characteristics	Placement Quality	Application	Reflection Writing	Reflection: Discussion	Diversity	Community Voice
Stereotyping/tolerance						
Personal development						
Interpersonal development						
Closeness to faculty						
Citizenship						
Learning/understanding and application						
Problem solving/critical thinking						
Perspective transformation						

■ = program characteristic was a significant predictor of most measures of this outcome.

■ = program characteristic was a significant predictor of some measures of this outcome.

▦ = characteristic was a mixed predictor of this outcome; some positive, some negative.

▨ = program characteristic was a negative predictor of some measures of this outcome.

Source: Based on data from the FIPSE-sponsored survey and interview studies reported in this book.

productive situations for students as well as genuine resources useful to the community. The service is where service-learning begins. The academic connections are also critical for success, but first comes service and the anchoring of learning in community experience. As one student interviewed noted, "I think the classroom is more of a support for the service and not the other way around. I just think that everything that has been valuable to me has been on the personal level with individuals." He weighed the community and academic elements of the process and then continued: "I'm not devaluing the academic part of it. I think it's necessary once you experience those things." In support of the importance of the academic, he talked about all the things he did in his service-learning class, including exploring social causes of the problem he was working with, the history of previous social movements, learning about change and how change is possible, and learning what others have done. But with all this serious academic work, he came back again to the roots of learning in the service: "I think the thing that hit me hardest about community service and the things that I'll remember the most are the things that I actually experienced firsthand—the service part." If the service does not work well for the student, the learning may not be productive.

The qualities that clustered together in our survey and were characterized as placement quality are consistent with earlier work on placements by Conrad and Hedin (1980) and others (Moore, 1981; Hursh and Borzak, 1979; Owens and Owen, 1979; Eyler, 1992). Placement quality provides a context in which students can exercise initiative, take responsibility, and work as peers with practitioners and community members. Students who worked with newly literate adults to collect reading materials to support future literacy efforts, those who helped a community center design brochures and a grant proposal, and those who planned an evaluation of an after-school program all experienced these challenges. A quality placement provides the real-world setting for learning that theorists from Dewey to cognitive scientists such as Resnick have found useful for acquiring knowledge and abilities that can be used to solve actual problems (Resnick, 1987b).

Placement quality affects personal and interpersonal development. Placement quality was most consistently associated with impact on personal and interpersonal outcomes. It was a positive predictor of virtually all of our measures of tolerance and stereotyping—such personal development as knowing the self better, spiritual growth, and reward in helping others, and interpersonal outcomes, such as leadership and communication skill and ability to work with others.

Application

Application refers to the degree to which students can link what they are doing in the classroom to what they are experiencing in the community and vice versa.

Application predicts academic learning outcomes. There were hints that application might be an important factor in the impact of service-learning in previous studies. Conrad and Hedin (1980) found that high school students performed better on problem-solving tests when the problems they experienced in their field placement were similar to those tested. Hamilton and Zeldin (1987) found that students learned more when the issues discussed in their class seminar matched those being observed in a legislative session. Batchelder and Root (1994) found a similar link in a small study of college classes; students performed more sophisticated and complex analyses of a social problem when the problem was related to their service. Given these findings, we sought to test whether this link would hold up across a larger, more diverse group of college students and programs.

Application was associated with virtually every one of the academic learning outcomes in our studies. It was often the strongest predictor of learning outcomes, problem solving and critical thinking, and perspective transformation. Application predicted such survey outcomes as student reports that they learned more and were more intellectually stimulated by their service-learning than by other classes, as well as specific learning outcomes such as deeper understanding of subject matter, understanding the complexity of issues, and knowing about the work of specific social agencies. Students who studied medical care policy while escorting AIDS patients to clinics and helping them obtain medical equipment for their homes, those who helped immigrants newly arrived in the community while studying multicultural issues, and those who helped plant trees in deforested areas while studying environmental issues all told us they saw these connections. Application also predicted critical thinking outcomes, such as issue identification and ability to see consequences, and perspective transformation outcomes, such as seeing issues in a new way and a belief in the importance of using public policy to attain social justice. Integration of service and learning that included both reflection and application was a consistent predictor of student performance on problem analysis outcomes such as complexity of analysis and quality of strategic thinking, as well as on critical thinking in the interview study.

Reflection

Reflection is sometimes described as the hyphen in service-learning; it is the link that ties student experience in the community to academic learning. At its simplest, reflection is being able to step back and be thoughtful about experience—to monitor one's own reactions and thinking processes. Some people are naturally contemplative, wondering how what they are doing fits with what they already know or pursuing questions that pique their curiosity in the course of their community service. Some readily share and reflect informally with roommates, friends, parents, and others, and some community service offers built-in reflection as staff and volunteers meet and discuss issues and strategies. But for many students, it takes explicit attention to the reflection process before they become thoughtful about what they do, and reflection is not routinely built into most community work (Moore, 1981). Some students we interviewed commented that their service raised questions that interested them but that they did not pursue because "I had these questions, but the class was over, and so that was that." This seemed to be the case when the service project was not discussed throughout the class but was an extra project to submit at the end of the semester.

In our reflection interviews when we asked what the student had gained from service, we found that students who had been engaged in volunteer service activities tended to talk about the people they had met and feelings about their experiences; when they talked about what they took from service, it was usually in terms of personal and interpersonal growth—gratitude for their own good fortune, greater tolerance, greater appreciation of other cultures, or learning to work with others. Students who had been engaged in service-learning that included opportunities for structured reflection also talked about these things, but often went beyond to talk about what they learned and how they could apply it to the real world. Involvement in reflective activities moved students to link the personal and the academic.

Reflection predicts academic outcomes. Reflection has long been considered central to effective service-learning, but there has been sketchy evidence to support this practitioner wisdom. In high school studies, Conrad and Hedin (1980) found that having a formal seminar to discuss the service was the most important predictor of student outcomes; Rutter and Newman (1989) found such seminars to be important for positive interactions between students and community members; Waterman (1993) found service-learning that included a reflective seminar to be associated with self-esteem and social responsibility. In Chapter Three we discussed several studies that found a relationship between service-learning and academic outcomes in college, but there have been only a couple of small studies in which reflection is isolated from other aspects of the experience. In a study of internships that included, but was not limited to, community service internships, Eyler (1993) found that extensive reflection was a positive predictor of transfer of curriculum-related concepts to a new situation but that regular but modest levels of reflection were not. In the study most relevant to service-learning, Myers-Lipton (1994, 1996) compared volunteers, students in an intensive two-year service-learning program, and students who were nonparticipants; he found that intensive service-learning had a positive impact on measures of international understanding, civic responsibility, and decreased racism, which was not the case for volunteer work or for nonparticipants. In both the Myers-Lipton and Eyler studies intensive reflection was necessary for impact, and in Myers-Lipton's study, this effect was measurable only at the end of a two-year period.

In our survey amount and quality of reflection—writing or discussion, or both—was a modest but significant predictor of almost all of the outcomes we examined. It was associated with at least some of the outcome measures in each outcome category except interpersonal development: leadership and communication skills and working well with others. The quantity and quality of reflection was most consistently associated with academic learning outcomes: deeper understanding and better application of subject matter and increased knowledge of social agencies, increased complexity of problem and solution analysis, and greater use of subject matter knowledge in analyzing a problem. This also included students' reports that they learned more, were more intellectually stimulated, and were motivated to work harder by service-learning than in other classes. Reflection was also a predictor of openness to new ideas, issue identification skill, problem-solving and critical thinking skill, and such perspective transformation outcomes as seeing issues in a new way, increased commitment to use of public policy to achieve social justice, and a more systemic locus of problem causes and solutions. Reflection is a useful tool for most service-learning goals, but it is central to a question for improved academic outcomes.

In the problem-solving interviews we compared levels of reflection intensity; the highly integrated service-learning classes were characterized by the centrality of the service to the day-to-day work of the class. These classes continuously reflected on the relationship between the service experience and the subject matter of the class; the less integrated classes were less likely to hold reflective discussion, and in several, the experience was never brought into the whole class for discussion but was an extra assignment, with reflection confined to assignments completed individually by the student participants. Just as Myers-Lipton and Eyler found that the level of reflection was important, we found that the centrality of reflection to the academic enterprise had a significant impact on problem solving and critical thinking and on the complexity of students' problem analysis and issue understanding.

There was an interesting pattern linking writing—a reflection variable that combined classroom writing assignments and journal writing—and outcomes that seemed quite divergent. Writing was most consistently linked to such personal outcomes as reductions in stereotyping and increased tolerance and to the academic outcomes of problem solving and critical thinking and perspective transformation. Although they seem at somewhat opposite poles of service-learning outcomes, they may represent one of the many ways in which these elements are in fact linked in student development. The self-exploration that often occurs in journals and in dialogue with faculty through journals is particularly useful for helping students come to understand themselves and others better. These early reflections on service in journals may stimulate the kinds of questions and insights that lead students to improved problem solving and new ways of looking at the world—in other words, perspective transformation. The kind of disciplined analytic work that is often integral to written classroom assignments may help to cement this growth. Personal development does not necessarily lead to academic development, but it is also not in conflict with it; service-learning is a vehicle for integrating the personal and the intellectual.

Written Reflection

Among the eleven hundred service-learning students we surveyed, about 60 percent kept a journal, with about 25 percent of the eleven hundred writing in it "very often"; nearly 70 percent completed a written assignment, with 30 percent reporting that this type of assignment was completed "very often." Students we interviewed sometimes had a love-hate relationship with the use of written assignments for reflection during service-learning. Students who are by temperament active learners may be less than enthralled by writing, but some noted that in spite of the work of sitting down to write, this was a productive process for several reasons. It helped them think more clearly, as this student noted: "I don't like to keep a journal, . . . but the assignment that really helped me get things clear in my mind was the journal keeping . . . taking the issues and turning them around and making them personal to the experiences we were having in our service project. It was taking the academic and making it personal." It provided the occasion for taking the time to process the experience: "The most important thing has been the journals. . . . I really hated having to force myself to write in a journal when I didn't feel like it, but there were times at the homeless shelter when I really needed that space. That was my world that I could retreat into, and it was times like that where the most internalization of the issues took place."

Writing, particularly journal writing, creates a permanent record of the service-learning process that many students find helpful, as this student put it: "Journals are the most helpful, because sometimes you can't remember everything. So when it's written down, it's there in black and white, and it's never going anywhere." A written record is useful as the students think about how they or their community project has changed over the course of the semester. This student noted about her journal, "You write it the day you do your service, and you can go back and look and you can see progress.

You can look back and say, 'How did this person progress? What did I do to help?'" These observations then serve as raw data for later reflection activities. As another student explained, "I think it's good for me to write things down. Writing the journal was great because it was a form of expression and memory. . . . I'll forget what I was experiencing, and when I was writing the paper, it was interesting to go back and recall the trouble I had in the very beginning and then my impression later and how it had changed."

The discipline imposed by having to put thoughts into written words was also viewed as a way to clarify thought by many of the students in the reflection interviews. One noted, "After I write down my thoughts and everything, I can look back and find answers to questions that I thought were impossible to find. . . . I've found answers to some questions through just writing what happened." Another said, "When you put something down on paper, it helps you straighten out your thoughts—or it helps me anyway. If I am confused about something or bungled up in my mind, if I can get it written down on paper and see exactly what experience I have had . . . , it straightens out my thinking."

Discussion Reflection

Nearly 70 percent of the service-learning students in our survey reported some formal discussion of their service, but relatively few reported frequent discussion; 18 percent reported meeting to share feelings "very often." There were also relatively few who reported discussions that went beyond sharing feelings and observations; only about 15 percent reported frequent discussions for analysis or for application of service to course subject matter. Discussion was a popular choice for "most useful" form of reflection because it is so flexible; it can occur formally in class or informally with friends, colleagues, or community partners, and it is easy to do compared to the discipline of taking up pen and paper. The social aspects of the process are also valued as a way of gathering new insights. One student thought that the "journals are pretty effective, but the problem with journals is that it's so self-contained, and you can't share your reflections with other people. Sometimes it takes like one word— where you're like, 'Wow!'—from someone else's mouth that really helps you reflect more. I think it's really sharing . . . ideas within the group, verbalizing them, when everyone learns. Everybody gains."

Discussion is easy, but there is a danger that it will get stuck at the level of sharing feelings and experiences and not move beyond. In our survey study, 97 percent of the instructors of the service-learning classes claimed to provide at least some time for sharing feelings and experiences from the service component of the class; only about 70 percent reported discussions of related issues, and 70 percent reported application of service experience to what was going on in the class. Although about 15 percent of the classes engaged in substantial issue or application discussion, devoting at least 10 percent or more of class time to integrative discussion, 30 percent engaged in none at all. Attention needs to be given to linking experience and academic subject matter during the reflective process and sharing feelings is only the first step in this process. This is another area where use of the Kolb cycle or similar models helps push discussion beyond what happened and what the participants' feelings are about it to deeper understanding and application.

Diversity

Diversity was measured by asking students if they had an opportunity to work with people from diverse ethnic groups during the course of their service-learning. Nearly two-thirds reported having this opportunity at least fairly often. There are, of course, other dimensions of diversity, and many of the students we interviewed talked about religious diversity, working with people from different income levels, and gender issues. Practitioners who are advocates of diversity or multicultural education do not necessarily agree on goals. For some, diversity should lead to greater tolerance and understanding within the present status quo—a sort of human relations perspective; for others, the goal is social transformation, which allows the contributions of different cultural perspectives to change the status quo of the university as well as the society (Rhoads, 1998).

Diversity predicts both tolerance and transformation. The results of our survey showed a connection between diversity during service-learning and both types of goals: the mainstream or assimilationist view and the transformational view. Diversity was a predictor of most measures of stereotype reduction and tolerance and personal development, such as belief that community partners were "like me," greater cultural appreciation, better self-knowledge, spiritual growth, finding reward in service, and valuing a future career that includes service. At the level of problem solving and critical thinking and perspective transformation, diversity was a significant predictor of most of the outcomes measured in these categories, including openness to new ideas, issue identification skill, the ability to see social issues in a new way, and commitment to social justice. Thus whether a program's goal is to create better relations among people from different backgrounds or to begin the process of questioning current social arrangements and transforming society, it is important to create opportunities for diversity.

The role of diversity was less clear in students' reports of learning and application of subject matter. Diversity had a mixed relationship to academic learning; students in highly diverse situations were less likely to find the experience intellectually stimulating or that it increased their ability to apply what they were learning. On the other hand, diversity did contribute to their sense that they learned more than in regular classes and that they better understood the complexity of social problems.

Community Voice

We measured community voice by asking students if the work they did "met needs identified by members of the community." About 30 percent felt this was the case very often, and 66 percent felt that it was the case fairly or very often. Because higher education practitioners tend to focus on student development as their primary goal, there has been criticism and concern that both community needs and community participation in decision making get short shrift in service-learning (Sigmon, 1996). Using the community as a laboratory rather than working with the community on jointly useful projects may stunt the development of partnerships that offer continuous benefits to both parties. It may also ironically make it more difficult to create situations for learners that facilitate learning, critical thinking, and perspective transformation. For a number of the students we interviewed, valuing community voice represented a goal of service—something that stretched them and helped them to grow as individuals and as citizens. One student observed, "I've learned that my goals are not what I should be working for there. If I am going to be of service to them, then I need to hear what their goals are, not my own." Appreciating the importance of this perspective and involvement in projects where this perspective was honored had a positive impact on some of the outcomes we measured.

Community voice predicts personal development. In our survey, community voice was most consistently a significant predictor of personal growth outcomes. It predicted tolerance, cultural appreciation, reward in service, valuing a career of service, and realizing that community partners "are like me." Community voice was also connected to a few other outcomes, all of which seemed to involve being closer to and having a better understanding of the community; for example, it was a predictor of feeling connected to community, of believing that people should do volunteer service, and of a more systematic locus of social problems.

Like diversity community voice was also a negative predictor of intellectual stimulation during service-learning; students who reported that their service met needs identified by community members were less likely to report that their class was intellectually stimulating. There may be a tension between doing what a community group plans and wants done and meeting student interest and learning needs. In genuine partnerships, students and community members may work and plan together; when students simply complete tasks identified by community groups, they may feel less engaged than when doing tasks they have chosen themselves or chosen to fulfill a particular academic goal. It is easy to see that students who are being useful to the community by completing a community wish list by picking up trash, painting a shelter, or stuffing envelopes for a mailing might find the work not well connected to their academic interests. Awareness of this possible outcome should alert practitioners to build joint planning into community projects.

Other Factors

In our analysis we controlled for gender, age, minority status, family income, and other service, so that differences between comparison groups on these factors would not account for outcome differences. Women outnumbered men about two to one in all three of our samples, which is fairly typical of service-learning programs. We did find for many outcomes that being female was a significant predictor of positive changes over the course of the semester of service over and above the impact of program characteristics. The other factor associated with some positive outcomes was involvement in other community service outside the service-learning experience. Some of the benefits of service-learning are intensified by the addition of volunteer service, and of course those who choose more service are more likely to report that it has value. The minority variable combines all non-Caucasians for purpose of analysis; minority students made up about 16 percent of the survey sample. There were few effects of minority status, family income, or age on the outcomes measured. Separate analysis contrasting African American students with all other students also showed no independent effect of race.

Program Characteristics and Closeness to Faculty

Having a close relationship with at least one faculty member is associated in the higher education literature with most of the positive outcomes of the college experience, from staying to graduate to academic achievement. Many of the key program characteristics we identified had an impact on whether students did become close to faculty members as a result of their service. We found that within service-learning, good placement quality as well as placements that were made by the faculty member rather than by the student or service office, application of service to the academic subject matter, and both written and oral reflection were significant predictors that students would become closer to faculty. Well-designed service-learning provides opportunities for students to get to know faculty informally, sometimes as they work alongside each other in the service site. It also creates reflective classes with high faculty-student interaction, with students getting to know the instructor better than in most traditional lecture-oriented classes. Regression tables that use closeness to faculty as a predictor of outcomes are in Resource D; Table E.4 in Resource E shows the relationship of program characteristics to the outcome of faculty closeness during service-learning.

Requiring Service-Learning?

As service requirements for high school or college graduation have become more popular, there has been a backlash of activism and even lawsuits by people who feel that it is not legitimate to require service and that, indeed, "requiring volunteer work" is a contradiction in terms. Even within our group of eleven hundred service-learning students there was not agreement; 61 percent believed that it was appropriate to require community service, but 17 percent were opposed to the idea. Whether service or service-learning should be a required part of the college experience will depend on the institutional mission and on how decision makers see the role of community service in education.

There are two rationales for requiring service. One argument is that service is part of civic duty and contributes to the development of citizenship; the other is that it is a useful component of academic development, leading to skills and knowledge beyond what is commonly acquired in the classroom. Since preparation for citizenship is part of the mission of public schools, it seems consistent with that mission to require practice in service, especially if students have considerable control over where their efforts are applied. Not everyone agrees with this. Although the legitimacy of requiring community service as citizenship in public high schools, colleges, and universities is debatable, private institutions may include service as part of their mission and select students for admission who endorse that commitment.

A stronger rationale for requiring community service is found in the academic value of service-learning explored in this book. Simply requiring service hours has a tenuous link to student outcomes, but community service that is well integrated with an academic course of study contributes to personal and interpersonal development, learning and application of knowledge, critical thinking ability, and perspective transformation, all of which are relevant to citizenship participation as well as scholarship. Service-learning is often better academic learning and thus a legitimate requirement of an academic program.

In our survey, we found that the students who participated in service-learning differed significantly from those who did not participate on almost every outcome we measured (Eyler, Giles, and Braxton, 1997). Thus students who are most in need of the developmental opportunities afforded by service-learning may be less likely to choose such course options voluntarily. This is compounded by the fact that we also found that high school and family experiences with social and community service activities also predicted which students would become active in community service during the college years (Eyler-Walker, 1997). Thus the students most active in high school tend to maintain that activity in college and are also more likely to choose service-learning.

Summary: Some Principles of Effective Service-Learning

Although all the program characteristics we have examined here are important, it is clear that the quality of application and reflection is central to achieving academic goals of higher education. When we listened to what students had to say about the reflection that worked for them and examined the relationship between integrated service-learning and the problem solving demonstrated by students, a series of reflection principles emerged for us. Effective service-learning reflection can be summed up in the Five C's: connection, continuity, context, challenge, and coaching.

Connection

Connection is a central concept of effective service-learning. At its heart, service-learning rests on the assumption that learning cannot be compartmentalized between the classroom and the use of what is learned later, in the community, or between affective and cognitive learning. Service-learning connects people—students and their diverse peers, students and community partners, and students and faculty. It also connects college and community, experience and analysis, feeling and thinking, now and future. Effective programs maximize these connections. Requiring participation may help build these connections for those who would not select them otherwise.

Continuity

The principle of continuity was central to Dewey's thinking; learning is never finished but is a lifelong process of understanding. Reflection must be continuous: throughout a service-learning course, across the four college years, throughout life. For college administrators, that means thinking of service-learning and community service components of the academic and social programs over the entire course of the college experience. For the instructor, care should be given to reflection before, during, and after service experience. It is through multiple opportunities for service and reflection that students have the opportunity to test and retest their ways of understanding and thus to grow and develop.

Context

Reflection is not just about thinking, but about thinking about something. People do not become good problem solvers or experts in the abstract; they become expert about particular subject matter and learn to solve particular kinds of problems. The messiness of the community setting is not just noise; it is integral to learning. Knowledge and skills are contextual; we learn in ways that prepare us for using knowledge by using it on real problems in the real world. This is why application is such an integral element of the reflective process and central to academic learning outcomes. Service-learning allows students to think and learn with the tools, concepts, and facts of the particular learning situation.

Context is also a consideration in selecting the style and place for conducting reflection. Conducting reflection sessions in the community with community partners can be a powerful tool where the reflective process is designed to be meaningful for all participants. Matching the formality of the reflection to the situation is also important. Students in service-learning classes will probably find structured reflection and written assignments helpful and legitimate; volunteer situations may require a lighter touch to keep students involved in reflection.

Challenge

The central event in learning from a constructivist perspective is the challenge of new experiences and information to the way things are believed to be. Growth rests on puzzlement, on challenge to current perspectives, and on the challenge to resolve the conflict. Students develop more complex and adequate ways of viewing the world when they are challenged but not overwhelmed by new experiences. The challenge has to match the needs of the student.

Coaching

Challenge is central to growth, but without adequate support it is likely either to discourage the student or lead to the rejection of new insights and information so that the student falls back on previous ways of viewing the world. Students need considerable emotional support when they work in settings that are new to them; there needs to be safe space where they know that their feelings and insights will be respected and appreciated. As their service develops and their questions become more sophisticated, they need intellectual support to think in new ways, develop alternative explanations for experiences and observations, and question their original interpretations of issues and events.

One of the most difficult challenges for faculty is to provide the interaction and feedback necessary to offer both challenge and support to students. It entails not only the usual grasp of the academic content of the course, but also detailed awareness of the students' service experience and ample opportunity for interaction. This can be difficult without adequate institutional support for faculty engaged in service-learning.

9

Strengthening the Role of Service
in the College Curriculum

*I didn't know why I was here at this university until I
joined [the service-learning program]. I felt like I was
lost and I was just a number, and I didn't really want
this to be my life, and I had never really heard of
service-learning. Then education really started to
make sense for me. . . . It enhanced what I learned
in books, not just memorizing before a test, but it's
made it stick and click for me.*

We began with the skeptic's question: "Where's the learning
in service-learning?" and the believer's question: "What
types of learning are found in which types of service-learning experiences?" Through the course of our studies we found a consistent
pattern of evidence that addresses concerns of both skeptic and
believer. The growing body of empirical support here and elsewhere
and the match between the outcomes of service-learning and many
of the goals identified in the higher education reform literature provide a solid base for institutions to consider how to strengthen the
role of community service as part of their academic mission.

We have found that the quality of service-learning makes a difference. This chapter is designed to help those on college campuses
take stock of their service-learning programs and strengthen them
in ways consistent with empirical evidence.

The Difference That Service-Learning Makes

Our focus has been primarily on the impact of service-learning on students. There is an empirical fit between our goals for students and the outcomes of service-learning. If we want students who are lifelong learners, can use what they know, and have a capacity for critical analysis, then programs like service-learning, which help them construct knowledge from experience and reflection, should form the core of their educational experience. Service-learning, and especially programs with good community placements, application of service to course work, extensive reflection, diversity, and community voice, make a difference in student learning. There are other goals of higher education as well that may be affected by service-learning.

The strengthened bonds among faculty and students may lead not only to greater academic success but also to better student retention and graduation rates. Community service projects can strengthen the links between a college and its surrounding community. And service-learning may put processes in motion that help in institutional transformation. The collaborative efforts necessary to build and sustain service-learning may also help to build and sustain more flexible and creative campus response to other issues.

Among the criticisms of higher education is the compartmentalization of knowledge and the barriers to interdisciplinary work for both faculty and students. Service-learning programs may create working relationships among faculty in different departments as they collaborate on interdisciplinary service-learning courses, methods for sharing community service resources, and action research projects. Service-learning is built on a foundation of inquiry or continuous learning and discovery, with the potential for creating awareness and respect for a broader vision of scholarship to add to the traditional scholarship of discovery, what Boyer (1990) identified as the scholarship of teaching, application, and synthesis.

Developing Quality Service-Learning Programs

A number of program characteristics make a difference, and the place to start is by assessing whether current programs conform to what is known about effective service-learning.

Quality of Academic Service-Learning Programs

Service makes a contribution to student development, but service-learning affects learning and cognitive development as well. Current service-learning opportunities on a campus can be assessed by asking the following questions:

- Do students have opportunities to do important work and take important responsibilities in community service placements?

- Are there close connections between academic subject matter and what students are doing in the community?

- Is reflection about the service integrated into classes through frequent opportunities for discussion and written analysis or projects?

- Does reflection challenge students to go beyond description and sharing of feelings to analysis and action planning?

- Do students work with people from diverse backgrounds and cultures?

- Are community projects developed in partnership with the community?

Some people are hesitant about service-learning because of the heavy demands it places on faculty and other institutional resources.

It is useful to remember that effective education is often labor intensive; this is not an attribute of just service-learning. Lecture methods were implemented partly because they are a cheap method to
deliver content to large numbers of students; there is ample research
to suggest that much learning acquired in this manner is inert and
soon forgotten. Howard (1998) cites research showing that during
lectures, students are not attending to the speaker nearly half the
time and that four months after such a course, students knew only
about 8 percent more than students who had never taken a course
on the topic. Service-learning is not the only pedagogy that engages
students in an active, constructive process of learning, but the other
approaches that do, such as Socratic dialogue or classroom simulations, are also labor intensive. Education that stimulates and challenges often involves the kind of reflective dialogue that is at the
heart of good service-learning, and this takes extraordinary effort.

Some of the questions in our list refer to program qualities that
require sustained work with community agencies in developing
placements that offer students stimulating responsible positions.
Reflection activities that tie experience and theory must be developed by faculty with skill as well as enthusiasm. And attention to
diversity and community voice is a continuous process. All of these
characteristics are time-consuming to construct and carry out, but
they are associated with positive outcomes for students. Institutions
that are serious about high-quality service-learning in classroom and
community must provide the infrastructure to support these faculty
efforts.

Creating High-Quality Placements

As faculty members and staff attempt to create community placements, they need to work with agencies willing to try to provide situations with the following characteristics:

- Students do meaningful work.

- Students have important responsibilities.

- Students have varied or challenging tasks.

- Students work directly with community partners.

- Students receive support and feedback from agency staff.

- The service continues over a sustained period.

Placements that include these elements are hard to establish for a single class during a single semester. Creating long-term relationships between community groups and the college makes feasible quality placements that also contribute to the community. Where appropriate, students should be involved in the negotiations and planning for service projects; this provides not only good experience for developing leadership and planning skills, but also reinforces that the service process is a partnership in which both student and community have something to give and take.

If instructors are going to do a good job of integrating service and learning, they need to have an understanding of the students' experience, and this may entail continuous effort and on-site presence. One student in a failed service placement made this point: "The key, I think, is for the professor to be able to have time—I think it must be very time-consuming—to know what she's putting her students into. My professor didn't have a clue. She went to this first meeting, and it was all sunshine and happiness. I think she didn't know what we were getting into." Difficult placements can be productive as students, community members, and faculty or staff struggle to work things out, but students sometimes feel that they are left to sink or swim without adequate site development or preparation. Having institutional support for the creation of a continuing relationship between community groups and the college or university should make it easier for faculty to meet both student academic needs and community needs. It is difficult to accomplish without this broader support and resources.

Preparation for service, sometimes called "preflection," or reflection before service experience, is also integral to a quality community experience. Students need to know what to expect and to have the skills necessary for the service they are asked to perform. It was not uncommon for students to feel set adrift: "I went into the classroom without any preparation or anything. They just sent me in there, and I wish I kind of knew what I was supposed to do before I got there." Many community agencies offer orientations and preparation for service; sometimes this takes a larger time commitment than students can make. Part of the selection of the type of service to be included in a class will depend on the demands that can be made on particular students and their levels of commitment.

Building Application into Service-Learning

When designing a service-learning experience, practitioners need to pay attention to creating connections:

- Close connections between the subject matter of the class and issues raised by service

- Close connections between the specific tasks the student performs in the community and the goals of the class

Finding service that roughly matches the course content is fairly straightforward; however, there are a number of barriers to matching tasks with course goals, and it takes energy to create a strong working relationship with a community group. Instructors who hope to integrate the service and learning need to have a good grasp of what the students are doing—through either extensive work in the field or extensive interaction with the students around their service experience or through reading student journals carefully and frequently. A faculty member who has little understanding of what students are doing in the community will have some difficulty in facilitating application.

The purpose of some classes may be served by requiring students to simply sign up for a few hours of service of their choosing each week, but this add-on approach is not likely to result in well-integrated service and learning. There are many projects or activities that students can undertake that do provide firmer links. Chemistry students can perform experiments and demonstrations for school children or tutor high school students in chemistry; education students can tutor; policy students might help a school district perform a needs analysis; those studying adult development or gerontology might help elderly members of the community create personal histories for their families, provide meal or household services, or tutor in an adult literacy program; students studying poverty issues might work with social agencies that provide food, housing, or job support; those studying foreign cultures might work on projects with immigrants from those regions of the world; accounting students might assist community members with tax preparation; a class in dance might organize dance classes for children at a local community center. There are dozens of ways to create opportunities that provide a needed service for the community—opportunities for close personal interaction between community members and students, and work that provides skill and knowledge relevant to the academic focus of a class. When the placement is chosen for its applicability to the academic work, it is easier to provide the structured reflection that pulls the experience together for students.

Planning for Reflection

There are many ways to build opportunities for reflection into a service-learning class. Choices depend on the goals of the course; the class size; what students bring in the way of abilities, interests, and experience; and faculty interests and skills. When planning a course, faculty should consider whether reflection would be enhanced by including the following elements:

- Opportunities to reflect on expectations before the service begins

- Frequent opportunities for discussion of service

- Frequent classroom application of theory to service experience and vice versa

- Written assignments with increasing demands for analysis as service progresses

- Frequent feedback on journals, work, projects, and other work

- Critical reflection that challenges student assumptions

Using Kolb's Model to Facilitate Reflection

Dewey's focus on the iteration between thought and experience is the touchstone for most service-learning practitioners; his emphasis on action-reflection and then action again underlies most models of reflection. Learning is a continuous construction of reality; it is never done because each new thing learned brings us to a new place with new possibilities for puzzlement. Kolb's model for the learning cycle (1984), derived from Dewey's constructivist theory of how the learning process takes place, suggests how the integration of feeling and action with abstract and systematic thought might be accomplished. Service-learning practitioners have embraced it because it is intuitive and easy to remember and apply to instructional practice. It also suggests methods for adapting instruction to the diverse needs of students with different learning styles.

The basic cycle begins with concrete experience (CE); once students have immersed themselves in experience, they pull back and attempt to describe that experience through reflective observation (RO). RO becomes the grist for the next stage of abstract conceptualization (AC), in which attempts are made to derive meaning from the experience and integrate observations with other sources of knowledge and understanding. This may include material from classroom texts or traditional academic research. At this stage students may form hypotheses or action strategies that may again be tested in the community through a process of active experimentation (AE).

The cycle, like Dewey's continuous quest from uncertainty and doubt to understanding to new sources of confusion and doubt, is iterative. Knowledge and understanding are under continuous construction as we increase our experience, knowledge base, and ideas about how old conceptions and new information fit together to explain the world. One moves from feeling, to observing, to thinking, to doing; the full cycle integrates the personal and the affective with the intellectual and academic. By honoring feelings first, the movement toward analytic thought may be enhanced for many students. Kolb would probably agree with the student we quoted earlier who commented, "I think people will do more thinking once they have felt."

Because this is a simple, intuitive, and easy-to-remember process, which also contains specific implications for reflective activities, many reflection techniques have developed using the model or borrowing from it. For example, one of the more popular reflection devices has been the "What? So what? Now what?" model of reflection popularized by the Campus Outreach Opportunity League (COOL). In this approach students are encouraged to describe events during their service, then to interpret those events, and then suggest next steps for further study or community action. It is often used in informal discussion settings like alternative spring breaks or other volunteer service programs where there is a low tolerance for classroomlike reflection assignments. Some students used the model for conversations in the van while returning from service sites. Several of our reflection interview students mentioned techniques very much like this one that were used to structure journals or discussions. One student noted that a particular advantage was that feelings, which often dominate service-learning discussions, were explicitly separated from more neutral observation: "It was difficult, but I think it was necessary to split that apart because commonly people put those two together—what they observed and their feelings—and come up with something in the middle. To separate them is difficult, but it aids in introspection and understanding."

The Kolb model is particularly easy to embed in both journals and essay assignments. Prompts or questions for the journal can be based on the learning cycle to encourage students to describe before they begin to make judgments or draw inferences, and the journals themselves can serve as observational data for later use in more complex written analysis. Examples of how to use this model are included in *A Practitioner's Guide to Reflection in Service-Learning* (Eyler, Giles, and Schmiede, 1996).

Combining Reflection Modalities

Instructors may combine discussion and writing or create activities that incorporate several modes of reflection. Role plays, panels that report on projects, and special projects developed for the community may include reflective components. A student who participated in a role-play activity based on one student's experience noted that "we were able to use our analysis from our own experiences in the service curriculum prior to that—like an analysis of how they work, was it successful, what could have been done differently in terms of leadership skills—and we were able to incorporate that too." The role plays provided the opportunity for repeated application of a set of analysis skills and organizational information—precisely the kind of repeated application that cognitive scientists have linked to better transfer of learning (Bransford and Vye, 1989).

Projects for the community may involve students in using a variety of organizational skills and also provide opportunities for reflection and feedback throughout the project. Students we interviewed talked about doing research for political action, writing grant proposals, planning community education efforts, and performing a needs assessment for a school district. One student struggled to develop a program and commented on the usefulness of the coaching and reflection built into the process: "I thought my program made sense. And then the acting director comes along, and he asked me some questions—'What's this?' and 'What's that?'—and I just had to stop and actually think and redesign the program so that the goals and the objectives and the strategies and the outcomes are all linked. I had to stop and think and rework the entire program." Community projects can offer an optimal integration of service and learning since the product is real work of use to the community and not just a reflective activity for a class assignment.

Although journals are thought of us as a solitary introspective form of reflection, one student talked about how her professor used student journals to focus class discussion. A student would be asked to read a passage from his or her most recent journal entry, but "we seldom get through a whole report because he fires questions at us. He wants to stimulate us to think. . . . And the whole class benefits because you may not even be called on during a particular week, but you hear the types of questions that were asked this week and you say, 'I better make sure that I make this type of observation or incorporate this into my reflection.'" This kind of activity reinforces the value of the journal as a tool for learning and also might be used to provide feedback in a class setting too large to allow for wide individual feedback. By making two or three student journals the focus for class discussion and exploration, fifty other students might be able to benefit, and without as frequent an individual faculty response as might be desirable.

Using application assignments to blend classes where some are and some are not doing service was also described by several students. Many students we interviewed felt that because only some classmates did service, it was ignored by the instructor in class, and sometimes this link was so tenuous that the students themselves did not see how their service would be interesting or relevant to the rest of the class. Others saw the value of different team members' bringing different expertise to the table. For example, in a class where learning teams consisting of both service and nonservice participants prepared presentations on social issues, a student remarked of her instructor: "She had us together—the research people and the service people. We were supposed to bring out common themes from . . . our work and bring out something we learned that we all learned. For our group, it was really easy since we'd identified early what our goals were and what our themes were. . . . Our group talked about poverty and homelessness and political strategies. The service people talked about how welfare was actually affecting people's lives—real specific stories. . . . Those doing research would bring in the numbers and the data."

Critical Reflection

An apocryphal tale from service-learning has the teacher stunned when one of his twenty-year-old students returns from a service project at the local soup kitchen saying, "This was a great experience; I hope my kids will be able to do community service at a place like this someday." Reflection can help students learn by integrating concepts and theories and their community experience, but if we want them to go beyond merely assimilating to the status quo, we need to encourage critical reflection. Critical reflection is about pushing students to explore the assumptions that underlie their own perceptions and the way that society is organized. In a critically reflective classroom, students will discuss not only effective ways to provide emergency aid for the poor but also ask, "Why do we need soup kitchens?" Critical reflection is the process that may lead to transformational learning—changes in how students understand the social order—and to action to right social wrongs. The process of critical reflection begins with a disorienting dilemma— something that does not fit. Community service, by bringing students into situations unlike those they have already experienced, creates many opportunities to deal with dissonance.

Coaching and feedback are important to all reflection, but especially demanding for critical reflection. Serious exploration of assumptions about the social order also requires sustained instruction about the nature of social change. The students we interviewed who were concerned about social justice and change were often those who were involved in programs where explicit attention was given to critical analysis and social transformation.

Faculty Coaching

Learning through reflection on experience, and particularly critical reflection, requires a balance between challenge and support. Growth occurs when students confront puzzling issues and have enough support to identify alternative ways of looking at and understanding the puzzle. Without guidance, students may become discouraged or reject dissonance by falling back on comfortable old ways of looking at issues. A student frustrated by work with the homeless told me "It's really important that when you are experiencing things like that to have some kind of support system around you. I think I've gotten more out of it because there were people around me going through similar things, [people] that I could talk to about those things, and I could hear viewpoints about similar experiences." Students learn and develop when they are dealing with challenges they can manage.

Coaching and feedback are often built into reflection assignments, but this is not always the case. Only 21 percent of our surveyed students reported frequent feedback from faculty on their service journals. In classes where service is optional, there may be little feedback or support. This student's experience with reflection and feedback appears typical for such classes: "In the class I took, we actually didn't do anything. We got the assignments at the start of the quarter, and we never talked about it. We handed the assignment in and that was it."

Students were appreciative of instructors who could be flexible and recognize teachable moments to use student experience in advancing the academic agenda of the course. One student described such a class as energetic: "Everyone was interested. It wasn't like half the class was asleep while the teacher was lecturing. We sat in a circle, and it was give and take." This teacher was able to respond to student curiosity and link their experiences to the subject matter of the course: "The teacher was really interested and could deal with any issue that came up. . . . He was very understanding. Some days we wouldn't really do what he had in mind, because an issue came up that week. He'd listen to it and somehow make it apply—asking, for example, 'How does that relate to the reading?'—and he would bring it way back into scope. What we were doing always pertained to what we were learning."

This ability to integrate student service experience smoothly into the course is the essence of service-learning. As the semester unfolds, initial support and encouragement can give way to more complex analysis. One student said that "for the first couple of weeks, she gave us little prompts like, 'What is your first impression?' 'What is different than you first expected?' 'How did you feel about the people?'" and then noted that later in the course, "we had to analyze a few of the situations according to sociological perspectives that we learned, like conflict theory . . . , and we had to define our problem as a social problem." A student in a literature class described the teacher as taking a fictional character and then asking how "this guy's experience would relate to the people you are working with."

In larger classes teams of students involved in the same type of service can provide feedback for each other as they work to apply what they are experiencing in the field. In one class, a student noted that "our team tries to talk at least once or twice a week. Usually our experiences are different. So one person might be in the first stage of a theory, and another person might be in the third stage. I say, 'Okay, I have this experience with my mentee,' and then someone else will say, 'We did this' and 'This is my experience.' So we each see how far the theory has gone with each person." Teams can help each other apply the material.

Creating a Climate for Honest Reflection

While waiting for a panel of service-learning students to share their experiences and insights with a student group, we chatted with a former student who was to appear on the panel. She told us that her recent service-learning experience had been a disaster; she had chosen the site because it was convenient, but she had not found the work very interesting or the site very well organized, and she had often failed to follow through; she was embarrassed at what she considered a waste of time because of her low effort. As the panel stories unfolded with one heartwarming story after another of emotional connection and personal transformation, we thought, "Well, at least we will see another perspective when Jean gets her turn." When Jean did get her turn, what we heard was another story about how this experience "had been fantastic," among the "most powerful" of her life and something that she had looked forward to each day she volunteered. She was not about to look like a failure among those inspiring tales that had preceded her. It left us impressed with the power of peer pressure and faculty expectations on how students present their service experience. It also made us wonder about the extent to which we, with our enthusiasm as true believing service-learning professionals, may block honest reflection by our students who do not want to hurt our feelings with any dissenting view of the process.

This topic came up quite spontaneously during several of our reflection interviews. One student commented, "One problem we have on this campus is that [the faculty sponsor]—I know she thinks we're all being really honest when we're reflecting, but if we're in a room and it's all the student leaders and their professors who are grading them, we're not going to be honest. I would never tell [the faculty member] that I didn't think she was being very effective. . . . Obviously we're all going to say that it's a great experience." If we want to use student feedback to improve service-learning, students have to feel that criticism is welcome and potentially productive.

At another university, a student echoed these thoughts but raised an even more important issue for learning when he addressed the tendency he saw of students to censor their own observations of what they experience: "Can you imagine someone writing, 'I hated this and this was horrible; these people deserve to be like this; they don't try to help themselves and it's their own fault and I'm never going back there and I can't believe you made me volunteer and I can't believe that this university is giving me credit for doing this, just like a basket weaving course!'? Is it that people never have these thoughts, or that they don't feel like they can express them?" This student was a strong advocate of service-learning but felt that many students were cut off from learning by barriers to expressing unpopular thoughts about their experience. Part of the process of critical reflection is to confront uncomfortable observations and try to figure out why things are the way they are and why we interpret them the way we do. Feeling alienated or disgusted by people students meet in the community is not uncommon, especially for those new to service; but it can be the first step in beginning to understand the difficult dynamics of social problems and beginning to rethink some assumptions about how society is arranged. If we want to make full educational use of the advantages of immersing students in complex and messy real-world situations, we cannot create classrooms where it is unacceptable to share shock, disappointment, or confusion. Learning occurs when there is puzzlement or conflict; if our enthusiasm discourages students from sharing their honest observations, then we block critical analysis and prevent growth.

Explicit discussion of steps of the reflective process and encouraging identification of alternative perspectives may elicit frank discussion. Techniques that allow students to pose questions or make observations anonymously on cards may help surface uncomfortable issues. When the instructor acknowledges from the beginning that community service is difficult and may bring the student into situations that are uncomfortable, students may feel freer to express their disappointments or concerns in ways that are productive.

When students can voice their dismay when residents of a community throw trash where the students have just cleared up old trash, then the way is cleared to explore why people might behave this way. Use of a systematic reflective process that moves from descriptions to feelings to analysis may create a climate where these issues are not papered over.

Preparation for Diversity and Dealing with Conflict

Certainly preparation for service is always important. Students commented on the particular importance of being prepared to work with people from cultures or with experiences that are dramatically different from those they have known. Many students do not realize that the same experience or language can have different meaning for people from different backgrounds; they need exposure to how misunderstanding may occur. One student noted, "A lot of the things we study in classes that have to do with cultural diversity are really important before going out and doing service. . . . When you go and do service, there's such a diverse population. That sort of information—just knowledge about how different people work—is really important."

In addition to understanding the nuances of language and behavior, students need continuing support to explore and deal with the conflicts that arise. One of the advantages of service-learning is that it gives students the chance to meet on equal ground, to become friends, to understand and walk in the shoes of people different from themselves. It affords the opportunity to see differences constructively, as in our earlier example where a white student came to appreciate, though not agree with, the view of her African American classmate that voluntary segregation of black students was a useful tool for building community among black students. On the other hand, situations where tensions are not explored and honest discourse is discouraged may reinforce stereotypes and allow hostilities to persist. If the goal is tolerance, then a lack of honest discourse can subvert that; if the goal is transformative, then suppressing rather than dealing with difference prevents the struggle to resolve conflict that is central to reconstructing perspectives.

Stopping and exploring how a particular incident may look from the perspective of different cultures and experiences can allow issues to surface. Establishing ground rules for discussing issues of controversy and conflict may help students value the process of sorting out disagreement. One student noted that she and others tended to avoid surfacing tense issues because "I think one of the problems why people don't talk more is that when they disagree, they don't know how to disagree well. They don't know how to talk and state their side and listen to the other side. . . . It just becomes a big screaming match . . . or it just becomes something where people just stomp out the door and ignore the other one."

Adapting Service-Learning to Student Differences

Faculty planning for service-learning need to be aware of student differences that may affect how they respond to service-learning. In reviewing course plans, faculty should ask themselves:

- Do course activities take into consideration the differing levels of service experience among students?

- Are reflection activities geared to the different levels of cognitive development likely to be present in the classroom?

- Are class activities varied to build on strengths of students with different learning styles?

The pathways students take as they become more involved and skilled in community service vary; these differences in service experience will also shape the activities and the insights they are ready for and the kind of challenge and support they need. It is not unusual to have students in a class who are doing service for the first time and those who are self-styled activists. While some are overwhelmed by the emotional power of the experience and focused on new friendships or shocked by what they see, others may be organizing political action. Faculty members need to be sensitive to the challenge this presents for feedback and instruction.

We were struck by two students' description of the same community-related activity in their policy class. One found observing in the juvenile court stimulating and listed half a dozen questions that came to mind; he cited it as an example of a powerful experience that led to effective reflection. A second student in the same class offered a different view of the same event. He noted first that "even the experience is problematic because it wasn't really engaging. . . . I'd suggest that the people who studied violence work with victim-offender reconciliation. I think that would have been a great experience. Instead, they went to the juvenile court to observe the hearings. That's just not a good experience." He noted that involvement in doing real service instead of observations would have entailed training and a larger commitment, but that this would pay off in the level of engagement and learning. These two students gave two spontaneously offered examples of the same activity; one offered it as a good example and the other as a cautionary tale. One student was relatively new to community service; one was a student leader with a sustained commitment to community action and service-learning. The same activity had very different meaning for two students at different stages in their development as community participants.

Differences in the capacity for understanding and using complex information also affect how students respond to a particular service-learning experience. As we saw in Chapter Five, the process of justifying a position by examining evidence for and against competing views requires a high level of cognitive development. Reflection activities that seem challenging and important to some students may seem pointless to others because they do not yet have the capacity to understand and deal with ambiguity and complexity. A student who still sees issues as cut and dried may not realize that there is a problem worth discussing. If perspectives can be sorted into right and wrong, then conflict may be viewed as illegitimate or, at best, a matter of educating those who are wrong and moving on. Repeatedly sharing impressions and opinions may simply seem like a waste of time.

One of the students we interviewed complained about the attempts made to develop a reflection opportunity for the community service she had elected as a class option. The instructor did not integrate the service into classroom discourse but tried to create a discussion session at the service site. Students in the program were involved with children in inner-city schools, and the thirty-five-minute reflection period was built into the school day: "We were supposed to be there from 8:45 until 9:20 and have like a reflection group with our leader. . . . She was really nice, but every week she asked us the same questions because I don't think she remembered which group she was with, and so progressively we all started getting there like 5 after 9 and later and later. . . . We tried to skip the sessions because they were terrible. It was the same thing, and it had nothing to do with what we were doing."

Perhaps the questions were poorly chosen, and this was poor reflection management. But it is also possible that questions that seemed irrelevant or repetitive were more appropriately matched with students with a more advanced developmental level. Sharing opinions and experiences may seem pointless to a student who is at Perry's dualistic stage or at stage three or four in the King and Kitchener model of development discussed in Chapter Five. If a student does not see a difference between structured and ill-structured problems, attention needs to be given to problem analysis and exposure to different ways of viewing the problem. Students who are more advanced may need more emphasis on how to evaluate conflicting information and draw warranted inferences. By using reflective activities that are too far ahead of where the students are working, instructors may create situations where students simply do not see the value of the process. If instructors are not sensitive to these intellectual development issues, they may not help students see that a repeated question may push them to new answers, insights, and questions.

Differences in learning styles are easily accommodated in service-learning because of the continuous cycle of active experiential and reflective intellectual activities. The complete learning cycle Kolb identified honors the importance of the contributions of different student styles from abstract conceptualizers to those who like to jump in and try things out. Everyone should feel comfortable with some part of the learning process.

How Do We Know? Why Do We Believe?

These two section questions, taken from the title of an essay on reflective judgment (King, 1992), are appropriate here because they reflect both the ending and beginning of our journey, and we hope our readers' journeys, in the discovery of the learning in service-learning. We have discovered that the learning in service-learning is in the questions. It is in the questions that service situations inherently pose, in the guided reflection provided by skilled teachers and facilitators and by the interplay of existing knowledge with new and dissonant experiences.

For many of the students whom we interviewed, it was a journey of new questions, new but tentative knowledge, and then new, and often puzzling and disturbing, doubts. This form of inquiry is the hallmark of effective service-learning and the cognitive development it produces.

At the end of the journey, the skeptic's question, "How do we know?" is answered by the believer's sense of evidence and the convergence of outcomes across many situations. While acknowledging the gaps and occasional anomalies that are yet to be understood, the believer answers the skeptic by pointing to the rich and powerful view of learning that emerges here. The believer also sees the link from this learning to effective citizenship.

But the believer's knowledge is tempered by the skeptic's new questions of whether the learning holds up over a lifetime and whether there might be other factors yet unimagined that might explain the learning in service-learning. Both the skeptic and the believer acknowledge that the learning and benefits for others who are not college students are largely unexplored. As reflective practitioners and teachers, we ask, "How can service-learning be designed so as to ensure these types of learning outcomes?" That question will direct our work as we create our guide to designing effective service-learning experiences, which will be a companion to this book.

We end this part of our journey of inquiry with a set of new questions about faculty learning, community development, long-term institutional change, and the future of service-learning itself. As T. S. Eliot (1971) wrote.

> We shall not cease from exploration
> And the end of all our exploring
> Will be to arrive where we started
> And know the place for the first time.

Resource A: College and University Participants in the Studies

Alma College
Antioch College
Augsburg College
Bentley College
Berry College
California Polytechnic at San
  Luis Obispo
California State University at
  Monterey Bay
Calvin College
Carson-Newman College
Clark-Atlanta University
College of the Ozarks
Colorado State University
Concord College
Cornell University
Covenant College
De Pauw University
Earlham College
East Tennessee State University
Gettysburg College
Guilford College
Indiana University
Indiana University/Purdue
  University at Indianapolis

Marquette University
Maryville College
Michigan State University
Morehouse College
Nazareth College
Northeastern University
Oberlin College
Rhodes College
Rollins College
San Francisco State University
Santa Clara University
Stanford University
Temple University
University of Cincinnati
University of Colorado
University of Florida
University of Michigan
University of Missouri
University of Oregon
University of San Diego
University of Utah
University of Washington
Vanderbilt University

Resource B: Sample and
Methods of the Studies

The primary data for this book come from two national research projects that we conducted between 1993 and 1998. In four data-gathering waves, including pilot surveys, we interviewed or surveyed nearly four thousand students across the country.

In the spring 1995 survey, 1,535 of the 2,462 students who completed the protest also completed the posttest for a pre-post match rate of 63 percent. The one-time reflection practices interview, also completed during the spring of 1995, totaled 67. During the spring 1996 problem-solving interviews, 100 students were interviewed before and 66 after their service-learning courses or programs, for a pre-post match of 66. The data reported in this book are based on these three samples.

The National Survey

The Comparing Models of Service-Learning project is a national study of the impact of service-learning programs on students' citizenship values, skills, attitudes, and understanding.

Sample

The data discussed here were gathered from 1,544 students at twenty colleges and universities during the spring of 1995. Students completed surveys at the beginning and end of their service-learning experience. Colleges were selected that had a variety of service-learning activities and represented different types and geographical locations. Included were six private universities, five small liberal arts colleges, and eight public universities. Five were located in the East, six in the Midwest, three in the South, and five in the West. All students in classes that agreed to participate in the study were surveyed. There were 1,131 pre- and postsurveys from students who participated in service and 404 from classmates who did not select service classes or options within classes.

Classes included service internships, professional classes such as those in education and social work that included service-learning, and special service-learning seminars, as well as traditional arts and sciences classes with a service-learning component. About two-thirds of the students surveyed were in traditional arts and sciences classes.

Measuring Outcomes

Survey measures focused on the many types of learning identified in Chapter One: personal and interpersonal development, understanding and application of subject matter learning, critical thinking and perspective transformation, and citizenship skills and values. These are among the most frequently expressed goals of service-learning programs (Giles, Honnet, and Migliore, 1991).

Students' assessments of their leadership skills, communication skills, and tolerance are based on items developed in an early version of a citizenship skill measure developed as part of the Measuring Citizenship Project of the Walt Whitman Center for the Culture and Politics of Democracy at Rutgers University (1993). Leadership skills are measured with items that, for example, ask students to compare their ability to "lead a group" or "know whom to contact to get things done"; communication skills draw on items that refer to "listening" or "communicating with others"; tolerance items include "respecting views of others" and "empathetic to all points of view." These three scales had Cronbach alphas ranging from .71 to .80. The ability to identify social issues and critical thinking skills are measured by single items, as are the values outcomes. Students' ratings of how they value such future roles as "careers helping people," "community leadership," and "influencing public policy" are drawn from measures developed by Markus, Howard, and King (1993). The focus of these value items is on the students' own definition of how they will live their lives.

Some of the personal and interpersonal development items related to citizenship include a sense of personal efficacy in affecting community issues, a belief that the community itself can be effective in solving its problems, and feeling connected to the community. These scales developed by Scheurich (1994) yielded alphas with this sample ranging from .46 for community connectedness to .64 for personal efficacy. In Scheurich's original development of the scale with students at a single college, the scales had somewhat higher consistency; the extreme diversity of this sample may have affected reliability.

The items that measured perspective transformation focused on students' commitment to systemic change and political action. Locus of community problems measures whether students take a systemic view of social problems or tend to assign blame narrowly to the individuals facing the problem. The alpha for this scale was .72. Students' beliefs that social justice is a critical issue for the community, that it is important to have an impact on the political structure, and that changing policy is the most important approach were measured by single items. The final scale in this set of measures focused on the tendency of students to reach closure quickly on an issue or to remain open to other views and information; this scale had an alpha of .50.

Data Analysis

Data were analyzed using hierarchical multiple regression with controls for age, gender, minority status, family income, and other community service during college.

Demographic Profiles

The 1,535 students in this sample came from 109 different courses and programs at twenty colleges and universities (they are listed in Resource A). Sample size per class ranged from 1 to 310 students. In this sample, 1,131 students were participating in service-learning at the time of the survey; the other 404 were either in comparison classes or had not chosen the service option in a class. The gender breakdown for the total sample was 68 percent female. There was no significant difference in service-learning/no service, with 69 percent of the service-learning sample being female. We deliberately selected a sample that would mostly reflect a traditional college age population; 95 percent of those in the sample were between seventeen and twenty-five years of age. The racial and ethnic makeup included 17 percent minority students. There was no difference in the sample between minority and nonminority students on the service-learning/non-service-learning choice, with an identical split of 83 percent and 17 percent. By design we focused on undergraduate students; 99 percent of the total sample were undergraduates distributed as follows: freshmen, 30 percent; sophomores, 24 percent; juniors, 24 percent; seniors, 21 percent. Table B.1 shows the distribution of majors by service-learning and no service.

Service Experiences

For most of the students in our sample, the pathways in service began before their college years. Only 22 percent had not had any service experiences in their junior or senior year of high school. They reported slightly lower levels of service involvement by their parents; 70 percent reported that their parents had some involvement in community service activities, and 23 percent reported parental involvement in service at least two or three times a month. There was an association between higher levels of students' high school service and parental involvement in community service.

Service during college was reported by 67 percent of our sample; this is slightly higher than we expected, as we had explored the drop

Table B.1. College Major by Service-Learning and No Service.

Major	No Service	Service-Learning
Humanities/English	59	171
Social Sciences	66	268
Math/Science/Engineering	132	250
Business	66	127
Education/Human Development	54	168
No information	27	147
Total	404	1,131

from high school to college service elsewhere (Giles and Eyler, 1994a). Freshmen were the least likely to report service activities while in college; for the freshmen in our survey, they were asked this question during the first week or two of their second semester in school, and only 47 percent of them reported service involvement prior to their service-learning class. This is in contrast to 82 percent of the seniors in our sample reporting college community service activities. This suggests that the path to service is more frequently traveled as college students progress through their undergraduate years. Students who choose service are more likely to have higher scores on the pretest measures for citizenship, political attitudes, and social opinions. These are related to high school service involvement and are mediated by the increased likelihood of doing service in college (Eyler-Walker, 1997). All of this suggests the importance of service and service-learning in high school for both postsecondary involvement and lifelong active citizenship.

Qualitatively, the path of service begins most frequently with direct service to children, with 62 percent of the almost 1,200 students who performed community service in their junior year in high school reporting that as their start. Senior year experiences were similar, with direct service to children reported at 60 percent. This was followed by service to adults in both the junior and senior years, accounting for 12 percent of the service experiences. Direct service was by far the most common high school service activity, with 60 percent in the junior year and 57 percent in the senior year.

During the college semester measured here, direct involvement with children was the top form of service (36 percent). In fact, direct involvement with all populations accounted for 90 percent of all service activities, with the rest being special projects, indirect administrative work, and planning and organizing service events. The modal number of hours served per week was one to three hours for 48 percent of the sample. The next most frequently reported amount was four to six hours a week. Only 14 percent reported doing more than six hours a week of service. Most students engaged in service for the biggest part of the semester, with 40 percent doing service for five to eleven weeks and 35 percent serving for more than eleven weeks. Only 23 percent reported serving for one to four weeks.

Problem-Solving Interviews

Recognizing the limitations of survey responses to assess student learning, we also conducted intensive interviews with a smaller number of students at the start and end of the semester. This allowed us to look at how students' understanding of social problems as well as their critical thinking abilities changed as the result of their service-learning.

Sample

Sixty-six students who were enrolled in courses with community service components were interviewed at the beginning and end of the 1996 spring semester. These courses were located at six colleges and universities and included both private and public institutions: University of Colorado, Indiana University/Purdue University at Indianapolis, Michigan State University, California State College at Monterey Bay, Nazareth College, and Vanderbilt University. In two large courses where service was an option rather than a requirement of the course, a sample of students who did not select the service option were interviewed as a control group. There were sixteen students in this control group.

Data Gathering

The interview protocol included general questions about community service and a series of questions that asked the students to analyze the causes of and solutions to a problem related to their service and to justify their reasoning. The interviews lasted approximately fifty minutes, and the same interviewer conducted the pre- and postinterview for each student. The interview protocols are in Resource C.

Data Analysis

Interviews were transcribed and scored. Although it was not possible to disguise whether interviews were pre or post because of internal cues, the coders were not aware if particular transcripts represented students from the control group or the highly reflective or less intense service-learning experiences. Transcripts were shuffled, and interviews from particular times and schools were not coded sequentially. Coding for problem analysis was based on themes from the expert-novice literature, as well as pilot work done prior to the study (Eyler, Root, and Giles, 1998). Categories included issue knowledge application, causal and solution complexity, causal and solution locus, and personal political strategy. (Coding categories are included in Resource C after the posttest interview protocol.) The critical thinking analysis was based on the reflective judgment model developed by King and Kitchener (1994). Cindy Lynch adapted questions and scoring techniques based on that theoretical approach to the needs of this study and advised on the scoring of critical thinking.

Data were analyzed using hierarchical multiple regression with controls for age, gender, and previous community service. The first analysis examined the impact of these background characteristics on the pretest measure of reflective judgment. The second analysis examined the impact of participation in service on problem-solving and critical thinking outcomes. The third analysis used only the fifty students who participated in service and examined the effects of an intensive reflective service-learning experience compared to participation in a less intensive experience. Intensive classes were those where the service was required and central to the daily class discourse; these classes focused on analyzing the service experience and relating it to the subject matter. Less intensive classes made service an option or were less likely to focus class activities on analysis of the experience.

Data from five of the six colleges were used for the problem-solving analysis; the sixth program was measured after students had already participated in service for a semester, and thus there were no pretest students. All sixty-six interviews were used for the critical thinking analysis.

Demographic Profiles

This sample of sixty-six matched pre- and postinterviews was done in the spring of 1996 with students from six colleges and universities. This also was a young, traditional age group, with 92 percent ranging from eighteen to twenty-five years old. The majority of the sample, 73 percent, was female. Undergraduates made up 98 percent of this group: freshmen, 38 percent; sophomores, 30 percent; juniors, 24 percent; and seniors, 6 percent. Table B.2 shows the distribution of the students' majors.

Service Experiences

This group reported high levels of previous service experiences, with 89 percent having had at least one previous experience. The average number of previous experiences was 2.6. Once again, working with children was the most common previous service experience (33 percent), followed by working with adults (24 percent) and then indirect service with agency staff (17 percent). Direct involvement with people was the most frequent form of service activity (50

Table B.2. College Major: Problem-Solving Interviews.

Major	Students
Undefined	7
Humanities/English	4
Social Sciences/History	9
Math/Science/Engineering	23
Education/Human Development	21
Business	2
Total	66

percent). This group reported that 71 percent had previous service-learning courses, with 29 percent of the sample having had more than one previous course.

In this sample we gathered data about the category of service because we were asking questions about problem solving that we geared toward the actual service involvement. These topics and the numbers of students providing service under each are presented in Table B.3. In most of these cases the category of service was also a theme or major content area of the service-learning course, such as AIDS policy, cultural diversity, or children. Again in this sample as with the others, direct involvement with children was the most frequently reported service activity, at 42 percent, and direct involvement with adults second, at 11 percent. Indirect kinds of service accounted for 25 percent of the reported activities. The number of weeks of service ranged from one to thirty-two, with the average of ten weeks. Hours served per week ranged from two to forty, with four as the mode and three hours per week as the median.

Reflection Interviews

The reflection interviews were designed to explore what students value in their service-learning and to enable us to share with practitioners reflection ideas that work well for students. These interviews were funded by the Corporation for National Service

Table B.3. Categories of Service: Problem-Solving Interviews.

Category	Number of Students
AIDS	8
Environment	8
Poverty	3
Prison project	1
Cultural diversity	10
Homelessness	2
Youth crime	3
Children	17
Mental illness/psychology	3
Other	11
Total	66

and were the source of ideas for *A Practitioner's Guide to Reflection in Service-Learning* (Eyler, Giles, and Schmiede, 1996). The primary use of these data in this book is to illustrate with student voices some of the points made with quantitative data.

Sample

After conducting our pilot interviews at Vanderbilt and the University of Tennessee, we selected six colleges and universities from the list of Corporation for National Service grantees to participate in the study: Bentley College, the University of San Diego, the University of Colorado, East Tennessee State University, Clark-Atlanta University, and the University of Washington. While we could not begin to represent the diversity of the types of higher education in such a small sample, we selected colleges and universities that varied in size, geographic location, type of service-learning program, history, and traditions (for example, historically black, private, public, liberal arts, preprofessional).

Although we were primarily interested in structured reflection that occurs in the classroom, we also wanted to explore reflection activities that occur in cocurricular programs, as well as self-directed reflection; we therefore selected a sample of forty-six students who had taken specific courses with service-learning options and twenty-one who had previously been involved only in cocurricular service projects. The data presented in this text focus primarily on the students who had the more structured reflective experiences.

Data Gathering

It was clear to us from the very beginning that the only research methodology appropriate for this project was to use in-depth, personal semistructured interviews. No other data-gathering method was capable of capturing the richness of the experience while providing a consistent approach to inquiring about modes of reflection. After several pilot interviews, we settled on an interview guide consisting of five basic areas of questioning (see Resource C for the reflection interview guide). Each interview was tape-recorded and lasted an average of about forty-five minutes. Interviewers were trained to probe for specific examples of helpful reflection experiences and techniques. Interviewees also filled out a brief service-learning history sheet that was used to gather data on background characteristics and previous experiences.

Data Analysis

The project's data analysis involved entering the transcribed interviews into a word processing database. We used qualitative analysis software (Ethnograph) to perform content analysis and to code themes and types of reflection.

Demographic Profiles

We interviewed sixty-seven students: sixty of the students represented the traditional student age range of nineteen to twenty-two years, but seven students were older. The gender ratio among participants was forty-five women and twenty-two men, which is consistent with existing evidence about the gender ratio among

Table B.4. Previous Community Service Experience, by Type of Service and People Worked with: Reflection Interviews.

People Worked With	Direct Involvement with People	Special Project for Group	Type of Service Indirect Service	Supervise Volunteers/ Manage Program	Plan/Organize Program	Total
Children	45	4	3	5	5	62
Teens	10	7	7	3	6	33
Adults	25	21	14	5	11	76
Peers	8	4	1	1	7	21
Agency staff	1	0	10	1	0	12
Total	89	36	35	15	29	204

Note: Sixty-seven students were interviewed. These data represent the variety of previous service activities they reported. Some students were involved in several activities, so totals exceed sixty-seven.

participants in most service programs nationwide. Of the sixty-seven students, forty-eight were Caucasian, eleven were African American, five were Asian American, and three were Latino. The class years were freshmen, 19 percent; sophomores, 12 percent; juniors, 27 percent; seniors, 34 percent.

Service Experiences

All of the students in this sample had previous as well as current service experiences. We measured this by coding each year of service experience as a service year unit. For example, if someone had three different concurrent service experiences of a year's duration each, we coded this as three service years. The number of service years ranged from one to thirty-seven; 8 percent had one service year, with the average being five and a half service years. Only 10 percent had more than nine service years. Like the previous sample, the most common form of early service experience was working directly with children. As Table B.4 illustrates, this group had a variety of previous community service experiences, including a mix of direct and indirect involvement, with serving children directly the most frequently mentioned service experience.

We deliberately sampled for students with extensive service and reflection experiences; as a result, 79 percent of the students in this group reported having at least one previous service-learning class. Thirty-four percent reported having just one service-learning class, and 17 percent had four or more previous service-learning classes.

Resource C: Survey and Interview Instruments

FIPSE Survey Instrument: Pretest

This is the survey administered to students before the service-learning semester in spring 1995.

Service Experiences Survey

Student ID #_____

About the Survey

The Service Experiences (SE) survey is a national project to find out more about what college students think about various community service projects. Some students have been involved in these projects since high school; others have been more involved with work, family, or their studies and haven't participated in these projects. We are interested in the activities and views of both. This questionnaire asks about your past experiences and for some of your opinions and self-assessments; we will ask questions about your 1995 experiences at the end of this term.

   Participation in the survey is completely voluntary. We hope that you will agree to complete the questionnaire fully so that we may have as accurate a picture as possible. Your student identification number is requested so that we may match up this questionnaire with information you may give in follow-up surveys; your responses will be confidential, and no one on your campus will have access to your individual answers. All results will be reported as grouped data only.

The project is being conducted by Dr. Janet Eyler and Dr. Dwight Giles of Vanderbilt University and is sponsored by the Fund for the Improvement of Postsecondary Education (FIPSE). The information we are collecting will help colleges plan for the most effective kinds of community service opportunities for their students.

Instructions for the SE Survey

1. Along with this booklet you should have a number two pencil and a BLUE computer scoring sheet for the questions. On both the top of this booklet and on the BLUE answer sheet, please fill in your student identification number. Blacken the appropriate numbers in the column below the number on the sheet.

2. Mark all answers with a NUMBER TWO PENCIL on the BLUE ANSWER SHEET provided. Where appropriate write open-ended responses on this booklet, in the space provided. Return the blue sheet and the booklet together.

3. Consider each statement carefully, but don't spend a lot of time deliberating about a single item.

4. For each subsection, read the statement at the beginning of the section. Then read each question and decide which response best represents your experience, actions, or opinions. Blacken the corresponding number on the answer sheet.

THANK YOU FOR YOUR PARTICIPATION.

Your Previous Activities

Think back on your high school and college experience and indicate your usual level of involvement in these activities.

Always (each week)   = 5

Often (2–3 times a month)   = 4

Sometimes (1 time a month)   = 3

Seldom (1–2 times a term)   = 2

Never   = 1

1. High school clubs/groups	1	2	3	4	5
2. High school junior year community service	1	2	3	4	5
3. High school senior year community service	1	2	3	4	5
4. High school athletic teams	1	2	3	4	5
5. Work for pay in high school	1	2	3	4	5
6. College athletic teams	1	2	3	4	5
7. College campus clubs/groups	1	2	3	4	5
8. College-community service	1	2	3	4	5
9. Religious clubs/groups	1	2	3	4	5
10. Work for pay in college	1	2	3	4	5
11. At home, my parents were active in community service	1	2	3	4	5

Types of Previous Service

Choose the number from the lists below to describe whom you worked with and what you did in service activities. If you worked in several activities describe the *one most important to you*. If you weren't active, leave that item blank.

Whom You Worked With

Children   = 1

Teens   = 2

Adults   = 3

Peers   = 4

Agency staff = 5

12. High school junior year	1	2	3	4	5
13. High school senior year	1	2	3	4	5
14. College (college before previous term)	1	2	3	4	5
15. Previous term in college	1	2	3	4	5

What You Did

Direct involvement with same person/group
   (e.g., tutor, coach, visit) = 1

Direct involvement with different people needing service
   (e.g., assist at shelter) = 2

Assist agency
   (e.g., clerical, physical labor) = 3

Special project for group
   (e.g., written brochure or fundraiser) = 4

Supervise other volunteers, organize program = 5

16. High school junior year	1	2	3	4	5
17. High school senior year	1	2	3	4	5
18. College (before previous term)	1	2	3	4	5
19. Previous term in college	1	2	3	4	5

Your Opinions

These are issues that people disagree on; please respond based on your honest reaction to each item. Please answer every item and choose the answer that makes sense to YOU, not what you think others would say.

Strongly agree   = 5

Agree   = 4

Uncertain   = 3

Disagree   = 2

Strongly disagree = 1

20. Adults should give some time for the good of their community.   1   2   3   4   5

21. I feel that social problems are not my concern.   1   2   3   4   5

22. Having an impact on community problems is within the reach of most individuals.   1   2   3   4   5

23. People who work in social service agencies can do little to really help people in need.   1   2   3   4   5

24. Government should get out of the business of solving social problems.   1   2   3   4   5

25. People who receive social services largely have only themselves to blame for needing services.   1   2   3   4   5

26. I feel that social problems directly affect the quality of life in my community.   1   2   3   4   5

27. Social problems are   1   2   3   4   5
more difficult to solve
than I used to think.

28. The problems that cause   1   2   3   4   5
people to need social
services are frequently the
result of circumstances
beyond their control.

29. If I could change one   1   2   3   4   5
thing about society, it
would be to achieve
greater social justice.

30. The most important   1   2   3   4   5
community service is
to help individuals.

31. The most important   1   2   3   4   5
community service is to
change public policy.

32. I think our social   1   2   3   4   5
problems can be solved
by the community.

33. For the most part, each   1   2   3   4   5
individual controls
whether he or she is
poor or wealthy.

34. Communities should   1   2   3   4   5
provide social services
to their members
in need.

35. I feel that I can have   1   2   3   4   5
an impact on solving
the problems in my
community.

36. It is important to me   1   2   3   4   5
personally to influence
the political structure.

37. It is important to me   1   2   3   4   5
personally to volunteer
my time to help people
in need.

38. It is important to me   1   2   3   4   5
personally to be very
well off financially.

39. It is important to me   1   2   3   4   5
personally to become
a community leader.

40. High school students   1   2   3   4   5
should be required to
provide a certain
number of hours of
community service in
order to graduate.

41. We should reach out   1   2   3   4   5
to specific people in need
rather than create
programs to address
social problems.

42. I feel that I can play an   1   2   3   4   5
important part in
improving the well-
being of my community.

43. My problems are too   1   2   3   4   5
large for me to give time
to helping others.

44. It is important to me
personally to have a
career that involves
helping people.

1   2   3   4   5

45. I feel positive about
my community's ability
to solve its social
problems.

1   2   3   4   5

46. Skills and experiences
that I gain from
community service will
be valuable in my career.

1   2   3   4   5

47. Community service
will help me develop
leadership skills.

1   2   3   4   5

48. I feel uncomfortable
working with people
who are different from
me in such things as
race, wealth, and
life experiences.

1   2   3   4   5

Skills and Activities

Below is a list of skills and activities that people do in various situations. Please read each of the following, and rate yourself with respect to how well you do each of these compared to most people.

Much better than most   = 5

Better than most   = 4

About the same   = 3

Not as good as most   = 2

Much worse than most   = 1

49. Respecting the   1   2   3   4   5
    views of others

50. Participating in   1   2   3   4   5
    community affairs

51. Thinking critically   1   2   3   4   5

52. Communicating   1   2   3   4   5
    my ideas to others

53. Engaging in discussion 1   2   3   4   5
    with others

54. Ability to compromise 1   2   3   4   5

55. Listening skills   1   2   3   4   5

56. Moral or ethical   1   2   3   4   5
    judgment

57. Identification of social 1   2   3   4   5
    issues and concerns

58. Thinking about the   1   2   3   4   5
    future

59. Ability to take action 1   2   3   4   5

60. Tolerant of people who 1   2   3   4   5
    are different from me

61. Effective in   1   2   3   4   5
    accomplishing goals

62. Ability to see   1   2   3   4   5
    consequences of actions

63. Empathetic to all   1   2   3   4   5
    points of view

64. Ability to work with   1   2   3   4   5
    others

65. Thinking about others 1   2   3   4   5
    before myself

66. Ability to speak in public	1	2	3	4	5
67. Feeling responsible for others	1	2	3	4	5
68. Knowing where to find information	1	2	3	4	5
69. Knowing who to contact in order to get things done	1	2	3	4	5
70. Ability to lead a group	1	2	3	4	5

Describing Yourself

For each of these phrases, indicate whether they describe you very well or not at all well or somewhere in between.

Describes me very well = 5

Somewhat well = 4

Uncertain = 3

Not well = 2

Not at all well = 1

71. I often discuss political or social issues with my friends.	1	2	3	4	5
72. I sometimes find it difficult to see things from the other person's point of view.	1	2	3	4	5
73. I try to keep up with local and national news.	1	2	3	4	5
74. I usually make up my mind right away about something.	1	2	3	4	5

75. I read a newspaper   1   2   3   4   5
    or watch news shows
    daily.

76. I try to understand   1   2   3   4   5
    my friends better by
    imagining how things
    look from their point
    of view.

77. If I am sure I am right,   1   2   3   4   5
    I don't waste much time
    listening to other
    people's arguments.

78. I often participate in   1   2   3   4   5
    advocacy or political
    action groups.

79. I often try to persuade   1   2   3   4   5
    others to take my
    point of view.

80. Before criticizing some-   1   2   3   4   5
    body, I try to imagine
    how I would feel if I were
    in his or her place.

81. Once I have decided   1   2   3   4   5
    something, I am hard
    to convince otherwise.

82. I often change my   1   2   3   4   5
    opinion about social
    problems when I hear
    others talk.

83. I always vote in state   1   2   3   4   5
    and local elections.

84. I always vote in national elections.   1   2   3   4   5

85. I usually take a long time to consider things before I make up my mind.   1   2   3   4   5

86. I am active in political campaigns.   1   2   3   4   5

87. I have testified in public hearings or spoken at meetings held by public agencies.   1   2   3   4   5

88. Once I make up my mind, I fight for what I believe in.   1   2   3   4   5

89. I am active in campus politics.   1   2   3   4   5

Questions About You

Mark the bubble that corresponds to the correct choice under each item.

90. Gender   1. female   2. male

91. Age 1. 17–18 2. 19–20 3. 21–22 4. 23–25 5. 26 +

92. Class 1. fresh. 2. soph. 3. jr. 4. sr. 5. grad student

93. Ethnicity
    1. African American
    2. Asian American
    3. Caucasian
    4. Hispanic/Latino
    5. Native American
    — Other [write in _____]

94. What is your best estimate of your parents' total income last year? Consider all income from all sources:

1. $20,000 or less
2. $20,001–30,000
3. $30,001–50,000
4. $50,001–75,000
5. $75,001 or more

95. What is the highest level of education reached by your father?
    1. some high school
    2. high school graduate
    3. some college or other postsecondary schooling
    4. college graduate
    5. graduate degree

96. What is the highest level of education reached by your mother?
    1. some high school
    2. high school graduate
    3. some college or other postsecondary schooling
    4. college graduate
    5. graduate degree

97. What is your college major?
    1. humanities/English/communications
    2. social sciences/history
    3. math/science/engineering/health sciences
    4. education/human development
    5. business
    — Other [write in _____]

98. How many hours a week do you work for pay while you are in college?
    1. none   2. 1–5   3. 6–10   4. 11–20   5. 21 or more

99. Did you vote Nov. 8, 1994?   1. yes   2. no

100. How many courses have you had in college where you participated in community service to meet some of the course requirements? Include any current service-learning course.
    1. none   2. one   3. two   4. three   5. four or more

101. Have you done any volunteering/community service in the past twelve months?
1. yes   2. no (Go to question 104) If yes, continue.

102. Have you done any volunteering/community service in the past month?
1. yes   2. no (Go to question 104)
If yes, how many hours did you spend in volunteer work during the past month? [write in_____]

103. Have you done any volunteering/community service in the past seven days?
1. yes   2. no (Go to question 104)
If yes, how many hours did you spend in volunteer work during the past seven days? [write in_____]

104. What career do you plan to pursue when you graduate?
[write in_____]

105. Think about the problems that your community service this semester is designed to help with; briefly list any organizations or services that address this problem in the community: (write below on this form)

Thank you

FIPSE Survey Instrument: Posttest

This is the survey administered to students at the end of their service-learning semester, spring 1995.

Service Experiences Postsurvey

Student ID #_____

About the Survey

This is a follow-up to the survey you took at the beginning of this term about your views of community service. Participation is voluntary; we hope you will complete this survey fully so that we may have an accurate picture of your experiences and views.

MARK ANSWERS ON SCANTRON SHEET.
PLEASE COMPLETE THE SURVEY FULLY AND CAREFULLY;
IT IS IMPORTANT TO KNOW HOW *YOU* THINK ABOUT
THESE ISSUES *NOW!* THANK YOU!!

1. Are you filling this survey out for community service you did as part of *this* class or program? 1. yes 2. no
   If YES, go to question 3. If NO go to question 2.

2. Did you participate in community service this term outside of this class or program? 1. yes 2. no
   If YES go to question 3. If NO go to question 56.

3. How many weeks did you participate in this service project? 1. none 2. one 3. two to four
   4. five to ten 5. over eleven

4. How many hours per week did you participate?
   1. 1–3 2. 4–6 3. 7–12 4. 13–20 5. over 20

5. With whom did you *primarily* work (provide service to)?
   1. children 2. teens 3. adults 4. peers 5. agency staff

6. What did you usually do?
   1. direct involvement with people receiving service (e.g., tutor, coach, visit)
   2. special project for group (e.g., brochure or fundraiser)
   3. indirect service (e.g., clerical, physical labor, transport)
   4. supervise other volunteers/manage program
   5. create/plan/organize new program

7. Did you participate in service projects other than the one described above this semester/quarter? 1. yes 2. no

8. Will you participate in community service next semester?
   1. yes 2. no

9. How many hours per week do you plan to volunteer?
   1. none 2. 1–3 3. 4–6 4. 7–12 5. over 12

Describe Your Service

For each item, choose the number that best describes your service this term. If a feature *does not apply* to you (e.g., it is about assignments and your service was not part of a class), mark 1, for "never."

Very often   = 5
Fairly often   = 4
Sometimes   = 3
Once in a great while = 2
Never   = 1

During my community service:

10. Had important responsibilities	1	2	3	4	5
11. Had challenging tasks	1	2	3	4	5
12. Made important decisions	1	2	3	4	5
13. What I did was interesting	1	2	3	4	5
14. Did things myself instead of observing	1	2	3	4	5
15. Talked with people receiving service	1	2	3	4	5
16. Professionals at site took interest in me	1	2	3	4	5
17. Volunteers met for seminars/formal discussions of the service	1	2	3	4	5
18. Had variety of tasks to do at site	1	2	3	4	5
19. Was appreciated when I did a good job	1	2	3	4	5

20. Felt I made a real   1   2   3   4   5
    contribution

21. Free to develop and   1   2   3   4   5
    use *my* ideas

22. People receiving   1   2   3   4   5
    service helped plan
    service activities

23. Discussed experiences   1   2   3   4   5
    with faculty

24. Discussed experiences   1   2   3   4   5
    with other volunteers

25. Worked with people   1   2   3   4   5
    from diverse ethnic
    backgrounds

26. Project met needs   1   2   3   4   5
    identified by members
    of the community

27. Experience challenged   1   2   3   4   5
    my previous opinions

28. Applied things I   1   2   3   4   5
    learned in college to
    my service placement

29. Will apply things I   1   2   3   4   5
    learned during service
    to my college classes

30. Kept a journal   1   2   3   4   5

31. Coordinator or faculty   1   2   3   4   5
    member responded to
    my journal

32. Completed writing   1   2   3   4   5
    assignments about my
    project or site

33. Coordinator or faculty led discussions where we shared feelings	1	2	3	4	5
34. Coordinator or faculty led discussions where we analyzed community and organizational problems.	1	2	3	4	5
35. Coordinator or faculty led discussions where we related our service to what we were learning in class	1	2	3	4	5
36. Gave speech or presentation about my service activities	1	2	3	4	5

What You Learned from Service

Students have identified different things they learned from their community service. Please indicate how important each benefit was to you. Please don't select more than *three* items as "Most Important."

Most important   = 4

Very important   = 3

Somewhat important = 2

Not important   = 1

I learned:

37. Deeper understanding of things I already had learned about in my classes	1	2	3	4

38. To apply things I have learned in class to real problems	1	2	3	4
39. How complex the problems faced by the people I worked with are	1	2	3	4
40. That the people I served are like me	1	2	3	4
41. How rewarding it is to help others	1	2	3	4
42. Understand myself better/personal growth	1	2	3	4
43. How to work with others effectively	1	2	3	4
44. Specific new skills (e.g., carpentry, food preparation, computers)	1	2	3	4
45. To appreciate different cultures	1	2	3	4
46. Spiritual growth	1	2	3	4
47. To identify many community programs which address social problems	1	2	3	4
48. To see social problems in a new way	1	2	3	4

How You Learned from Service

Rate the importance of these activities in your learning; limit "Most Important" to *two* or *three* items.

Most important   = 4

Very important   = 3

Somewhat important = 2

Not important   = 1

Much of my learning came from:

49. Faculty and staff presentations	1	2	3	4
50. Providing real service to people	1	2	3	4
51. Reflection in journals or written assignments	1	2	3	4
52. Working with professionals in field	1	2	3	4
53. Informal sharing of experiences with other volunteers or classmates	1	2	3	4
54. Formal structured debriefing sessions or class discussions	1	2	3	4
55. Interaction with people I served	1	2	3	4

Relationships with Faculty and Other Students

These items refer to relationships with others at your school that have developed through *community service* activities and those that you have developed in activities *other than* service. If you have not participated in service mark 1 ("does not apply") for items that refer to service.

Strongly agree   = 5

Agree   = 4

Disagree   = 3

Strongly disagree   = 2

Does not apply   = 1

During Activities Other Than Community Service

56. I have developed a close   1   2   3   4   5
    personal relationship
    with at least one faculty
    member.
57. I am satisfied with the   1   2   3   4   5
    opportunities to interact
    informally with faculty.
58. I have developed close   1   2   3   4   5
    personal relationships
    with other students.
59. The student friendships   1   2   3   4   5
    I have developed are
    intellectually stimulating.

During Service Activities

60. During community   1   2   3   4   5
    service I have developed
    a close, personal
    relationship with at least
    one faculty member.
61. Community service has   1   2   3   4   5
    been a good opportunity
    for me to interact
    informally with faculty.
62. As a result of my   1   2   3   4   5
    community service I
    have developed close
    personal relationships
    with other students.
63. The student friendships   1   2   3   4   5
    I have developed during
    service have been
    intellectually stimulating.

Your Opinion About the Service This Term

64. I would rate my service experiences this term as:
    1. poor   2. fair   3. good   4. excellent

65. Compared to my regular classes I learned _____
    in my community service.
    1. much less   2. less   3. the same   4. more   5. much more

66. Compared to regular classes I found community service
    _____ intellectually challenging.
    1. much less   2. less   3. the same   4. more   5. much more

67. Compared to regular classes I found myself _____
    motivated to work hard during community service.
    1. much less   2. less   3. the same   4. more   5. much more

Your Opinions

These are issues that people disagree on; please respond based on your honest reaction to each item. Please answer every item and choose the answer that makes sense to YOU, not what you think others would say.

Strongly agree	= 5
Agree	= 4
Uncertain	= 3
Disagree	= 2
Strongly disagree	= 1

68. Adults should give some time for the good of their community.

    1   2   3   4   5

69. I feel that social problems are not my concern.

    1   2   3   4   5

70. Having an impact on   1   2   3   4   5
    community problems
    is within the reach of
    most individuals.

71. People who work in   1   2   3   4   5
    social service agencies
    can do little to really
    help people in need.

72. Government should get   1   2   3   4   5
    out of the business of
    solving social problems.

73. People who receive social   1   2   3   4   5
    services largely have only
    themselves to blame for
    needing services.

74. I feel that social problems 1   2   3   4   5
    directly affect the quality
    of life in my community.

75. Social problems are more   1   2   3   4   5
    difficult to solve than I
    used to think.

76. The problems that cause   1   2   3   4   5
    people to need social
    services are frequently the
    result of circumstances
    beyond their control.

77. If I could change one   1   2   3   4   5
    thing about society, it
    would be to achieve
    greater social justice.

78. The most important   1   2   3   4   5
    community service is
    to help individuals.

79. The most important   1   2   3   4   5
community service is
to change public policy.

80. I think our social   1   2   3   4   5
problems can be solved
by the community.

81. For the most part, each   1   2   3   4   5
individual controls whether
he or she is poor or wealthy.

82. Communities should   1   2   3   4   5
provide social services
to their members in need.

83. I feel that I can have an   1   2   3   4   5
impact on solving the prob-
lems in my community.

84. It is important to me   1   2   3   4   5
personally to influence
the political structure.

85. It is important to me per-   1   2   3   4   5
sonally to volunteer my
time to help people in need.

86. It is important to me   1   2   3   4   5
personally to be very
well off financially.

87. It is important to me   1   2   3   4   5
personally to become
a community leader.

88. High school students   1   2   3   4   5
should be required to
provide a certain number
of hours of community
service in order to graduate.

89. We should reach   1   2   3   4   5
    out to specific people in
    need rather than creat-
    ing programs to address
    social problems.

90. I feel that I can play an   1   2   3   4   5
    important part in
    improving the well-
    being of my community.

91. My problems are too   1   2   3   4   5
    large for me to give
    time to helping others.

92. It is important to me   1   2   3   4   5
    personally to have a
    career that involves
    helping people.

93. I feel positive about my   1   2   3   4   5
    community's ability to
    solve its social problems.

94. Skills and experiences   1   2   3   4   5
    that I gain from
    community service will
    be valuable in my career.

95. Community service will   1   2   3   4   5
    help me develop
    leadership skills.

96. I feel uncomfortable   1   2   3   4   5
    working with people
    who are different from
    me in such things as race,
    wealth, and life
    experiences.

Skills and Activities

Below is a list of skills and activities that people do in various situations. Please read each of the following and rate yourself with respect to how well you do each of these compared to most other people.

Much better than most = 5

Better than most   = 4

About the same   = 3

Not as good as most   = 2

Much worse than most = 1

97. Respecting the views of others	1	2	3	4	5
98. Participating in community affairs	1	2	3	4	5
99. Thinking critically	1	2	3	4	5
100. Communicating my ideas to others	1	2	3	4	5
101. Engaging in discussion with others	1	2	3	4	5
102. Ability to compromise	1	2	3	4	5
103. Listening skills	1	2	3	4	5
104. Moral or ethical judgment	1	2	3	4	5
105. Identification of social issues and concerns	1	2	3	4	5
106. Thinking about the future	1	2	3	4	5
107. Ability to take action	1	2	3	4	5
108. Tolerant of people who are different from me	1	2	3	4	5

109. Effective in   1   2   3   4   5
accomplishing goals

110. Ability to see   1   2   3   4   5
consequences of actions

111. Empathetic to all points   1   2   3   4   5
of view

112. Ability to work   1   2   3   4   5
with others

113. Thinking about others   1   2   3   4   5
before myself

114. Ability to speak in public   1   2   3   4   5

115. Feeling responsible   1   2   3   4   5
for others

116. Knowing where to   1   2   3   4   5
find information

117. Knowing whom to   1   2   3   4   5
contact in order to
get things done

118. Ability to lead a group   1   2   3   4   5

Describing Yourself

For each of these phrases, indicate whether they describe you very
well or not at all well or somewhere in between.

Describes me very well   = 5

Somewhat well   = 4

Uncertain   = 3

Not well   = 2

Not at all well   = 1

119. I often discuss political   1   2   3   4   5
or social issues with
my friends.

120. I sometimes find it difficult to see things from the other person's point of view.   1   2   3   4   5

121. I try to keep up with local and national news.   1   2   3   4   5

122. I usually make up my mind right away about something.   1   2   3   4   5

123. I read a newspaper or watch news shows daily.   1   2   3   4   5

124. I try to understand my friends better by imagining how things look from their point of view.   1   2   3   4   5

125. If I am sure I am right, I don't waste much time listening to other people's arguments.   1   2   3   4   5

126. I often participate in advocacy or political action groups.   1   2   3   4   5

127. I often try to persuade others to take my point of view.   1   2   3   4   5

128. Before criticizing somebody, I try to imagine how I would feel if I were in his or her place.   1   2   3   4   5

129. Once I have decided   1   2   3   4   5
something, I am hard to
convince otherwise.

130. I often change my opinion   1   2   3   4   5
about social problems
when I hear others talk.

131. I usually take a long time   1   2   3   4   5
to consider things before
I make up my mind.

132. I am active in political   1   2   3   4   5
campaigns.

133. I have testified in public   1   2   3   4   5
hearings or spoken at
meetings held by public
agencies.

134. Once I make up my   1   2   3   4   5
mind, I fight for what I
believe in.

135. I am active in campus   1   2   3   4   5
politics.

FIPSE Preinterview Questionnaire

This is a questionnaire completed by each interview subject before the first interview.

Your Community Service History: Preliminary Questionnaire

Please give us a little background information about your service history:

1. Year in school (circle one) a. freshman   b. sophomore
    c. junior   d. senior   e. graduate student

2. How many classes have you taken which include service as part of the course requirements?
a. none   b. one   c. two   d. three   e. four or more

3. Have you taken a service internship or independent study?
a. yes   b. no

4. List service experiences:
When_____
What did you do?_____
With whom? _____
How long?_____
Class related?_____

5. In college service-learning experiences have you:
A. participated in formal discussions where you shared feelings about the experience?
a. yes   b. no
B. participated in formal discussions where you linked your service experiences to theories being studied in class?
a. yes   b. no
C. participated in role play or simulation about service issues or social problems related to your service?
a. yes   b. no
D. kept a journal?
a. yes   b. no
E. completed written assignments about the service problem?
a. yes   b. no
F. completed a written project for the people you were helping?
a. yes   b. no
G. made an oral presentation describing your service or project?
a. yes   b. no
H. made an oral presentation analyzing a service problem or issue?
a. yes   b. no

Other formal or informal activities that helped you reflect on your
service:

FIPSE Problem-Solving Interview Protocol: Preinterview

*This is the interview protocol used to question students before their
service-learning semester. It focuses on previous service and on analyzing a problem related to their coming service experience.*

Preinterview Protocol

We appreciate your willingness to talk with us. We are interested
in how students doing service think about community issues. We
are also interested in how their thinking changes after experience
in the community in a course like this one. The information from
students will be used to help colleges plan better service programs.

Service History Questions

*Use the one-page questionnaire or casual interaction with the student
before the interview to identify the issues area the student is involved with.
If the student is not doing service this semester [control], then discuss his
or her previous service and ask why the student chose to take the particular course.*

Previous Service	*No Previous Service*
1. I noticed that you first did volunteer service in [or with] _____.	1. I noticed that this is your first volunteer service experience.
Would you tell us a bit about how you first got started in community service?	Why did you decide to get involved in service this semester?
Why did you decide to get involved in community service?	What do you expect to get out of your service course this semester?
Why did you decide to get involved in service this semester?	
What do you expect to get out of your service course this semester?	

Questions About Understanding Social Problems

Now we want to explore the way you think about the kinds of issues you will be involved with in your service this semester. Community problems are always controversial; people don't agree about what causes them, how to solve them, or even how we can know when we are on the right track. We want to explore your views and how you arrived at them.

You will be working with _____ in your project this semester. Let's see if we can identify an issue to talk about. *Go to statement of issue below.*

Sample Issues [may add issues as appropriate]

A. *Children* [for those tutoring or working with children's groups]. People in the community are concerned about children who are falling behind in school and those who eventually drop out before graduation. Evidence exists to support different opinions about why this is happening.

B. *Homeless*. People agree that homelessness is a problem for the community, but they disagree on why it has grown so dramatically in recent years.

C. *AIDS*. People in the community are very concerned about the continuing spread of AIDS, although they differ widely in their views about why it is a problem and why it continues to spread.

D. *Juvenile Delinquency/Youth Violence*. Many people in the community are concerned about violence and crime committed by young people. There is disagreement about why this is a growing problem.

E. *Poverty*. In spite of many attempts to eliminate poverty, many people are poor. There is evidence to support several different views about why poverty has persisted and why it is a growing problem for children in this community.

F. *Environment/Global Warming*. There is evidence to support different points of view about whether we are experiencing global warming and if so, whether it is a problem created by the activities of people.

G. *Diversity*. People in the community disagree about the extent and the source of racial and ethnic conflict, but they are very concerned about it.

2. Imagine that you have been put in charge of a community task force to develop a plan to deal with this problem. What would be the first things you would do as you tried to develop your plan? [*or*] Imagine you were holding your first meeting. What would you say to the group first? What do you think your task force would talk about at that first meeting?

Possible Probes [use as needed; be neutral, and let the
student shape this response without cueing]

Can you say more about that?

Why would that be important to do?

What would you do next? Why?

And then you would?

We've been talking about the problem generally; now let's focus
specifically on what causes the problem. [*or*] You mentioned some
causes of the problem; let's talk more about that. Are there other
causes? [*Do NOT restate or summarize their definition of the problem;
if there are summaries, the student needs to do them.*]

3. What do you think causes this problem?

Probes

Anything else?

Do other things contribute?

Tell me more about that.

[*May ask if appropriate:*] Can you briefly summarize what you
   have said about the causes of the problem?

Now I'd like to know a little bit more about how you came to
hold these opinions. I will push you to explain exactly why and how
you came to believe what you do; this is because it is important to
understand HOW people think about these issues, not just WHAT
they think. When you give your opinion, I know that all sorts of
things have gone into it that I can't see, so when I push you to
explain, it is not to suggest that your response is wrong or should
change; I just want to see clearly how you have arrived at your
view—sort of put a transparent window over this process of thinking that we can't see.

Has Point of View	Has No Point of View
How do you know that it/those is/are the cause(s)?	Do you have any ideas of possible causes?
On what do you base your view? [Encourage justification.]	Could you ever say that these are the causes? How would you come to be able to say that? [or Why can't you say that?]
Can you ever know for sure that your position is correct? How? [or Why not?] [Important to probe for detailed reasons for being sure or not.]	Will we ever be able to know for sure what the causes are? How? [or Why not?]

Focus on how they know; use their responses to frame questions, for example, "You mentioned reading articles. If you find articles with different points of view, how do you decide which is better?"

4. Let's explore some other possible points of view on this and what you think about those views. What are some other opinions about the causes of these problems? [If the student can't identify competing views, the interviewer may suggest a couple.]

Why do people have different points of view about the factors related to this problem? [framing] [This is a controversial issue, and we are interested in how people decide on one position rather than another.]

[*Focus on how they know what is right or better; if experts:*] How do you decide which view is right when experts disagree? [*If readings, research, or something else is used:*] How do you know which research and articles are on the right track?

When people have different opinions about causes, is one right and the others wrong?

[*If yes*] Why or why not?

[*If no*] Is one better than the others? What do you mean by better? [recognizing, resolving/justification]

What does it mean when experts have different points of view about the causes of a problem?

Why do they disagree?

And how do you decide which one to accept? [*nature of problem/framing*]

We've been talking about the causes of _____. Let's shift our focus and think about what can be done about it.

5. What should be done to try to solve this problem? [*framing, resolving*]

[*Probes: Use as appropriate. Start with very neutral probes, and shift to the structured probes only if necessary.*]

Probes

Could you say more about that?

What factors should be considered? Why?

What information would need to be gathered? Why? How would you find it?

What would you do with that information? [*framing/tools, resolving*]

What other resources would be needed? How would they be used?

6. How confident are you that your approach would work? [*If the interviewee is uncertain, ask:*] What are the sources of that uncertainty? What could you do to be more confident about the viability of your solution?

7. What are some other opinions about possible solutions to this problem? Why do you think people have different views about how to solve the problem? [*framing*]

When people disagree, is one solution better than the others? [*If no*] Why not? [*If yes*] What do you mean by better? [*recognizing, resolving/justification*]

How do you decide which solution is better? [*or*] When experts disagree on what to do, how do you decide which way is better?

Personal Strategies for Community Action

We have been talking about the problem as a community issue and how it might generally be resolved, but we are also interested in how you think individual citizens can become active in helping solve social problems like [*issue being discussed*]. We are interested in your personal strategy.

8. How would you personally go about getting something done about the problem in this community?

Probes

What would your personal strategy be?

What exactly would you do? And then what next?

How would you do that?

[*Possible variation to get them laying out specifics:*] If you were going to advise a friend like yourself who wanted to get involved in this or other community issues what would you suggest?

9. Are there some rules of thumb or guidelines that you think people should follow if they want to help solve community problems?

What would your practical recommendations be for someone who wants to solve community problems?

We appreciate your sharing your views with us. I hope you found this a useful chance to reflect on the issues you will be dealing with this semester.

We will get in touch toward the end of the course about getting together again to talk about your experiences on your project and new thoughts you might have about _____. Thank you for your time. I enjoyed having the chance to talk with you.

FIPSE Problem-Solving Interview Protocol: Postinterview

This is the interview protocol used to question students at the end of the service-learning semester. Students analyze a problem related to the service they have just completed.

Postinterview Protocol

We appreciate your willingness to talk with us again; we want to hear how your service-learning went this semester. And it will be interesting to see what you are thinking about [*issue from first interview*] now that you have been involved with it during your community service.

[*Use the information form the students filled out to get a sense of their classroom/service activities. Use this information to probe a bit about the reflection activities they engaged in.*]

1. Tell me a little about your service this semester.

    Probes
    _____

    What kinds of things did you do?

    Whom did you work with?

    What do you think you learned from your service?

    Probes
    _____

    Are there things you learned from the service that you wouldn't have learned in the classroom?

    Are there things you learned in class that you understand better because of your service?

    How was the service used in class?

    Probes
    _____

    Were there particular activities or assignments or discussions where you reflected on the service and applied it to what you were learning?

What was most effective for you?

What do you wish had been done?

Were there any events or experiences that surprised you during service?

What is your overall reaction to your service-learning experiences?

Did the service this semester change the way you think about issues? How?

Questions About Understanding Social Problems

Now we want to explore again the way you think about the issues you were involved in this semester. As we said before, community problems are always controversial; people don't agree about what causes them, how to solve them, or even how we can know when we are on the right track. We want to explore your views now and how you arrived at them.

During our last discussion we talked about your views on _____. Let's explore how you think about it NOW.

[*Please be very open-ended with these questions using neutral probes to encourage full development of response, but do not cue.*]

2. Imagine that you have been put in charge of a community task force to develop a plan to deal with this problem. What would be the first things you would do as you tried to develop your plan? [*or*] Imagine you were holding your first meeting. What would you say to the group first? What do you think your task force would talk about at that first meeting?

> *Possible Probes [use as needed; be neutral; let the student shape this response without cueing]*

Can you say more about that?

Why would that be important to do?

What would you do next? Why?

And then you would?

Anything else?

We've been talking about the problem generally; now let's focus specifically on what causes the problem. [or] You mentioned some causes of the problem; let's talk more about that. Are there other causes? [Do NOT restate or summarize the student's definition of the problem. It may be useful to summarize before proceeding, but if there are summaries, the student needs to do them.]

3. What do you think causes this problem?

Probes

Anything else?

Do other things contribute?

Tell me more about that.

[*May ask if appropriate:*] Can you briefly summarize what you have said about the causes of the problem?

Now I'd like to know a little bit more about how you came to hold these opinions. I will push you to explain exactly why and how you came to believe what you do; this is because it is important to understand HOW people think about these issues, not just WHAT they think. When you give your opinion, I know that all sorts of things have gone into it that I can't see, so when I push you to explain, it is not to suggest that your response is wrong or should change; I just want to see clearly how you have arrived at your view—sort of put a transparent window over this process of thinking that we can't see.

[*If the student says, "It's like I said before," meaning during the first interview, stress the importance of his or her full development of a response now. Some of the student's thinking may have changed in subtle ways, and we are interested in what he or she thinks now.*]

Has Point of View	Has No Point of View
How do you know that is/those are the causes(s)?	Do you have any ideas of possible causes?
On what do you base your view? [*Encourage justification.*]	Could you ever say that these are the causes? How would you come to be able to say that? [*or*] Why can't you say that?
Can you ever know for sure that your position is correct? How? [*or* Why not?] [*Important to probe for detailed reasons for being sure or not.*]	Will we ever be able to know for sure what the causes are? How? [*or* Why not?]

[*Focus on how the student knows; use the responses to frame questions, e.g.,* You mentioned reading articles. If you find articles with different points of view, how do you decide which is better?]

   4. Let's explore some other possible points of view on this and what you think about those views. What are some other opinions about the causes of these problems? [*If the student can't identify competing views, you may suggest a couple.*]

   Why do people have different points of view about the factors related to this problem? [*framing*]

   [This is a controversial issue; we are interested in how people decide on one position rather than another.]

   [*Focus on how they know what is right or better. If experts:*] How do you decide which view is right when experts disagree? [*If readings or research is used:*] How do you know which research and articles are on the right track?

   When people have different opinions about causes, is one right and the others wrong?

   [*If yes*] Why or why not?

   [*If no*] Is one better than the others? What do you mean by better? [*recognizing, resolving/justification*]

What does it mean when experts have different points of view about the causes of a problem?

Why do they disagree?

And how do you decide which one to accept? [*nature of problem/framing*]

We've been talking about the causes of _____. Let's shift our focus and think about what can be done about it.

5. What should be done to try to solve this problem? [*framing, resolving*]

Could you say more about that?

What factors should be considered? Why?

What information would need to be gathered? Why? How would you find it?

What would you do with that information? [*framing/tools, resolving*]

What other resources would be needed? How would they be used?

6. How confident are you that your approach would work?

[*If the interviewee is uncertain, ask:*] What are the sources of that uncertainty?

What could you do to be more confident about the viability of your solution?

7. What are some other opinions about possible solutions to this problem?

Why do you think people have different views about how to solve the problem? [*framing*]

When people disagree, is one solution better than the others?

[*If no*] Why not?

[*If yes*] What do you mean by better? [*recognizing, resolving/justification*]

How do you decide which solution is better?

[*or*] When experts disagree on what to do, how do you decide which way is better?

Personal Strategies for Community Action

We have been talking about the problem as a community issue and how it might generally be resolved, but we are also interested in how you think individual citizens can become active in helping solve social problems like [*issue being discussed*]. We are interested in your personal strategy.

8. How would you personally go about getting something done about the problem in this community?

Probe

What would your personal strategy be?

What exactly would you do?

And then what next?

How would you do that?

[*Possible variation to get them laying out specifics:*] If you were going to advise a friend like yourself who wanted to get involved in this or other community issues what would you suggest?

9. Are there some rules of thumb or guidelines that you think people should follow if they want to help solve community problems?

What would your practical recommendations be for someone who wants to solve community problems?

We appreciate your sharing your views with us. I hope you found this a useful chance to reflect on the issues you worked with this semester. Thank you for your time. I enjoyed having the chance to talk with you again.

Problem Analysis Coding Categories

These are the categories used to score the problem-solving interviews for problem and solution complexity, locus of problem and solution,

knowledge application, and personal strategy. Critical thinking was scored
using principles based on reflective judgment analysis.

Problem Analysis Coding Categories

Locus of Problem and Solution

1. Problem Locus [probloc]
   0. no problem locus
   1. individual mental state/individual behavior
   2. individual focus/some placement within broader systems
   3. systemic locus without extensive development
   4. extensive, well-developed systemic locus
   5. process focus with systemic locus [emphasis on need to assess problem as well as place within broader systemic context]
2. Solution Locus [solloc]
   0. no solution locus
   1. solution focused on individual mental state/individual behavior/individual failure/solution to meet immediate need of individuals
   2. solution involves correcting systems failure/addressing root causes of problem
   3. combined individual/systemic locus of solution well elaborated
   4. process focus [emphasis on need to assess problem and explore alternative solutions within broader systemic context]

Causal Complexity

3. Assess Complexity of Cause [causcomp]
   0. no causal analysis
   1. Low: simple/no context/one cause/low elaboration of reasons for problem

2. Medium: extensive elaboration of single cause/more than one cause with moderate elaboration

3. High: multiple causes well elaborated/situated in context/multiple stakeholders/integrated—causes linked

Solution Complexity

4. Assess Complexity of Solutions [solcomp]

    0. no solution

    1. Low: noncontextualized/naive/often individual action without analysis unconnected to current service infrastructure

    2. Medium: some context/mention needs assessment/awareness of current efforts/may cite current program as model

    3. High: systemic approach/connected to causes and needs assessment/multiple solutions or complex solutions/contextualized/supported with analysis

5. Sophistication of Personal Action Strategy [perstrat]

    0. no personal strategy

    1. Low: noncontextualized/naive/unaware of current programs/unaware of practical processes for connecting with programs and community/"just tell them" or "I'll start a program"

    2. Medium-low: unclear strategy but recognition of need for process to identify strategy, e.g., vague information-gathering strategy

    3. Medium: aware of current programs and need to work with others/need to assess community/realistic "practical rules of thumb"/elaborate needs assessment strategy

    4. High: highly contextualized/aware of volunteer and policy processes/targeted plan/systematic approach/clearly practical awareness of community/characterized by clear, detailed knowledge of processes and programs

Knowledge Application

6. Knowledge [know]
   0. no information about issue supplied
   1. Low: little specific information about social issue discussed
   2. Medium: some concrete grasp of issue/some specific issue information
   3. Medium-high: considerable information about issue/references to other resources/mentions reading or information from class
   4. High: very detailed and specific information and multiple resources about issue

Corporation for National Service (CNS) Reflection Interview

This is the interview protocol used to explore student experience with reflection. It was used one time and provided data for the practitioner's guide.

Reflection Interview Guide

Interview Number:_____ Date:_____
Interviewer:_____

We are interested in your experiences with community service and your views about how this service has contributed to your understanding of social problems and issues. We are also interested in the specific kinds of learning experiences that may have influenced your understanding. We hope to be able to share the insights of students about service-learning with people who are planning programs, so we want to explore your learning process in some detail.

Personal Service History

First I'd like to ask you about your personal history of service. I see that your first service experience was _____.
Tell me more about_____. [*Warm-up*]

How did you first get involved? Why did you do this? [*probe for motivation*]

[*Refer to subsequent experiences; ask about others. If they differ, ask:*] I notice that you have worked with different issues/types of projects. Can you tell me how you got involved with these projects?

How would you describe this change in your involvement?

Were there specific events or moments when you realized you wanted to do something different?

Probes

Describe the moment.

Was anyone else involved in this process? Who?

What has kept you doing service?

[*If they are all of the same type, ask:*] I notice that you seem to have been involved with [*issue/problem*] for some time. Can you tell me what keeps you involved with this issue?

Thinking About Social Issues and Problems

Now I'd like to ask you about your thinking about community and social issues.

Has your thinking about social issues or the people you work with in the community changed over time?

Probe

Which? Both?

Can you think of times when you were *surprised* by something in your service, that is, when you suddenly looked at a situation or an issue in a way that you hadn't before and when you realized that you needed the answers to some new questions?

[*Ask for each incident:*] Please describe the incident. What made this situation different? A puzzle? What made you want to find out more about the situation? How did it influence your thinking? What helped you reflect on this issue?

Probe

Were there structured discussions, projects, or assignments that helped you think about the issues?

Reflective Program Experience

Now I'd like to find out more about some of the experiences you've had in different service programs.

[*Refer to any mentioned as critical incidents above and on service history sheet.*]

Of these experiences you've had, were there programs or classes where you had opportunity for formal reflection?

[*If yes, use probes in column A. If no, use the probes in Column B.*]

Column A	Column B
Journals? How structured?	Just talking with others? Who?
Written assignments?	Personal journals?
Discussions?	Discussions?
Making presentations?	Group activities?
Projects?	Reading?
Reading?	Listening to others?
Training/orientation?	Training/orientation?
Lectures? Other?	Other?

Were there other reflection experiences? Please describe.

Reflections on Reflection

[*Ask for both informal and formal as reported in "Reflective Program Experiences" above.*]

[*If no reflective experiences are reported, go to "Summary of Learning."*]

Now I'd like to find out if and how these experiences affected your thinking, if they helped you understand issues more fully.

Can you think of an example of an assignment in a service-learning class or programs that helped you understand the issues you were working with more clearly?

Probes [for each example]

Did it help you to understand something as more than just a theory?

Did it help you to apply some of the things you were learning in the classroom to community issues?

Were there any assignments or activities that left you with new questions?

[*Be alert to redundancy here from incidents mentioned in "Thinking About Social Issues and Problems." May need to probe further from examples given there.*]

Of all the experiences that shifted your way of understanding community issues and service, which was the most valuable for you? Why?

From your experience, what would you say is the most effective type of reflection? Why?

Summary of Learning

What have you learned from community service that you might not have learned in the classroom alone?

Is there anything else we should know to help us understand the impact of service learning on those who participate?

Thank you.

Resource D: Survey Regression Tables: Impact of Service-Learning

276

Table D.1. Impact of Service-Learning on Personal and Interpersonal Outcomes over a Semester.

	Tolerance	Personal Efficacy	Leadership Skills	Communication Skills	Career Skills	Want Career Helping
Service-learning	.08***	.14***	.05*	–.01	.02	.09***
Closeness to faculty	–.09***	.09***	.11***	.11***	.05*	.04
Pretest	.45***	.38***	.66***	.62***	.41***	.60***
Gender	.08***	–.08**	.00	–.06**	–.16***	–.04
Other college service	.03	.09***	.00	.00	.13***	.08***
Age	.01	.01	.06**	.01	.01	–.03
Minority	.01	.02	.00	–.01	–.02	–.05*
Family income	–.05*	–.05	–.01	–.01	–.07	–.04

Note: Analysis is hierarchical multiple regression; data shown are standardized Betas. Students in service-learning, $n = 1,131$; nonservice students, $n = 404$. *$p < .05$, **$p < .01$, ***$p < .001$. Negative Betas for gender indicate that women are more likely to score higher than men on the outcome variable when controlling for all other variables; positive Betas for minority indicate minorities score higher.

Table D.2. Impact of Service-Learning on Changes in Critical Thinking and Perspective Transformation Outcomes over a Semester.

	Identifying Issues	See Action Consequences	Open to New Views	Systemic Problem Locus	Important to Change Policy	Importance of Social Justice	Important Influence on Political Structure
Service-learning	.04	−.01	.08***	.12***	.06*	.06*	.06*
Closeness to faculty	.06*	.07**	−.04	.01	.01	.01	.12***
Pretest	.45***	.41***	.56***	.61***	.32***	.47***	.56***
Gender	.00	−.03	−.03	−.09***	−.03	−.09**	.02
Other college service	−.03	.04	−.01	.06**	.00	.03	.02
Age	.09***	.01	−.03	.04	.04	.02	.02
Minority	.03	−.03	−.03	.02	.04	.04	−.02
Family income	.01	.00	−.05*	−.03	−.03	−.04	.00

Note: Analysis is hierarchical multiple regression; data shown are standardized Betas. Students in service-learning, n = 1,131; nonservice students, n = 404. *p < .05, **p < .01, ***p < .001. Negative Betas for gender indicate that women are more likely to score higher than men on the outcome variable when controlling for all other variables; positive Betas for minority indicate minorities score higher.

Table D.3. Impact of Service-Learning on Changes in Service to Community Outcomes over a Semester.

	Community Efficacy	Important to Volunteer My Time	Everyone Should Volunteer	Important to Be Community Leader	Require Service in School
Service-learning	.11***	.15***	.15***	.05	.06*
Closeness to faculty	.08**	.04	.05*	.09***	.05
Pretest	.43***	.41***	.44***	.51***	.60***
Gender	.05*	-.10***	-.28***	.00	-.05*
Other college service	.07**	.14***	.09***	.05*	-.03
Age	.01	.02	.01	-.03	.02
Minority	-.01	-.02	-.01	.00	.00
Family income	-.03	-.03	-.05*	-.06*	.03

Note: Analysis is hierarchical multiple regression; data shown are standardized Betas. Students in service-learning, $n = 1,131$; nonservice students, $n = 404$. $*p < .05$, $**p < .01$, $***p < .001$. Negative Betas for gender indicate that women are more likely to score higher than men on the outcome variable when controlling for all other variables; positive Betas for minority indicate minorities score higher.

Resource E: Survey Regression Tables: Impact of Program Characteristics

Table E.1. Impact of Program Characteristics on Students' Comparison of Value of Service-Learning and Regular Classes (n = 1,131 service-learning participants).

	Service-Learning Was High-Quality	Learned More in Service-Learning	Intellectually Challenged in Service-Learning	Motivated to Work Harder in Service-Learning
Placement quality	.47***	.21***	.15***	.32***
Application	.10**	.29***	.32***	.16***
Reflection/discussion	.12***	.18***	.22***	.11**
Reflection/writing	.01	−.03	−.03	−.03
Diversity	.05*	.05*	−.07*	.02
Community voice	.01	.00	−.10**	−.03
Gender	−.02	−.07**	−.08**	−.03
Other service	.01	−.03	.01	.06*
Age	−.01	.05	.02	.00
Minority	−.03	−.02	−.06*	.00
Family income	.02	.03	.00	−.03

Note: Analysis is multiple hierarchical regression; numbers are Betas. *p < .05, **p < .01, ***p < .001. Negative Beta for gender means women were more likely to show outcome; negative Beta on "minority" means Caucasians were more likely to show outcome during service-learning.

Table E.2. Impact of Program Characteristics on Students' Perceptions of Personal and Interpersonal Benefits of Service-Learning (n = 1,131 service-learning participants).

	Needy Are Like Me	Appreciate Cultures	Know Self Better	Spiritual Growth	Rewarding to Help	Learn to Work with Others
Placement quality	.11**	.03	.15***	.11**	.19***	.22***
Application	.09*	.13***	.19***	.18***	.11**	.03
Reflection/discussion	.04	.02	.08*	-.01	-.09*	.09**
Reflection/writing	.07*	.01	.08*	.13***	.11***	.03
Diversity	-.03	.39***	.08*	.09**	.05	.05
Community voice	.07*	-.05	.01	-.03	.07*	.02
Gender	.01	-.05	-.08*	.04	-.07*	-.07*
Other service	.00	.01	.06	.03	.06	.11***
Age	-.01	.01	.03	-.02	-.05	.01
Minority	-.02	-.03	.05	-.02	-.03	.04
Family income	-.07*	-.07*	-.01	-.07*	-.05	.00

Note: Analysis is multiple hierarchical regression; numbers are Betas. *p = .05, **p < .01, ***p < .001. Negative Beta for gender means women were more likely to show outcome during service-learning.

Table E.3. Impact of Program Characteristics on Students' Perceptions of Academic Learning Benefits of Service-Learning (n = 1,131 service-learning participants).

	Understand Subject	Apply Material	Empathy/ Complexity of Issues	Specific Skills	Know About Agencies	See Issues New Way
Placement quality	.01	.03	.03	.15***	.04	.08*
Application	.38***	.41***	.27***	.01	.13**	.18***
Reflection/discussion	.09**	.09**	.05	.10**	.07*	.11**
Reflection/writing	.10**	.11***	.00	.07*	.15***	.07*
Diversity	-.07*	-.13***	.09**	-.03	-.03	.09**
Community voice	.02	.03	.04	.00	.03	.01
Gender	.00	-.04	-.08**	.02	-.07*	-.09**
Other service	-.01	-.03	.01	.03	.03	.02
Age	.01	.01	.04	-.01	-.05	.03
Minority	-.09**	-.08**	.02	.05	.05	.04
Family income	-.03	.00	.00	-.02	-.07*	.02

Note: Analysis is multiple hierarchical regression; numbers are Betas. *p < .05, **p < .01, ***p < .001. Negative Beta for gender means women were more likely to show outcome; negative Beta on "minority" means Caucasians were more likely to show outcome during service-learning.

Table E.4. Impact of Program Characteristics on Building Close Relationships with Faculty, Other Students, and Community (n = 1,131 service-learning participants).

	Close to Faculty During Service-Learning	Close to Other Students During Service-Learning	Feel Connected to Community After Service-Learning
Placement quality	.18***	.09*	.06
Application	.08*	.03	-.01
Reflection/discussion	.32***	.28***	.03
Reflection/writing	.09**	-.06	.00
Diversity	.01	.02	.02
Community voice	-.07*	.04	.10**
Pretest measure	N.A.	N.A.	.31***
Gender	.00	-.03	-.10***
Other service	.02	.13***	.12***
Age	.03	-.01	-.02
Minority	.04	.01	-.05
Family income	-.02	.01	-.05

Note: Analysis is multiple hierarchical regression; numbers are Betas. *p < .05, **p < .01, ***p < .001. Negative Beta for gender means women were more likely to show outcome; negative Beta on "minority" means Caucasians were more likely to show outcome during service-learning. N.A. = not applicable.

Table E.5. Impact of Program Characteristics on Changes in Personal and Interpersonal Outcomes over One Semester of Service-Learning (n = 1,131 service-learning participants).

	Tolerance	Personal Efficacy	Leadership Skills	Communication Skills	Career Skills	Career Helping
Placement quality	.12***	.15***	.14***	.14***	.07*	-.02
Application	.04	.06*	.02	.03	.21***	.04
Reflection/discussion	-.02	.04	.04	.01	.09**	.11***
Reflection/writing	.02	.01	.02	.00	-.03	-.02
Diversity	-.03	.05	.00	-.03	.05*	.05*
Community voice	.07*	.05	-.02	.01	.01	.05*
Pretest measure	.56***	.37***	.61***	.59***	.32***	.57***
Gender	-.09***	-.07**	.00	-.08**	-.13***	-.05*
Other service	.00	.04	-.01	-.03	.08**	.07**
Age	.01	.00	.06*	.01	-.03	-.05
Minority	.02	-.01	-.04	.00	-.03	-.05
Family income	-.05*	-.05	-.02	-.01	-.06*	-.04

Note: Analysis is multiple hierarchical regression; numbers are Betas. $*p < .05$, $**p < .01$, $***p < .001$. Negative Beta for gender means women were more likely to show outcome; negative Beta on "minority" means Caucasians were more likely to show outcome during service-learning.

Table E.6. Impact of Program Characteristics on Changes in Critical Thinking and Perspective Transformation Outcomes over One Semester of Service-Learning (n = 1,131 service-learning participants).

	Thinking Critically	Identifying Issues	See Action Consequences	Systemic Problem Locus	Important to Change Policy	Importance of Social Justice	Important Influence on Political Structure
Placement quality	.03	.02	.00	.04	.01	.03	.00
Application	.00	.11***	.08*	.03	.12**	.09**	.06*
Reflection/discussion	.06*	.07*	.04	-.05	.05	.07*	.08**
Reflection/writing	-.01	.03	.09*	.01	.05	.08**	.01
Diversity	.00	-.04	.06*	-.01	.03	.06*	.00
Community voice	.03	.05	.01	.08**	.02	.00	.00
Pretest measure	.47**	.43***	.43***	.63***	.31***	.45***	.58***
Gender	.01	-.02	.00	-.09***	-.03	-.03	.02
Other service	.02	-.05	-.06*	.05*	.00	.01	.01
Age	.04	.07*	.06*	.01	-.04	-.01	.01
Minority	.00	.02	.00	.01	.02	.03	.00
Family income	.02	.02	.01	-.01	-.02	-.02	.04

Note: Analysis is multiple hierarchical regression; numbers are Betas. *p < .05, **p < .01, ***p < .001. Negative Beta for gender means women were more likely to show outcome; negative Beta on "minority" means Caucasians were more likely to show outcome during service-learning.

Table E.7. Impact of Program Characteristics on Changes in Community Service Outcomes over One Semester of Service-Learning (n = 1,131 service-learning participants).

	Community Efficacy	Important to Volunteer My Time	Everyone Should Volunteer	Important to Be Community Leader	Future Volunteer Time Commitment	Require Service in School
Placement quality	.10**	.05	.07*	.03	.09*	.01
Application	.07*	.09**	.07*	.08*	.05	.06*
Reflection/discussion	.07*	.03	.05	.08*	.11***	.08**
Reflection/writing	−.05	−.05	−.06*	−.08**	−.09**	−.02
Diversity	.06*	.05*	−.04	.01	.08*	.00
Community voice	.01	.06*	.05	−.01	−.05	.00
Pretest measure	.39***	.42***	.43***	.53***	N.A.	.62***
Gender	−.04	.08***	−.09**	.04	−.02	−.06**
Other service	.02	−.07**	.03	.01	.25***	−.04
Age	−.02	−.03	.00	−.01	−.03	.02
Minority	−.03	−.02	−.02	−.02	.02	.00
Family income	−.03	.00	−.05	−.04	−.01	.02

Note: Analysis is multiple hierarchical regression; numbers are Betas. *p < .05, **p < .01, ***p < .001. Negative Beta for gender means women were more likely to show outcome; negative Beta on "minority" means Caucasians were more likely to show outcome during service-learning. N.A. = not applicable.

Resource F:
Interview Regression Tables:
Impact of Well-Integrated
Service-Learning

Table F.1. Integration of Service and Learning as a Predictor of Changes in Understanding Social Issues and Knowledge Application.

	Causal Complexity	Solution Complexity	Knowledge Application	Personal Strategy
Integration of service-learning	.31*	.35**	.33**	.51***
Previous service	−.05	−.01	.02	.10
Age	.11	−.03	.30**	.16
Gender	.02	−.28*	−.06	−.11
Pretest measure	.20	.36**	.31**	.41***

Note: Analysis is multiple hierarchical regression; *$p < .05$, **$p < .01$, ***$p < .001$. Negative Beta for gender means women were more likely to show outcome. Analysis of pre- and postinterviews of fifty-seven college students.

288

Table F.2. Integration of Service and Learning as a Predictor of Changes in Perspective Transformation and Critical Thinking/Problem Solving.

	Systemic Problem Locus	Systemic Solution Locus	Solution Strategy	Critical Thinking Level
Integration of service-learning	.27**	.43***	.32*	.27*
Previous service	.03	.01	.13	.00
Age	.22*	.08	.13	.22*
Gender	−.05	−.08	−.08	.12
Pretest measure	.47***	.31**	.13	.46***

Note: Analysis is multiple hierarchical regression; *p* < .05, **p* < .01, ***p* < .001. Negative Beta for gender means women were more likely to show outcome. Analysis of pre- and postinterviews of fifty-seven college students, sixty-six for critical thinking..

References

Alt, M. A., and Medrich, E. A. "Student Outcomes from Participation in Community Service." Paper prepared for the U.S. Department of Education Office of Research, 1994.

Anderson, J. R. "Acquisition of Cognitive Skill." *Psychological Review*, 1982, 89, 369–406.

Ansley, F., and Gaventa, J. "Researching for Democracy and Democratizing Research." *Change*, 1997, 29(1), 46–53.

Association of American Colleges. *The Challenge of Connecting Learning*. Washington, D.C.: Association of American Colleges, 1991.

Astin, A. W. "Student Involvement in Community Service: Institutional Commitment and the Campus Compact." Paper presented at the Wingspread Conference on Service Learning Research, Racine, Wis., 1991.

Astin, A. W. *What Matters in College: Four Critical Years Revisited*. San Francisco: Jossey-Bass, 1992.

Astin, A. W., and Sax, L. "How Undergraduates Are Affected by Service Participation." *Journal of College Student Development*, 1998, 39(3), 251–263.

Astin, A. W., Sax, L., and Avalos, J. "Long-Term Effects of Volunteerism During the Undergraduate Years." *Review of Higher Education*, forthcoming.

Bandura, A. *Self-Efficacy: The Exercise of Control*. New York: Freeman, 1997.

Barber, B. "Service, Citizenship and Democracy: Civic Duty as an Entailment of Civil Right." In W. Evers (ed.), *National Service Pro and Con*. Stanford, Calif.: Hoover Institution Press, 1990.

Barber, B. *An Aristocracy of Everyone*. New York: Ballantine Books, 1992.

Barber, B., and Battistoni, R. "A Season of Service." *PS: Political Science and Politics*, 1994, 26, 235–262.

Batchelder, T. H., and Root, S. "Effects of an Undergraduate Program to Integrate Academic Learning and Service: Cognitive, Prosocial Cognitive and Identity Outcomes." *Journal of Adolescence*, 1994, *17*, 341–356.

Bellah, R. L., and others. *Habits of the Heart: Individualism and Commitment in American Life*. New York: HarperCollins, 1985.

Boss, J. A. "The Effect of Community Service Work on the Moral Development of College Ethics Students." *Journal of Moral Education*, 1994, *23*, 183–198.

Boyer, E. L. *The Undergraduate Experience in America*. New York: HarperCollins, 1987.

Boyer, E. L. *Scholarship Reconsidered: Priorities of the Professoriate*. Princeton, N.J.: Carnegie Foundation for the Advancement of Teaching, 1990.

Boyer, E. L. "Creating the New American College." *Chronicle of Higher Education*, Mar. 9, 1994, p. A48.

Bransford, J. D. "Who Ya Gonna Call? Thoughts About Teaching Problem Solving." In P. Hallinger, K. Leithwood, and J. Murphy (eds.), *Cognitive Perspectives on Educational Leadership*. New York: Teachers College Press, 1993.

Bransford, J. D., and Vye, N. J. "A Perspective on Cognitive Research and Its Implications for Instruction." In L. Resnick and L. E. Klopfer (eds.), *Toward the Thinking Curriculum: Current Cognitive Research*. Alexandria, Va.: Association for Supervision and Curriculum Development, 1989.

Braxton, J. M., Sullivan, A.V.S., and Johnson, R. "Appraising Tinto's Theory of College Student Departure." In *Higher Education Handbook of Theory and Research*, Vol. 12. New York: Agathon Press, 1997.

Braza, J., and Kreuter, M. W. "A Comparison of Experiential and Traditional Learning Models in Studying Health Problems of the Poor." *Journal of School Health*, 1975, *45*(6), 353–355.

Brown, A. L., Bransford, J. D., Ferrara, R., and Campione, J. "Learning, Understanding, and Remembering." In J. Flavell and E. Markham (eds.), *Mussen Handbook of Child Psychology*, Vol. 1. New York: Wiley, 1983.

Campus Compact. *Service Matters: Engaging Higher Education in the Renewal of America's Communities and American Democracy*. Providence, R.I.: Campus Compact, 1998.

Chickering, A., and Gamson, Z. F. "Seven Principles for Good Practice in Undergraduate Education." *AAHE Bulletin*, Mar.-Apr. 1987.

Clohsey, W. W. "Altruism and the Endurance of the Good." Paper presented at the International Society for Third Sector Research Conference, Geneva, July 1998.

Cohen, J., and Kinsey, D. "Doing Good and Scholarship: A Service-Learning Study." *Journalism Educator*, 1994, 48(4), 4–14.

Conrad, D., and Hedin, D. *Executive Summary of the Final Report of the Experiential Education Evaluation Project*. Minneapolis: Center for Youth Development and Research, University of Minnesota, 1980.

Conrad, D., and Hedin, D. *High School Community Service: A Review of Research and Programs*. Madison, Wis.: National Center on Effective Secondary Schools, 1989.

Cooper, D. "Reading, Writing and Reflection." In R. Rhoads and J. Howard (eds.), *Academic Service Learning: A Pedagogy of Action and Reflection*. San Francisco: Jossey-Bass, 1998.

Cooper, D., and Julier, L. (eds.). *Writing in the Public Interest: Service-Learning and the Writing Classroom*. East Lansing: Michigan State University, 1995.

Daloz Parks, S., Keen, C. H., Keen, J. P., and Parks Daloz, L. A. *Common Fire: Lives of Commitment in a Complex World*. Boston: Beacon Press, 1996.

Delve, C., Mintz, S., and Stewart, G. (eds.). *Community Service as Values Education*. New Directions for Student Services, no. 50. San Francisco: Jossey-Bass, 1990.

Dewey, J. *School and Society*. (2nd ed.) Chicago: University of Chicago Press, 1933.

Dewey, J. *Experience and Education*. New York: Collier Books, 1938.

Ehrlich, T. "Civic Learning: Democracy and Education Revisited." *Educational Record*, Summer-Fall 1997, pp. 57–65.

Eliot, T. S. "Little Gidding." In *Four Quartets*. Cambridge, Mass.: Harvard University Press, 1971.

Eyler, J. "Citizenship Education for Conflict: An Empirical Assessment of the Relationship Between Principled Thinking and Tolerance for Conflict and Diversity." *Theory and Research in Social Education*, 1980, 8(2), 11–26.

Eyler, J. "From Pedagogy to Andragogy: The Role of the Internship in the Transition to Adult Learning." *Experiential Education*, 1992, 17(4), 5, 22.

Eyler, J. "Comparing the Impact of Two Internship Experiences on Student Learning." *Journal of Cooperative Education*, 1993, 29(3), 41–52.

Eyler, J., and Giles, D. E., Jr. "The Impact of Service-Learning on Citizenship Development." Paper presented to the American Educational Research Association conference, San Francisco, 1995.

Eyler, J., and Giles, D. E., Jr. "The Importance of Program Quality in Service-Learning." In A. Waterman (ed.), *Service-Learning: Applications from the Research*. Hillsdale, N.J.: Erlbaum, 1997.

Eyler, J., Giles, D. E., Jr., and Braxton, J. "The Impact of Alternative Models of Service-Learning on Student Outcomes." Paper presented to the National Society for Experiential Education conference, New Orleans, 1995.

Eyler, J., Giles, D. E., Jr., and Braxton, J. "The Impact of Service-Learning on College Students." *Michigan Journal of Community Service Learning*, 1997, 4, 5–15.

Eyler, J., Giles, D. E., Jr., Lynch, C., and Gray, C. J. "The Impact of Different Models of Service-Learning on the Reflective Judgment of Postsecondary Students." Paper presented at the American Educational Research Association meeting, Chicago, 1997.

Eyler, J., Giles, D. E., Jr., and Schmiede, A. *A Practitioner's Guide to Reflection in Service-Learning: Student Voices and Reflections*. Nashville, Tenn.: Vanderbilt University, 1996.

Eyler, J., and Halteman, B. "The Impact of a Legislative Internship on Students' Political Skill and Sophistication." *Teaching Political Science*, 1981, 9, 27–34.

Eyler, J., Root, S., and Giles, D. E., Jr. "Service Learning and the Development of Expert Citizens: Service-Learning and Cognitive Science." In R. Bringle and D. Duffey (eds.), *With Service in Mind*. Washington, D.C.: American Association for Higher Education, 1998.

Eyler-Walker, K. "The Relationship of High School Activities to Citizenship Attitudes and Behavior." Unpublished paper, Comparing Models of Service-Learning project, Vanderbilt University, 1997.

Feynman, R. *Surely You're Joking, Mr. Feynman*. New York: Norton, 1985.

Feynman, R. *The Meaning of It All*. Reading, Mass.: Helix Books/Addison-Wesley, 1998.

Fischer, K. W., and Bidell, T. R. "Dynamic Development of Psychological Structures in Action and Thought." In R. M. Lerner (ed.), *Handbook of Child Psychology*, Vol. 1: *Theoretical Models of Human Development*. (5th ed.) New York: Wiley, 1997.

Fitch, R. T. "Differences Among Community Service Volunteers and Nonvolunteers on the College Campus." *Journal of College Student Development*, 1991, 32(6), 534–540.

Freire, P. *Pedagogy of the Oppressed*. New York: Herder & Herder, 1970.

Furco, A. "Service-Learning: A Balanced Approach to Experiential Education." In B. Taylor (ed.), *Expanding Boundaries: Serving and Learning*. Washington, D.C.: Corporation for National Service, 1996.

Gabelnick, F. "Educating a Committed Citizenry." *Change*, 1997, 29(1), 30–35.

Gamson, Z. F. "Higher Education and Rebuilding Civic Life." *Change,* 1997, *29*(1), 10–13.

Gamson, Z. F., and others. *Liberating Education.* San Francisco: Jossey-Bass, 1984.

Giles, D. E., Jr., and Eyler, J. "The Impact of a College Community Service Laboratory on Students' Personal, Social, and Cognitive Outcomes." *Journal of Adolescence,* 1994a, *17,* 327–339.

Giles, D. E., Jr., and Eyler, J. "The Theoretical Roots of Service-Learning in John Dewey: Towards a Theory of Service-Learning." *Michigan Journal of Community Service-Learning,* 1994b, *1,* 77–85.

Giles, D. E., Jr., and Eyler, J. "A Service-Learning Research Agenda for the Next Five Years." In R. Rhoads and J. Howard (eds.), *Academic Service Learning: A Pedagogy of Action and Reflection.* San Francisco: Jossey-Bass, 1998.

Giles, D. E., Jr., and Freed, J. B. "Service Learning Dimensions of Field Study: The Cornell Human Ecology Field Study Program." Paper presented at the National Conference on Service-Learning, Washington, D.C., 1985.

Giles, D. E., Jr., Honnet, E. P., and Migliore, S. (eds.). *Research Agenda for Combining Service and Leaning in the 1990s.* Raleigh, N.C.: National Society for Experiential Education, 1991.

Gore, J., and Nelson, H. "How Experiential Education Relates to College Goals and Objectives." *Evaluation and Program Planning,* 1984, *7,* 143–149.

Gose, B. "Many Colleges Move to Link Courses with Volunteerism." *Chronicle of Higher Education,* Nov. 14, 1997, pp. A45–A46.

Gray, M. J., and others. *Coupling Service and Learning in Higher Education: The Final Report of the Evaluation of Learn and Serve America, Higher Education Program.* Washington, D.C.: Corporation for National Service, 1998.

Greene, D., and Diehm, G. "Educational and Service Outcomes of a Service Integration Effort." *Michigan Journal of Community Service Learning,* 1995, *2,* 54–62.

Halliburton, D. "John Dewey: A Voice That Still Speaks to Us." *Change,* 1997, *29*(1), 24–29.

Hamilton, S. F. "Adolescents in Community Settings: What Is to Be Learned?" *Theory and Research in Social Education,* 1981, *9*(2), 23–38.

Hamilton, S. F., and Fenzel, L. M. "The Impact of Volunteer Experience on Adolescent Social Development: Evidence of Program Effects." *Journal of Adolescent Research,* 1988, *3,* 65–80.

Hamilton, S. F., and Zeldin, R. "Learning Civics in Community." *Curriculum Inquiry,* 1987, *17,* 407–420.

Hedin, D. "Students as Teachers: A Tool for Improving School Climate and Productivity." *Social Policy*, 1987, *17*(3), 42–47.

Holland, B. "Analyzing Institutional Commitment to Service: A Model of Key Organizational Factors." *Michigan Journal of Community Service Learning*, 1997, *5*, 42–55.

Honnet, E. P., and Poulsen, S. *Principles of Good Practice in Combining Service and Learning.* Wingspread Special Report. Racine, Wis.: Johnson Foundation, 1989.

Howard, J. "Academic Service Learning: A Counternormative Pedagogy." In R. Rhoads and J. Howard (eds.), *Academic Service Learning: A Pedagogy of Action and Reflection.* San Francisco: Jossey-Bass, 1998.

Hudson, W. E., and Trudeau, R. H. "An Essay on Institutionalization of Service-Learning: The Genesis of the Feinstein Institute for Public Service." *Michigan Journal of Community Service Learning*, 1995, *2*, 150–158.

Hursh, B. A., and Borzak, L. "Toward Cognitive Development Through Field Studies." *Journal of Higher Education*, 1979, *50*(1), 63–77.

Jacoby, B., and others. *Service-Learning in Higher Education: Concepts and Practices.* San Francisco: Jossey-Bass, 1996.

Kendall, J. C.., Duley, J. S., Little, T. C., Permaul, J. S., and Rusing, S. *Strengthening Experiential Education Within Your Institution.* Raleigh, N.C.: National Society for Internships and Experiential Education, 1986.

Kendall, J. C., and others (eds.). *Combining Service and Learning*, 2 vols. Raleigh, N.C.: National Society for Internships and Experiential Education, 1990.

Kendrick, J. R. "Outcomes of Service-Learning in an Introduction to Sociology Course." *Michigan Journal of Community Service Learning*, 1996, *2*, 72–81.

King, P. M. "How Do We Know? Why Do We Believe?" *Liberal Education*, 1992, *78*(1), 2–9.

King, P. M., and Kitchener, K. S. *Developing Reflective Judgment: Understanding and Promoting Intellectual Growth and Critical Thinking in Adolescents and Adults.* San Francisco: Jossey-Bass, 1994.

Kitchener, K. S., and Fischer, K.W. "A Skill Approach to the Development of Reflective Thinking." In D. Kuhn (ed.), *Contributions to Human Development*, Vol. 21: *Developmental Perspectives on Teaching and Learning Thinking Skills.* Basel, Switzerland: S. Karger, 1990.

Kitchener, K. S., Lynch, C. L., Fischer, K. R., and Wood, P. "Developmental Range of Reflective Judgment: The Effect of Contextual Support and Practice on Developmental Stage." *Developmental Psychology*, 1993, *29*(5), 893–906.

Knefelkamp, L., Widick, C., and Parker, C. (eds.). *Applying New Developmental Findings*. New Directions for Student Services, no. 4. San Francisco: Jossey-Bass, 1978.

Kolb, D. *Experiential Learning: Experience as the Source of Learning and Development*. Upper Saddle River, N.J.: Prentice Hall, 1984.

Lempert, D. H. *Escape from the Ivory Tower: Student Adventures in Democratic Experiential Education*. San Francisco: Jossey-Bass, 1995.

Levine, A., and Cureton, J. *When Hope and Fear Collide*. San Francisco: Jossey-Bass, 1998.

Levison, L. "Choose Engagement over Exposure." In J. C. Kendall and others (eds.), *Combining Service and Learning*. Raleigh, N.C.: National Society for Internships and Experiential Education, 1990.

Lynch, C. L. "Facilitating and Assessing Unstructured Problem Solving." *Journal of College Reading and Learning*, 1996, 27, 16–27.

Lynch, C. L., and Huber, G. *A Developmental Guide to Critical Reflection Skills and Problem Solving in Service-Learning Settings*. Final report of the Comparing Models of Service-Learning Research Project. Nashville, Tenn.: Vanderbilt University, 1998.

Lynch, C. L., and Wolcott, S. "A Developmental Guide for Evaluating Problem-Solving Efforts." Paper presented at a faculty workshop, California State University, Fresno, Apr. 1998.

Markus, G. B., Howard, J., and King, D. "Integrating Community Service and Classroom Instruction Enhances Learning: Results from an Experiment." *Educational Evaluation and Policy Analysis*, 1993, 15(4), 410–419.

Mezirow, J. *Transformative Dimensions of Adult Learning*. San Francisco: Jossey-Bass, 1991.

Mezirow, J. "Understanding Transformation Theory." *Adult Education Quarterly*, 1994, 44(4), 222–232.

Mezirow, J. "Contemporary Paradigms of Learning." *Adult Education Quarterly*, 1996, 46(3), 158–173.

Miller, J. "Linking Traditional and Service-Learning Courses: Outcome Evaluation Using Two Pedagogically Distinct Models." *Michigan Journal of Community Service Learning*, 1994, 1, 29–36.

Mintz, S. D., and Hesser, G. "Principles of Good Practice in Service-Learning." In B. Jacoby and others, *Service-Learning in Higher Education: Concepts and Practices*. San Francisco: Jossey-Bass, 1996.

Moore, D. T. "Discovering the Pedagogy of Experience." *Harvard Educational Review*, 1981, 51(2), 286–300.

Moore, D. T. "Knowledge at Work: An Approach to Learning by Interns." In

K. Borman and J. Reisman (eds.), *Becoming a Worker*. Norwood, N.J.: Ablex, 1986.

Moore, W. S. "The Learning Environment Preferences: Exploring the Construct Validity of an Objective Measure of the Perry Scheme of Intellectual Development." *Journal of College Student Development*, 1989, *30*, 504–514.

Morse, S. W. *Renewing Civic Capacity: Preparing College Students for Service and Citizenship*. ASHE-ERIC Higher Education Report no. 8. Washington, D.C.: School of Education and Human Development, George Washington University, 1989.

Morton, K. "The Irony of Service: Charity, Project, and Social Change in Service-Learning." *Michigan Journal of Community Service-Learning*, 1995, *2*, 19–32.

Myers-Lipton, S. J. "The Effects of Service-Learning on College Students' Attitudes Towards Civic Responsibility, International Understanding, and Racial Prejudice." Unpublished doctoral dissertation, University of Colorado, 1994.

Myers-Lipton, S. J. "Effect of a Comprehensive Service-Learning Program on College Students' Level of Racism." *Michigan Journal of Community Service-Learning*, 1996, *3*, 44–54.

Newman, M. "Response to Understanding Transformation Theory." *Adult Education Quarterly*, 1994, *44*(4), 236–242.

Niemi, R. C., and Associates. *The Politics of Future Citizens*. San Francisco: Jossey-Bass, 1974.

Ostrow, J. "Self-Consciousness and Social Position: On College Students Changing Their Minds About the Homeless." *Qualitative Sociology*, 1995, *18*(3), 357–375.

Owens, T. R., and Owen, S. K. "Enhancing the Quality of Community Learning Experiences." *Alternative Higher Education*, 1979, *4*(2), 103–112.

Pascarella, E. T., Ethington, C. A., and Smart, J. C. "The Influence of College on Humanitarian/Civic Involvement Values." *Journal of Higher Education*, 1988, *59*, 412–437.

Pascarella, E. T., and Terenzini, P. T. *How College Affects Students: Findings and Insights from Twenty Years of Research*. San Francisco: Jossey-Bass, 1991.

Pataniczek, D., and Johansen, C. "An Introduction to Internship Education: New Roles for Students and Faculty." *Journal of Experiential Education*, 1983, *6*(2), 15–19.

Perry, W. H. *Forms of Intellectual and Ethical Development in the College Years*. Austin, Tex.: Holt, Rinehart and Winston, 1970.

Pollack, S. S. "Early Connections Between Service and Education." In T. K. Stanton, D. E. Giles, Jr., and N. Cruz, *Service-Learning: A Movement's Pio-*

neers Reflect on Its Origins, Practice, and Future. San Francisco: Jossey-Bass, 1999.

Putnam, R. "Bowling Alone: America's Declining Social Capital." *Journal of Democracy,* Jan. 1995, pp. 65–78.

Reardon, K. M. "Undergraduate Research in Distressed Urban Communities: An Undervalued Form of Service-Learning." *Michigan Journal of Community Service-Learning,* 1994, *1,* 44–54.

Reardon, K. M. "Institutionalizing Community Service-Learning at a Major Research University: The Case of the East St. Louis Action Research Project." *Michigan Journal of Community Service-Learning,* 1997, *4,* 130–136.

Resnick, L. *Education and Learning to Think.* Washington, D.C.: National Academy Press, 1987a.

Resnick, L. "The 1987 Presidential Address: Learning in School and Out." *Educational Researcher,* 1987b, *16*(9), 13–20.

Rhoads, R. "Critical Multiculturalism and Service Learning." In R. Rhoads and J. Howard (eds.), *Academic Service Learning: A Pedagogy of Action and Reflection.* San Francisco: Jossey-Bass, 1998.

Rifkin, J. "The Future of the Workplace." Speech to the Federal Highway Administration, Washington, D.C., Apr. 1, 1996. Videotape no. 96-05-02-18-1. West Lafayette, Ind.: C-SPAN Public Affairs Video Archives, Purdue University.

Roose, D., and others. *Black Student Retention Study.* Oberlin, Ohio: Oberlin College, 1997.

Rose, M. *Lives on the Boundary: The Struggles and Achievements of America's Underprepared.* New York: Free Press, 1989.

Rutter, R., and Newman, F. "The Potential of Community Service to Enhance Civic Responsibility." *Social Education,* 1989, *53*(6), 371–374.

Sax, L. J., and Astin, A. W. "The Benefits of Service: Evidence from Undergraduates." *Educational Record,* Summer-Fall 1997, pp. 25–33.

Scheurich, J. "Citizenship Responsibility Scales." Unpublished manuscript, University of Texas, 1994.

Schön, D. *The Reflective Practitioner: How Professionals Think in Action.* New York: Basic Books, 1983.

Schön, D. "Knowing in Action: The New Scholarship Requires a New Epistemology." *Change,* 1995, *27*(6), 27–34.

Serow, R. C., and Dreyden, J. L. "Community Service Among College and University Students: Individual and Institutional Relationships." *Journal of Adolescence,* 1990, *25*(9), 553–566.

Shulman, L. "Taking Learning Seriously." Plenary address at the American Association for Higher Education conference, Mar. 22, 1998, Atlanta. Video-tape. Gaithersburg, Md.: Visual Aids Electronics Corp.

Shumer, R. "Academic Learning Plus Experiential Learning Equals Complete Learning." Paper presented at the National Society for Experiential Education conference, San Francisco, 1993a.

Shumer, R. *Describing Service-Learning: A Delphi Study.* Minneapolis: University of Minnesota, 1993b.

Shumer, R., and Cady, J. M. *Youth Works–Americorp Evaluation: Second-Year Report, 1995–1996.* St. Paul: Department of Work, Community, and Family Health, University of Minnesota, 1997.

Sigmon, R. "Service-Learning: Three Principles." *Synergist,* 1979, 8, 9–11.

Sigmon, R. "The Problem of Definition in Service-Learning." In R. Sigmon and others, *The Journey to Service-Learning.* Washington, D.C.: Council of Independent Colleges, 1996.

Sigmon, R., and Edwards, D. "North Carolina: Early Leaders in Service Learning." In J. C. Kendall and others (eds.), *Combining Service and Learning.* Raleigh, N.C.. National Society for Internships and Experiential Education, 1990.

Silcox, H. (ed.). *A How-To Guide to Reflection: Adding Cognitive Learning to Community Service Programs.* Philadelphia: Brighton Press, 1993.

Sirianni, C., and Friedland, L. "Civic Innovation and American Democracy." *Change,* 1997, *29*(1), 14–23.

Smith, M. W. "An Assessment of Intended Outcomes and Perceived Effects of Community Service-Learning for College Students: Striking a Chord in the Key of C." Unpublished doctoral dissertation, Department of Educational Leadership, University of Maryland, 1993.

Stanton, T. K. "Service-Learning: Groping Toward a Definition." *Experiential Education,* 1987, *12*(1), 2,4.

Stanton, T. K. "Liberal Arts, Experiential Learning and Public Service: Necessary Ingredients for Socially Responsible Undergraduate Education." In J. C. Kendall and others (eds.), *Combining Service and Learning.* Raleigh, N.C.: National Society for Internships and Experiential Education, 1990.

Stanton, T. K., Giles, D. E., Jr., and Cruz, N. *Service-Learning: A Movement's Pioneers Reflect on Its Origins, Practice, and Future.* San Francisco: Jossey-Bass, 1999.

Suelzle, M., and Borzak, L. "Stages of Fieldwork." In L. Borzak (ed.), *Field Study.* Thousand Oaks, Calif.: Sage, 1981.

Sugar, J., and Livosky, M. "Enriching Child Psychology Courses with a Preschool Journal Option." *Teaching of Psychology,* 1988, *15*(2), 93–95.

Tennant, M. "Perspective Transformation and Adult Development." *Adult Education Quarterly*, 1993, 44(1), 34–42.

Tennant, M. "Response to Understanding Transformation Theory." *Adult Education Quarterly*, 1994, 44(4), 233–235.

Tinto, V. *Leaving College: Rethinking the Causes and Cures of Student Attrition*. (2nd ed.) Chicago: University of Chicago Press, 1993.

Voss, J., Greene, T., Post, T., and Penner, B. "Problem Solving Skills in the Social Sciences." In G. H. Bowers (ed.), *The Psychology of Learning and Motivation: Advances in Research Theory*, Vol. 17. Orlando, Fla.: Academic Press, 1984.

Voss, J., Tyler, S., and Yengo, L. "Individual Differences in Social Science Problem Solving." In R. Dillon and R. Schmeck (eds.), *Individual Differences in Cognitive Practices*, Vol 1. Orlando, Fla.: Academic Press, 1983.

Walt Whitman Center for the Culture and Politics of Democracy. *The Civic Skills Test: A Critical Examination Working Group Notebook*. New Brunswick, N.J.: Walt Whitman Center, Rutgers University, 1993.

Ward, K. "Service-Learning and Student Volunteerism: Reflections on Institutional Commitments." *Michigan Journal of Community Service Learning*, 1996, 3, 55–65.

Waterman, A. "Conducting Research on Reflective Activities in Service-Learning." In H. Silcox (ed.), *A How-To Guide to Reflection: Adding Cognitive Learning to Community Service Programs*. Philadelphia: Brighton Press, 1993.

Waterman, A. "The Role of Student Characteristics in Service-Learning. In A. Waterman (ed.), *Service-Learning: Applications from the Research*. Hillsdale, N.J.: Erlbaum, 1997.

Whitehead, A. N. *The Aims of Education*. Old Tappan, N.J.: Macmillan, 1929.

Whitehead, A. N. "Religion and Science." In M. Garner (ed.), *Great Essays in Science*. New York: Prometheus, 1994.

Zlotkowski, E. "Linking Service-Learning and the Academy: A New Voice at the Table?" *Change*, 1996, 28(1), 20–27.

Zlotkowski, E. (ed.). *Successful Service-Learning Programs: New Models of Excellence in Higher Education*. Bolton, Mass.: Anker Publishing, 1998.

Index

"What? So what? Now what?" reflection model, 195–196
Whitehead, A. N., 8, 64, 66
Widick, C., 118
Wolcott, S., 109, 111
Wood, P., 125
Work: authenticity of, 86–87, 89–91; as important, 89–91, 99–100; and political action, 103, 148; versus simulated exercises, 67, 89–90; types of community, 193, 196–197
Working with others: and caring, 87–89; as charity or for social justice, 17–18, 142, 148, 155; commitment to, 148; and disorienting dilemmas, 141–145; and engagement, 86–87, 89–91, 94, 143–144;

and interpersonal skills, 43–44, 276; and leadership skills, 44, 276; as peers, 41–43, 62, 143–144. *See also* People students worked with, categories of
Writing, reflection and journal, 33–34, 90, 121, 168, 174–176, 196, 197, 280–286

Y

Years of service, coding, 223
Youth crime service work, 87, 93, 220

Z

Zeldin, R., 61, 170
Zlotkowski, E., 2, 7